Poetic Realism in Scandinavia and Central Europe

Clifford Albrecht Bernd

Poetic Realism in Scandinavia and Central Europe

1820–1895

CAMDEN HOUSE

Copyright © 1995 by
CAMDEN HOUSE, INC.

Published by Camden House, Inc.
Drawer 2025
Columbia, SC 29202 USA

Printed on acid-free paper.
Binding materials are chosen for strength and
durability.

All Rights Reserved
Printed in the United States of America

ISBN 1-57113-010-1

Library of Congress Cataloging-in-Publication Data

Bernd, Clifford A.
   Poetic realism in Scandinavia and Central Europe, 1820–1895 / Clifford Albrecht Bernd.
      p.   cm. -- (Studies in German literature, linguistics, and culture)
   Includes bibliographical references and index.
   ISBN 1-57113-010-1 (alk. paper)
   1. German literature--19th century--History and criticism.
2. Danish literature--19th century--History and criticism
3. Swedish literature--19th century--History and criticism.
4. Scandinavian literature--Appreciation--Germany. 5. Realism in literature. I. Title. II. Series: Studies in German literature, linguistics, and culture (Unnumbered)
   PT345.B465 1995
   830.9' 12--dc20   94-24502
                                                                         CIP

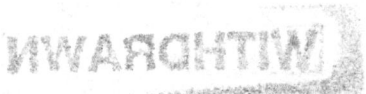

To Wolfgang Preisendanz,

*the champion of those who
have fought for the recognition of Poetic Realism
and furthered our understanding of it.*

Contents

Preface   xiii

Danish *Poetisk Realisme*   1

1. The curtain goes up: the inception of a new artistic style in Denmark   1
2. The father of *Poetisk Realisme:* Poul Martin Møller   4
   - Throwing away the compass of Romanticism   4
   - The new compass of *Poetisk Realisme:* "Glæde over Danmark"   5
   - Sowing the seed of *Poetisk Realisme*   15
   - Invoking the model of Boccaccio: *En dansk Students Eventyr*   17
   - Dropping the torch   21
3. The second apostle: Steen Steensen Blicher   22
   - *En Landsbydegns Dagbog*   24
   - The line forward to Theodor Storm   30
4. The golden touch: Thomasine Gyllembourg   33
   - Searching for a theory of the novella   35
   - *En Hverdags-Historie*   40
   - Pressing a parallel to Gottfried Keller   44
5. Further momentum: Carl Bernhard   46
6. *Poetisk Realisme* finds an extension in pictorial art: Christen Købke   49
   - *Parti af Østerbrogade i morgenbelysning*   50
   - *Efterårsmorgen ved Sortedamssøen*   52
7. *Poetisk Realisme* becomes overshadowed by newer forms of Danish art   53
   - Political and economic conditions   53
   - Hans Christian Andersen   54
   - N. F. S. Grundtvig   56
   - Meïr Goldschmidt   57
   - The visual arts: Thorvaldsen and Købke   59
8. *Poetisk Realisme* exhausts its creative vigor on Danish soil   61
   - The lengthening of the shadows   61

The light before the final eclipse: Bernhard Ingemann's conversion to *Poetisk Realisme*	62
Varners Sommer-Vandringer	63
Poetisk Realisme suspends its functions in Denmark and strikes out in different directions abroad	64

Swedish *Poetisk Realism*   72

1. The Danish movement spreads to other parts of Scandinavia   72
2. *Poetisk Realisme*'s failure to reach Norway   72
3. Swedish foreign policy favors the travel of Danish culture to Sweden   74
4. Conditions retarding the travel of *Poetisk Realisme* to Sweden   75
5. Thomasine Gyllembourg finds a Swedish successor in Fredrika Bremer   76
6. Johan Erik Rydqvist's manifesto for *Poetisk Realism*   77
7. Per Daniel Atterbom introduces the term *Poetisk Realist*   80
8. The triumph of theory over practice in Sweden   84
9. The blaze of glory in Finland: Johan Ludvig Runeberg   85
   - The conditioning factors enabling Runeberg to become a *Poetisk Realist*   86
   - The masterpiece: *Fänrik Ståls sägner*   89
10. *Poetisk Realism* comes to a halt in Finland   97
    - Runeberg's legendary status prevents others from following in his footsteps   97
    - Stepped-up Russian cultural oppression compels younger Finnish authors to write in a different vein   97
    - Zacharias Topelius and Aleksis Kivi ring down the curtain on *Poetisk Realism* in Finland   99
    - *Poetisk Realism* suspends its functions in Finland and migrates abroad   100

Scandinavian Poetic Realism travels to Germany   106

1. Political conditions abet the flow of Danish literature into Germany   106
2. Novellas of Danish *Poetisk Realisme* are translated into German en masse   110
3. Baron Constant Dirckinck-Holmfeld stirs German interest in the lyric of *Poetisk Realisme*   112

4. Jens Bergendahl von Schepelern, Adolph von Gähler, and other Dano-Germans add works of Swedish *Poetisk Realism* to the Danish literary current flowing into Germany ... 114
5. Carl August Hagberg and the Brothers Brockhaus introduce the term *Poetischer Realist* to the German literary scene ... 118
6. Swedish *Poetisk Realism* comes to the attention of German readers via other channels ... 120

German *Poetischer Realismus* ... 122

1. Julian Schmidt develops a theory of *Poetischer Realismus* at Leipzig ... 122
    Leipzig's importance for the reception of Scandinavian Poetic Realism ... 122
    Julian Schmidt moves to Leipzig and is attracted to Scandinavian Poetic Realism ... 123
    Schmidt's mission as a journalist ... 126
    Schmidt's theory unfolds ... 127
2. Schmidt's brother-in-arms Otto Ludwig ... 134
    Ludwig not Freytag ... 134
    Zwischen Himmel und Erde ... 137
    Ludwig's philosophical exercises on *Poetischer Realismus* ... 140
3. Continuing *Poetisk Realisme* on German-speaking soil: Theodor Storm ... 144
    Storm versus Schmidt ... 144
    Storm between Denmark and Germany ... 144
    Storm adapts the novella of *Poetisk Realisme* ... 147
    Immensee ... 148
    Aquis submersus ... 150
    Der Schimmelreiter ... 152
    Storm, the lyricist ... 155
    "Meeresstrand" ... 157
4. The little giant: Gottfried Keller ... 161
    Keller and Storm ... 161
    Keller's calling to *Poetischer Realismus* ... 161
    Romeo und Julia auf dem Dorfe ... 164
    "Abendlied" ... 170
    Der grüne Heinrich ... 173
    Wilhelm Petersen: fiction in reality and reality in fiction ... 178

5. The latecomer: Conrad Ferdinand Meyer ... 181
   Continuing the novella of *Poetischer Realismus* ... 181
   Der Heilige ... 183
   Continuing the lyric of *Poetischer Realismus* ... 186
   "Der römische Brunnen" ... 187
6. The Low German poet: Klaus Groth ... 190
   The reception of Groth's verse ... 190
   Early verse ... 192
   Quickborn ... 194
7. Experimenting with the diary novel: Wilhelm Raabe ... 198
   Die Chronik der Sperlingsgasse ... 198
   Moving away from *Poetischer Realismus* ... 203
8. Ringing down the curtain: Theodor Fontane ... 204
   Fontane's calling to *Poetischer Realismus* ... 204
   "Archibald Douglas" ... 206
   "Ausgang" ... 214
   Transforming *Poetischer Realismus* into social realism ... 215
   Unwiederbringlich ... 216
   Effi Briest ... 219

Works Consulted ... 233

Index of Names ... 239

Preface

THIS BOOK IS the outcome of writing its predecessor, *German Poetic Realism* (1981). At the completion of that task I felt that yet a larger one awaited me, that of dealing with this literary convention in its cross-national, cross-linguistic context. In the course of writing the earlier volume, I belatedly discovered that historians of Danish literature, as well as historians of Swedish literature, have addressed themselves no less to Poetic Realism within their respective language boundaries than have critics of German literature. While German literary historians refer to *Poetischer Realismus*, Danish critics consider a *Poetisk Realisme* and the Swedish critics *Poetisk Realism*. In different tongues, then, students of literature share an interest in a convention of the same name. To the students of each of these national manifestations of Poetic Realism, however, the namesakes in the other linguistic traditions have remained terra incognita. For instance, a scholar of no lesser stature than Richard H. Samuel, for many years the head of the flourishing School of Germanic Studies at the University of Melbourne, Australia, and one of the most eminent Germanists of our century, explicitly argued that Poetic Realism constituted "a specific German phenomenon" (in *AUMLA*, Journal of the Australasian Universities Modern Language Association, no. 2, August 1954, p. 2). Such a statement is patently untrue; the convention and even the term itself are as firmly embedded in the Danish and Swedish literary heritages as in German tradition.

The time has now arrived, I believe, when we must begin to hear the three individual voices as parts of a single chorus. The investigation of each should no longer be so tightly shuttered as to obstruct the fresh insights that can come from a familiarity with the others. There is an obvious gain in our perspective of literary history if we look at these comparable national traditions. For too long, I think, we have allowed Danish and Swedish literature to be studied at our universities out of charity; these disciplines should be encouraged now for the genuine poetic history they contain.

Reading important masterpieces of the three Poetic Realisms within the larger context of common European literary history and topography should be as rewarding as viewing a gallery of European Impressionist paintings collectively, rather than simply as national representatives. Suddenly, certain resemblances between the various national branches of the same convention become recognizable, just as common traits are distinguishable in members of one family, traits that may not be visibly expressed in like manner or with equal intensity and hence may be easily misunderstood or overlooked if an individual family member is viewed in isolation from the family as a whole.

Originally I had wanted to produce a unified synthetic overview of Danish-Swedish-German Poetic Realism, but the need to differentiate the shadings of the three linguistic segments and to show reasons for the literary movement's upsurge and decline in one national culture after another convinced me that a more appropriate method of presentation would be a historical-typological study, analyzing the evolution, step by step, of the three currents of Poetic Realism, beginning in Denmark, continuing in Sweden and Swedish Finland, and reaching the final apogee in the vast German-speaking world.

This method also gives me a better opportunity, I believe, to put before my readers a major thesis of this book: that Poetic Realism is quintessentially a Danish literary convention — not a specifically German phenomenon, as Germanists traditionally have thought. In Denmark Poetic Realism was born and flourished, and from Denmark its currents swelled and spilled over across that nation's frontiers to the adjacent Swedish- and German-speaking worlds, where they then flowed in ever widening ripples further eastward and southward. I like to think of this book, therefore, as wheel-shaped. The first part, on Danish *Poetisk Realisme*, is the hub of the wheel, and the subsequent chapters are the spokes; ideal readers will want to return occasionally to the discussion of the Danish tradition as they explore its evolving ramifications in different tongues, in different places, and at different times.

*

A preface is sometimes used as a device not only to allow an author to shed his air of assurance, but also to complain of his troubles, and to ask readers and reviewers to be lenient with him. I had to contend with only one problem serious enough to permit such an appeal: the progress in writing this book came to a halt again and again when I encountered difficulties in obtaining pertinent texts of Danish literature. The same thing held true for Swedish texts, although to a lesser extent. Often enough I discovered that volumes I wanted to consult were unavailable anywhere in the United States. Frequently I was frustrated by not finding a tome precisely at the time I needed to examine it in order to continue writing a particular segment of my manuscript. I had then to interrupt my work and put off the completion of that chapter or sub-chapter until the subsequent summer when I could return again to the Royal Library at Copenhagen (or visit the great libraries at Stockholm, Uppsala, and Helsinki). On other occasions my initial joy at successfully locating a text in the United States quickly turned sour when I received the notification that the particular volume was non-circulating. This happened most frequently with books at the New York Public Library, which holds the best collection of Scandinavian primary, secondary, and periodical literature in this country. The information that the volume was too old, too brittle, or too rare to go out on interlibrary loan left me with no alternative but to fly from California to New York. There, however, my frustration was further compounded — more than once — when, upon arrival at the Library's main building on Fifth Avenue, I was told that the book I wished to peruse had been removed to a storage facility in another part of the city. *Habent sua fata libelli!*

The many German anthologies and translations of the early nineteenth-century Danish literary works I consulted — in order to read in the forewords the reasons given as to why the German reading public at the time should be introduced to Danish literature — were also difficult to obtain. The Library of the German Society of Pennsylvania in Philadelphia holds a few of these. For others I had to search in Germany. Kiel's University Library was always the best place to start. As the most important German library within the kingdom of Greater Denmark in the early nineteenth century (from the Act of Incorporation uniting the duchy of Holstein with Denmark in 1806 until the Dano-German War of 1864), it had acquired large holdings of Danish literature in German translation. But many of these volumes burned in the flames of the Second World War. My library order slips were often returned stamped *verbrannt* (destroyed by fire). I had then to travel — literally — to libraries all over Germany to obtain the individual texts for which I was searching.

*

Portions of this book have appeared, in various other forms, in the aforementioned earlier book or in correlative articles. Many of the revisions owe their existence to the suggestions of colleagues and the incitement of students. The number of those who aided me extends far beyond any list of names I could set down here. I must single out for special thanks, though, my Danish friends Leif Ludwig Albertsen and Sven-Aage Jørgensen. My sincere gratitude also goes out to my Swedish friends Carl-Sture Packalén and Tore Wretö.

There is a certain sadness in recalling those who have not lived to judge how I profited from their advice. Børge Gedsø Madsen, my late colleague in Danish literature on the Berkeley campus of the University of California, was the first to encourage me to write this cross-national study. His encyclopedic knowledge also was a great help in developing my scaffolding of Danish *Poetisk Realisme*. I am particularly saddened that I cannot place this volume in the hands of Fritz Martini. Without his insistence the section "Ludwig not Freytag" would never have been written. Few critics of German literature may know that he possessed a surprising familiarity with Finnish letters. It was my good fortune to have been able to discuss with him Runeberg's place in literature. No author could have wished for a more expert, thoughtful, and energetic adviser than I found in him.

It remains for me to offer a word of appreciation to Camden House, especially to James Hardin for his unflagging fidelity to this book and to Holly Povis for her painstaking scrutiny of my manuscript. The experience Eline Bernd acquired while on the staff of the *Frankfurter Allgemeine* made her — once more — an invaluable editorial assistant.

Clifford Albrecht Bernd

University of California, Davis
June 21, 1994

DANISH *POETISK REALISME*

1. The curtain goes up: the inception of a new artistic style in Denmark

LET US BEGIN our study by looking to the earliest stirrings of Poetic Realism and considering its germination during the 1820s in Denmark. In that tiny nation, far removed from the crossroads of European artistic life at the time, a handful of authors and painters laid the foundation for a new inter-European style in art. Few critics outside of Denmark have taken note of *Poetisk Realisme*, as the style is known in Danish. Even in Denmark proper many years elapsed before any conscious effort was made to understand its particular aesthetic intent or its wider historical significance. Vilhelm Andersen (1864–1953), sometimes called the "dean of Danish literary historians," first directed critical attention to it in 1893.[1] Since then, a definite awareness of *Poetisk Realisme* has emerged in the land which gave it birth. As Danish scholars have continually mapped the crests and troughs in the stream of native artistic traditions, they have increasingly clarified the self-conscious, collective striving of the 1820s to introduce something new into literature as well as pictorial art. As a result, it is now fashionable in Danish historiography to speak of *Poetisk Realisme*.

Nowhere does the flourishing contemporary Danish interest in Poetic Realism become more apparent than in the modern standard history of Danish literature consulted in universities, schools, and libraries all across Denmark, the *Dansk Litteratur Historie* (A History of Danish Literature), published by Copenhagen's Politikens Forlag under the general editorship of Poul H. Traustedt. In this widely acclaimed, multi-volume work, superseding other comprehensive treatments of Denmark's literary legacy, Oluf Friis (1894–1979), one of the foremost modern critics of early nineteenth-century Danish literature, not only urges widespread recognition of *Poetisk Realisme* but in the 269-page discussion has endowed it with an importance hitherto not credited to it. No other study of Denmark's liter-

---

[1] Vilhelm Andersen, *Danske Studier* (Copenhagen: Gad, 1893), 125.

ary legacy considers *den poetiske realismes* generation of writers so extensively or so solidly acknowledges it.[2]

Like many artistic movements, Danish Poetic Realism emerged out of a revolt against a preceding movement. That earlier movement, the ashes from which was born *Poetisk Realisme*, we call Danish Romanticism.

The dawn of the nineteenth century had seen the triumph in Denmark of a peculiarly Nordic form of Romanticism and the establishment of a virtual literary dictatorship under the aegis of the youthful, exuberant poet and dramatist Adam Oehlenschläger (1779–1850). He had championed a literature of sensational nostalgic fantasy, exulting in the ephemeral and bizarre. This literature had distinguished itself as a poetry of escape, carrying its action into fanciful and enchanting Arabian nightscapes and imaginary worlds of Nordic mythology. Its drama, either a comedy of grandeur or a valiant struggle culminating in heroic martyrdom, rarely, if indeed ever, gave an audience an opportunity to confront or consider the presence of any sorrow in real life.

Taken as a whole, Danish literature (as well as Danish pictorial art) at the threshold of the nineteenth century had reflected the bright and unrestrained optimism of the then rich Danish monarchy. At that time Denmark stretched from the northernmost tip of Norway to as far south as German-speaking Europe, with overseas possessions on all populated continents but Australia, extending from the coral strand of India in the east to as far west as the enchanted isles of the Caribbean, from the sultry lowlands of African Guinea in the south to as far north as Greenland's icy mountains. Indeed, the country had seemingly assumed a geographic reach equal to its mythically fantastic literature.[3]

Yet this exalted Romantic movement had barely taken root when Denmark unwittingly found itself entangled with the major contestants in the Napoleonic struggle for European dominance. Fatally, the British, to forestall a French invasion of their island from Danish ports, furiously bombarded the unsuspecting city of Copenhagen in 1807, not only bringing death and destruction but also throwing the embattled Danes into an alliance with the worst of all possible allies. Denmark became Napoleon's pitiful vassal-cohort. Denmark's trade, on which its economy relied, slackened with the loss of British markets and virtually was

---

[2] Oluf Friis, *Dansk Litteratur Historie*, ed. P. H. Traustedt. New, augmented ed., III (Copenhagen: Politiken, 1976), 11-278.

[3] For a delightful picture of Denmark and Danish literature around 1800, see the excellently written and handsomely illustrated volume by Leif Ludwig Albertsen, *On the Threshold of a Golden Age* (Copenhagen: The Royal Danish Ministry of Foreign Affairs, 1979).

extinguished as the British navy preyed on helpless Danish commercial vessels. The continental war itself ruled out alternate routes for Danish agricultural exports via the overland route to Germany. Consequently, the prices for agrarian products dropped drastically, in turn causing a precipitous fall in land prices and a concomitant difficulty in collecting taxes. The revenues that did continue to trickle in simply evaporated under the demands of heavy wartime expenditures. Before the war began to turn solidly against Napoleon, the immediate fate of Denmark, his sole remaining ally, was already sealed. In 1813, convulsed by economic disaster, the unhappy nation took the exceptional step of declaring a state bankruptcy. As a result, many Danes, including even the pompous Oehlenschläger himself, suddenly became paupers.[4] The peace treaty, signed in 1814, forced Denmark to pay dearly for having joined the losing side in the great European war, further aggravating the pathetic state of affairs. A nation that only a few years earlier had enjoyed flourishing prosperity suddenly found itself fettered by war debts and imprisoned in demoralizing destitution.

Denmark's swift transition from wealth to poverty radically altered the Danish outlook on life and the course of the nation's literature. When the Danes were compelled to relinquish visions of world dominance, and when they were no longer allowed the complacency of life and the prestige which their wealthy empire had afforded, the Romantics lost their compelling influence. As the defeated and impoverished nation writhed in despair, the splendid auras and eloquent declamations of the Romantics seemed a cruel deception, easily discredited. Lofty ideals and bright visions gallingly contrasted with the somber prospects of a new generation. Thus newly lit, their writings showed strange fantasy, naive optimism, and reckless delusion, certainly not pointing where Danish poets and writers now had to move.

The Danish Götterdämmerung ushered in a new artistic climate. The times called for a new response, a poetic vision to meet the challenge of the drastic upheaval in everyday Danish life. The placidly grandiose flights of Oehlenschläger and his fellow Danish Romantics to idealized realms of mythological fiction had to give way to a literature more consonant with the appalling political and economic realities of contemporary Denmark. Danish sensibilities not only favored but even demanded that artists abandon fecund fantasy and replace it with a more realistic view of the stifling circumstances of Denmark's new everyday life.

Oehlenschläger himself did not adapt well to the new tides, continuing to write in much the same vein. He was, of course, intelligent enough to realize how much the plight of the nation had dampened all enthusiasm

---

[4] Adam Oehlenschläger, *Meine Lebens-Erinnerungen*, III (Leipzig: Lorck, 1850), 83.

for poetic appeals to grandeur.[5] But rather than radically change his mode of writing, he found respite in traveling to the still flowering fields of Romanticism: in Germany, Italy, France, the Netherlands, and Sweden. To compensate for his declining popularity in a modern un-Romantic Denmark, he began, in the early 1820s, to compose poems in German, finding audiences in Germany more favorably disposed toward Romanticism than were his own countrymen.[6] As he found favor with German-speaking audiences, he increasingly delighted in calling himself "a German poet."[7] He so Germanized himself that by 1827 a prominent German newspaper, the *Dresdner Morgenzeitung*, could remark that he was no longer writing anything of importance in Danish and as a result had exiled himself from Danish literature.[8] This flight abroad, by the greatest force in Romanticism on the Danish scene, only hastened further that literary mode's rapid disintegration in Denmark, leaving the grittier realism of a new movement, *Poetisk Realisme*, to fill the ensuing vacuum.

2. The father of *Poetisk Realisme:* Poul Martin Møller

Throwing away the compass of Romanticism

The birth of the countermovement to Danish Romanticism can be pinpointed rather precisely. *Poetisk Realisme* began auspiciously in what at first seems an entirely inauspicious event: on the first day of November 1819 a young poet-clergyman named Poul Martin Møller (1794–1838)[9] sailed on a vessel of the Danish East India Company, seeking relief from the stultifying despair reigning throughout Denmark. He hoped to find refreshment in the semi-cloistered life of a clergyman, ministering to the

---

[5] Ibid.

[6] Ibid., IV, 18.

[7] Ibid., III, 65.

[8] *Dresdner Morgenzeitung*, 1827, Spalte 87.

[9] There is as yet no general study of Møller in English, but the essay by W. Glyn Jones, "Søren Kierkegaard and Poul Martin Møller," *Modern Language Review* 60 (1965): 73-82, offers an excellent introduction to his aesthetic principles. The most extensive study on this author is by Vilhelm Andersen, *Poul Møller, Hans Liv og Skrifter*, 3rd ed. (Copenhagen: Gyldendal, 1944). In German there is a good modern overview of Møller's work by Bernd Henningsen, *Poul Martin Møller oder Die dänische Erziehung des Søren Kierkegaard* (Frankfurt am Main: Akademische Verlagsgesellschaft, 1973).

spiritual needs of Danish sailors plying their trade in the China seas.[10] Quickly realizing, however, that he had little interest in theological or pastoral matters, he spent most of his time not reminding his seagoing flock of its eternal destiny within a divinely ordained order but, rather, according to his own words, "poring over literature, in silent reflection, and with his pen in his hand."[11]

This period of "self-imposed exile" (as Møller called it),[12] spent in concentration on the nature and function of literature, radically altered the course of Danish belles lettres. Møller, looking at Danish literature from a distance, allowing himself both perspective and calm, soon became convinced that the stifling scene in contemporary Denmark called for a new poetry, one that would be responsive to the current tenor of the vanquished Danish nation. The glittering palace of art, hung with Oehlenschläger's mythical brocade, had to be forsaken, he thought, in order to grapple with everyday Danish life on the darkling plain. At last, Danish literature had acquired the new pilot it so desperately needed. Møller threw away Denmark's Romantic compass. For a while he floundered on the ocean waves, but soon after his vessel had put into Manila Bay on July 16, 1820, he perfected the new compass.

The new compass of *Poetisk Realisme:* "Glæde over Danmark"

That compass, Møller's immortal poem "Glæde over Danmark" (Joy over Denmark),[13] as Oluf Friis rightly tells us, "opened up a new period in Danish literature ... called Poetic Realism."[14] Quite apart from its repre-

---

[10] It has been said on several occasions that Møller embarked on his high seas journey because of a Romantic attraction for exotic and distant lands, but this opinion aligns Møller all too closely with the magic-carpet-fever of the type of Romanticism that was shattered when the fantastic Danish empire went down in defeat in the Napoleonic conflagration. An intimate friend of the poet-theologian summed up the reasons more accurately: "Poul Møller went to China because he couldn't join a monastery, and if ruins can be built up again, I hope to see him some day refreshed" (quoted in Andersen, *Poul Møller, Hans Liv og Skrifter*, 101).

[11] Andersen, *Poul Møller, Hans Liv og Skrifter*, 104.

[12] Poul Martin Møller, *Efterladte Skrifter*, 2nd ed., VI (Copenhagen: Reitzel, 1848-1850), 71. All references to Møller's works and letters, unless otherwise cited, refer to this edition. Despite the publication date, it is still the most complete (and accurate) edition of Møller available.

[13] Detailed analyses of this poem are available only in Danish. The best one is by Hans Brix, "Glæde over Danmark," *Analyser og Problemer* 6 (1950): 170-82.

[14] Oluf Friis, "Outlines of Danish Poetry from Oehlenschläger to Johannes Jensen," *Edda* 21 (1924): 28.

sentative significance as the first key work of Poetic Realism, it is the best known of all of Møller's lyrics,[15] a recognition even weightier considering that the Danes count Møller's verses amongst "the pearls of Danish literature."[16]

Of those hailing this landmark poem, none is more revered in Denmark today than Søren Kierkegaard (1813–1855). He recorded that in 1838 he had attended the funeral service for Møller, at which time "Glæde over Danmark" was recited, and that he was strangely moved by the verses; they constantly echoed in his ears.[17] Six years later he dedicated his famous treatise *Begrebet Angest* (The Concept of Dread) to the memory of Møller, saluting the poet as both "the mighty trumpet of my awakening" and the composer of "Glæde over Danmark." Danish readers of Kierkegaard have acknowledged repeatedly the honor of this dedication. The attention of non-Danish readers, however, should also be directed to this celebrated poem:

> Glæde over Danmark
>
> Rosen blusser alt i Danas Have,
> Liflig fløiter vist den sorte Stær,
> Bier deres brune Nectar lave,
> Hingsten græsser stolt paa Fædres Grave,
> Drengen plukker af de røde Bær.
>
> Her imellem Havets dybe Kløfter
> Gives aldrig Vaar og Blomsterpragt,
> Hvalen kold og dum ved Skibet snøfter,
> Tause Fugl de brede Vinger løfter
> Med sit Bytte fra den vaade Jagt.
>
> Mine Venner i den danske Sommer!
> Mindes I den vidtforreiste Mand,
> Som saa langt fra Danas faure Blommer,
> Her, hvor Sydens Blæst paa Seilet trommer,
> Flakker fra sit elskte Fødeland?

---

[15] P. M. Mitchell, *A History of Danish Literature*, 2nd ed. (New York: Kraus-Thomson, 1971), 123.

[16] Valdemar Hansen, "Le Principe de Personnalité chez trois Penseurs Danois: Høffding, Kierkegaard, Poul Møller," in *Proceedings of the XIIth International Congress of Philosophy*, XII (Florence: Sansoni, 1961): 209-10.

[17] Walter Lowrie, *Kierkegaard*, I (New York & London: Oxford University Press, 1938), 143-44, 148-49.

Udi Øst og Vest, og hvor jeg vanker,
Drømmer jeg om Jer ved Danmarks Sund.
Selv iblandt Constantias fulde Ranker
Mindes jeg med længselfulde Tanker
Løvet i Charlottas Bøgelund.

Klærken raaber i Manillas Rønner:
"Danmark er et lidet, fattigt Land."
Det forsikrer Javas rige Sønner.
Selv Batavias skrantne Kræmmer stønner:
"Danmark er et lidet fattigt Land."

Morgenlandets Søn i Kaaber lange
Bag sin Vifte gisper efter Luft.
Han har spraglet Fugl, men ingen Sange,
Hierteløse Møer med gylden Spange;
Store Glimmerblomster uden Duft.

Kunde du ved Guld og Sølv at love
Kiøbe dig en nordisk Qvindes Tro,
Kiøbe dig et Pust fra Søens Vove,
Kiøbe dig et Ly af Thules Skove,
Og en Kløvermark til Middagsro?

Fattig Mand, som pløier danske Lande,
Ryster Æbler af sit eget Træ;
Har en kraftig Arm, en kløgtig Pande,
Korn paa Marken, Melk i sine Spande;
Quien staaer i Græsset over Knæ.

Ja vor danske Jord er sommerfrodig;
Der er Kræfter ved det danske Brød.
Derfor er den danske Mand saa modig;
Derfor var Normannens Kniv saa blodig;
Derfor er den danske Kind saa rød.

Lad kun Østens Drot blandt kjøbte Friller
Døsig strække sig paa Purpur ud,
Lytte paa den sorte Halvmands Triller,
Mellem Salens tempelhøje Piller,
Kold og gusten som en Marmorgud.

Under lyse Bøg den danske Beiler
Med sin herligvoxne Pige gaaer;
Over deres Hoved Maanen seiler;
Svanen i det klare Vand sig speiler;
Nattergalen høit i Busken slaaer.

Moder har ei danske Barn alene;
Men hvo anden paa den vide Jord,
Bringer over Altrets brede Stene
Gud sit Barn, som hun den blonde, rene?
Ingen anden paa den vide Jord.

Dersom sligt for Fattigdom du tyder,
Østens atlaskklædte, rige Mand,
Glad mit sorte danske Brød jeg bryder,
Takker Gud, mens fra min Læbe lyder:
"Danmark er et lidet fattigt Land!"[18]

(Roses proudly glow in Dana's bowers;
Horses graze where sleep heroic dead;
Bees distill the sweetness from the flowers;
Starlings scatter notes in silver showers;
Children gather berries, ripe and red.

Here between the shadows of the shifting
Ocean never come the budding springs;
Only heavy whales go slowly drifting,
While the silent seagulls hover, lifting
Quarry from the waves, with moveless wings.

Friends afar in shining Danish summer,
Do you hail your comrade any more?
Here the tropic wind, a tireless drummer,
Beats against the sails, and this newcomer
Dreams of native fields by Dana's shore.

East or west, however far I wander,

---

[18] The text of the poem is taken from its first, sensational printing: in the literary weekly *Tilskuerne* 1, no. 47 (1823): 374-76. Subsequent reprints have altered the text in innumerable ways.

I will think of you by Denmark's Sound;
Even where Constantia's vineyards squander
Splendid beauty, I imagine yonder
Bright Charlottë's beechwood, summer-crowned.

Monks in hovels of Manila grumble,
"Denmark is a little, beggar land."
Java's sons confirm it, even humble
Pedlars of Batavia scornfully mumble,
"Denmark is a little, beggar land."

Slaves of silk-clad Orientals hear them
Stir their fans in torrid discontent,
With their heartless, jeweled mates that fear them,
Gorgeous birds, but not a song to cheer them,
Gaudy tinsel flowers that have no scent.

Could you buy the faith of Northern maiden
With the promise of a golden boon?
Buy a gust of sea-waves fragrance-laden,
Clover fields for slumber, or a glade in
Denmark's fields to dream away the noon?

Poor men who have ploughed their Danish furrow
Shake the fruit from their own orchard trees;
Mind and body quick at work and thorough,
Corn and milk aplenty for to-morrow;
Heifers drowse in grass up to their knees.

Denmark's soil is rich, her sons laborious;
There are virtues in the Danish bread;
Wherefore Danish courage is so glorious,
Wherefore was the Northman's sword victorious,
Wherefore is the Danish cheek so red.

Let the Master of the East, reclining
With his purchased women, doze and nod,
Listen to the eunuchs' voices whining
Through the columns echoing and twining,
While he dozes, an exhausted god.

Underneath the beech, the Danish lover

> To the loveliest repeats his vows.
> Drifting moonlight showers white above her;
> Mirrored swans on haunted waters hover;
> Nightingales sing loudly in the boughs.
>
> If such things be poverty's true measure,
> Silk-clad eastern prince, I understand;
> Then I break my Danish bread at leisure,
> Thanking God, I too exclaim with pleasure,
> "Denmark is a little, beggar land!")
> Translated by Robert Silliman Hillyer[19]

Most strikingly this poem, at least to any student of Danish literary history, constitutes the very antithesis of everything Oehlenschläger and his brand of Danish Romanticism represented. If with Oehlenschläger the human mind supernaturally tempted men away from the visible world, if with Oehlenschläger poetry consisted of a powerful sensuousness embodying the freedom of the spirit unfettered by any worldly chains, then with Møller poetry is sustained in the face of reality, bowing to familiar sights and sounds instead of retreating to the impersonal arena of the gods of mythology.

In "Glæde over Danmark" one discovers no potent spirit to help the listener succumb to the nefarious power of a magical spell. Instead, we find a poetic convocation of specific things and places to which the everyday self can clearly relate. No metrical complications or irregularities of scansion draw attention to themselves. Our auditory sense only perceives the regular rhythm of short rhymed stanzas, naturally allowing us to concentrate all the more intensely on the weighty and precise imagery of the poem's story.

Particularly noticeable here are the sharply drawn pictures carefully chosen from the contemporary Danish landscape in its most luscious bloom. These are thrown into even sharper relief by an invidious comparison with the alien magic of the exotic Orient. In addition, a musical accompaniment consisting of a clear trochaic beat and a scheme of alternating masculine and feminine rhymes combines with the pictures to produce an enchanting hymn of joy to Møller's Denmark.

The complacency, however, into which the listener is lured by the combination of the metrical structure's lulling evenness and the rapture over the images of a delightful Denmark in the summertime becomes

---

[19] From *A Book of Danish Verse* (New York: The American-Scandinavian Foundation, 1922; reprint, 1976), 63-65. Reprinted courtesy of the American-Scandinavian Foundation.

thrice deceptive. On three separate occasions (in the twenty-second, twenty-fifth, and sixty-fifth verses) the poet hammers away at his lingering conclusion: Denmark is no longer the rich and vast empire it was before the war, but merely "a little, beggar land." On three occasions the poet deliberately shocks his listeners out of complacency, and each time he tortures them further, suffusing his disturbing refrain with a feeling of clenched frustration by piling into the three verses a series of gnashing dental sounds: "Danmark er et lidet, fattigt Land." What are we to make of a poet ostensibly attempting to inform us of his soaring delight at the thought of his native land, who then three times lets this disguise fall away? On the one hand, he seems intoxicated by his country and goes on at length to convince himself and us of how wonderful Denmark is. But on the other hand, he clearly knows that conditions in contemporary Denmark belie this happy thought. He certainly must be embarrassed to hear (in the fifth stanza) that in Asia people scorn the pitiable condition of his country. And when he not once, not twice, but three times confesses that Denmark has been reduced to a state of pauperism, he charges this realization with so much echoing significance that we must wonder whether he is truthful when speaking of Denmark as a bright abode. In short, we hardly know whether the poet smiles or weeps over conditions on the Danish home front. Is his joy over Denmark covertly mitigated by the flow of secret tears? Or does he try to cover up his tears with a forced smile?

We cannot believe Møller wholly succumbs to the joys of being a Dane, since, at least for the reader, no happy associations with Danish life lastingly tranquilize the breast: to let such associations invade us too completely would do violence to the poem and force out of its triply stressed position the haunting refrain calling attention to Denmark as "a little, beggar land." In view of this refrain, the poem's title, "Joy over Denmark," demands interpretation as ironic.

On the other hand, an impressive number of bright and happy pictures of Danish life do seem to be intentionally chiseled into the poem's structure, so many, indeed, as to make it difficult to imagine the poet utterly despairing over his nation's frailty. These pictures, no less than the poem's melody, argue for an interpretation altogether different from the one above and make us want to accept the title at face value, as something genuinely felt.

Two opposing responses to the actual situation in Denmark, then, seem to commingle in the poet's heart. Joy and sorrow appear simultaneously, interwoven with one another. Similarly, Møller's German contemporary Friedrich Schleiermacher (1768–1834), speaking of the sweet but sad mood of melancholia, sensed how much a person could know joy and sorrow at the same time.[20]

The characteristic unity of "Glæde over Danmark" resides in the poet's perception of this double perspective, underscored by the consistent double beat of the poem's unerring trochaic pattern and by the double nature of the regularly shifting interwoven masculine and feminine rhyme in each stanza. Every attentive reader senses the poet's powerful musical control over the message and his knowledge of orchestrating sounds to let an unmistakable dualism echo throughout the verses in counterpoint.

In sum, gathering up all the threads of its linguistic-metrical totality, this poem articulates a serious attempt by the poet to come to terms with the actualities of contemporary Denmark by accepting the positive as well as the negative experience of daily life, the joy as well as the frustration pervading the Danish scene to which the poet belongs. He rivets his gaze on the realities of his time and place, and he observes a plethora of things to lighten his heart. At the same time, however, he does not allow these pleasures to become a dulling opiate, for he is fully aware of the disillusionment caused by the political chaos of the day, from which there can be no escape. (The sole avenue of escape open to him, the flight to a foreign culture across the seas, proved fruitless, and strengthened his realization that he could only be at home in Denmark.)

As a poet, Møller is certainly a realist. A rigid objectivity of matter and manner serves as his central aesthetic standard throughout this poem. He observes the minutiae of daily life from a detached distance: the composed northern hemisphere from the perspective of life in the torrid heat and squalor of southeast Asia; the enchanting southern hemisphere from the viewpoint of life under the cooling winds of homey Denmark. He concludes that the only attitude realistically appropriate in the given historical situation must be either joyous without overlooking the sorrow of the day or doleful without forgetting the pleasures of the locale.

It would have been unrealistic for him to indulge only in a maudlin lament on the suffering Danish humanity of his day; such an exclusively doleful attitude would have implied an ignorance of the remaining sights of gladness in Denmark. But it would have been equally unrealistic for him to engage in a superficial reverie on the joys of Danish life, flagrantly disregarding the grief choking Denmark. Møller was realistic enough to know that the true state of affairs in Denmark required a calmness of judgment sustaining both tears and laughter.

---

[20] Friedrich Schleiermacher, *Über die Religion*, Philosophische Bibliothek 225 (Hamburg: Meiner, 1961), 166.

How radically these verses of Møller differed from the Romantic tide just then ebbing in Denmark! To comprehend fully the magnitude of the new wave battering against the shores of Danish literature with this novel poem, it would be helpful to backtrack in literary history and return once more to Oehlenschläger, that crusty crusader for everything in Danish literature to which Møller, after his voyage of self-imposed exile, took exception. Any comparison of these two literary opponents establishes Møller's particular achievement more clearly and helps us understand more vividly what stamped his poem peculiarly innovative.

Oehlenschläger had come to power on the Danish Parnassus twenty years earlier with an equally sensational poem: "Af 'Guldhornene'" (The Golden Horns). Like Møller's poem, it too had opened up a new chapter of Danish literary history, successfully liberating Danish literature from the philosophical eggshells of eighteenth-century Rationalism, replacing the latter with a heightened sense of awe and wonder for the most unfathomable pages of ancient Nordic history. With "Af 'Guldhornene'" the pendulum of Danish literature suddenly swung from pensive reflection to wondering empathy, from a philosophical preoccupation with the problems of life to an emotional appeal never to surrender to earthly bonds but to look instead for the light of supernatural splendor. This appeal was centrally anchored in the core of Oehlenschläger's programmatic poem (beginning with verse 100):

> For di sieldne Faae
> Som vor Gave forstaae,
> Som ei Jordlænker binde,
> Men hvis Siele sig hæve
> Til det Eviges Tinde,
> Som ane det Høie
> I Naturens Øie,
> Som tilbedende bæve
> For Guddommens Straaler ... [21]

> (The few who know
> The gift we bestow,
> Who never surrender
> To earthly bond;
> Who scale the splendour
> Of eternity,
> And through Nature see

---

[21] From *The Oxford Book of Scandinavian Verse* (Oxford: Clarendon, 1925), 53.

> The light beyond,
> Who trembling divine
> God's fires that shine ...)
> *Translated by Robert Silliman Hillyer*[22]

Not only does the poet invite us to accompany him on his ecstatic journey but his elevated, winged words carry us along. Nowhere, perhaps, does he better succeed in lifting us to such enchanted realms than in those verses which are repeated twice (verses 46-53 and 126-33) as a sign of choral intent. The incantatory effect of the repetition, the empyreal images of the chorus, and the artificial attempt to reproduce with the chorus the meters of ancient Icelandic heroic poetry (a meter conveying a feeling to which a more modern audience could hardly relate) all conspire magnificently to transport us on some sort of magic carpet to a most incredible land of dream-like wonder. We scarcely believe our ears and eyes when we hear and read:

> Hrymfaxe den sorte
> Puster og dukker,
> Og i Havet sig begraver.
> Morgenens Porte
> Delling oplukker,
> Og Skinfaxe traver
> I straalende Lue
> Paa Himlens Bue.[23]

> (Hrymfaxe the black
> Snorts, and plunges
> Into the tide.
> Delling flings back
> The bolts of dawn.
> The gate swings wide.
> Skinfaxe lunges
> Up from the dark
> On the heavenly arc.)
> *Translated by Robert Silliman Hillyer*[24]

---

[22] From *A Book of Danish Verse*, 18. Reprinted courtesy of the American-Scandinavian Foundation.

[23] From *The Oxford Book of Scandinavian Verse*, 51, 53-54.

[24] From *A Book of Danish Verse*, 16. Reprinted courtesy of the American-Scandinavian Foundation.

Passing from Oehlenschläger's poetry to Møller's we exit a fantastic imaginary carnival and enter the familiar world of the everyday citizen. From the realm of unleashed subjective emotion we step into the sphere of realistic fidelity to observable detail. The lofty poetic quest for the unattainable has yielded to an unabashed affirmation of the everyday world and a poetic representation of real life in both its joy and suffering. From poetic fantasy we move to Poetic Realism.

Møller emancipated Danish literature from Oehlenschläger's artificial bondage, rejecting the mighty and glorious world of the ancient Icelandic *Edda* and substituting for it areas of contemporary experience. To Møller, as we see in comparing his seminal poem with Oehlenschläger's verses, it was a fault to mistake eloquence for poetry. Not exuberance of expression, image, and meter, but the crisp restraint of emotion and a stringent intellectual discipline could produce a poetry truly responsive to the temper of life within Møller's reach.

Yet if in contrast to Oehlenschläger's verses Møller's poem makes the reader feel at one with the actual world, the physical nature of this actual world seems relatively unimportant. Møller's realism is not materialism or naturalism but, rather, something distinctly poetic. What counts is not the actual world, but the poet's response to it. Furthermore, Møller's realism exhibits no inordinate concern for the specific political and social questions of his day, although they certainly defined the challenge to compose poetry differing radically from the sparkling virtuosity of Oehlenschläger's. Primarily the temporal, ultimate values inherent in the political and social world about him interest Møller, and as the example of "Glæde over Danmark" shows, of these he finds most compelling the polarity of joy and sorrow in daily life. This polarity gives Møller's realism its poetic sanction and explains the singular hold the poem had on Kierkegaard and countless others ever since the debut of *Poetisk Realisme*.

Sowing the seed of *Poetisk Realisme*

The ship on which Møller had charted a new course for Danish literature dropped its anchor again in Copenhagen's harbor on July 14, 1821. When Møller disembarked, the greatest challenge of his life awaited him. Would he be able to win over enough converts to the new mode of realism to redraw the map of Danish literature? Much spoke in favor of this ambition. The new political and social climate of Denmark had led to the dethronement of Oehlenschläger and his fanciful consorts from their authoritative positions. Møller had no need to worry, therefore, about too much hefty opposition to his new ideas. The time, after all, was ripe for change. Moreover, in the solitude of reflection during the twenty-one months abroad, Møller had prepared well for the poetic rebellion he wished to incite, and in his pocket now he carried onto Danish soil the lyric manifesto for the new literary movement, "Glæde over Danmark." And not least, Møller was combative by instinct, making his task easier. Still, Romanticism, long firmly ensconced on the Danish Parnassus, resisted instant displacement.

Nevertheless, Møller set about his labor with vehemence and energy, engaging himself all over the Danish metropolis in fierce intellectual gladiatorship, cleaning what he considered the Augean stables of the Romantics. He contested everything in literature that seemed fantastic, exotic, or idealistic and argued instead for a new form of art based on the new reality of the Danish nation as "a little, beggar land." How much his personality had changed in his long absence utterly astonished his friends from former years.[25] His new missionary fervor had transformed him entirely, giving him conviction and purpose that knew no bounds. The formidable arguments he presented in his many contentious speeches, debates, and reviews echoed far and wide. The famous dictum lifted from one of these reviews — "All poetry that does not come from life is a lie"[26] — has been cited over and over; even down to the present, handbooks of Danish literature quote it.

But in face-to-face conversations he commanded his greatest influence. In them the weight of his pioneering spirit was best perceived; in them his polemical and satirical voice reverberated most clearly. As Oluf Friis has said, to these conversations Møller owed the forceful impact he made on Danish letters.[27]

In 1823, less than two years after his return to Denmark, Møller scored his greatest victory: he persuaded the polymathic editor of the popular literary weekly *Tilskuerne*, Knud Lyne Rahbek (1760–1830), to publish "Glæde over Danmark." The publication of *Poetisk Realisme*'s keynote poem in this important periodical brought it naturally to the attention of the widest possible circle of Danish literati who could take inspiration from it to compose in a similar vein. Only if other talented poets included some of the distinguishing qualities of this poem in their own creative writing would the seed of *Poetisk Realisme* sown by Møller come to fruition.

---

[25] Møller, *Efterladte Skrifter*, VI, 82.

[26] Møller, *Efterladte Skrifter*, III, 182; cf. also the commentary in Poul Møller, *Skrifter i udvalg*, ed. Vilh. Andersen, II (Copenhagen: Gad, 1930), 429.

[27] Oluf Friis in *Dansk Litteratur Historie*, III, 23.

Invoking the model of Boccaccio: *En dansk Students Eventyr*

Before the *Poetisk Realisme* of Møller's maiden poem could take root in Danish soil, however, Møller compulsively planted another seed. This time with a novella he helped usher in a new era of Danish literature. In February and March of 1824 he read to a captivated audience in the Student Society of Copenhagen's university from his newly written novella *En dansk Students Eventyr* (The Tale of a Danish Student), a work now acknowledged as his chef d'oeuvre.[28] Though sensational and seminal, this novella remained Møller's unfinished cathedral. He spent years writing and revising it, but before he could crown it with a satisfactory conclusion, the challenge of other commitments overtook him, demanding he put the work aside. He never returned to it, and it remained in its uncompleted manuscript form until published posthumously in 1843. But this novella assuredly had provided stimulus for the spread of *Poetisk Realisme* a decade earlier, when he read it in the academic arena of the Student Society, for we know Møller scored his greatest triumphs in oral engagement.

Of all the characteristics of *En dansk Students Eventyr* contributing to the unique position it holds in the history of Danish literature and the topography of inter-European Poetic Realism, none proved more significant than the form Møller chose for his prose masterpiece: the novella. An ancient Oriental genre, the novella had entered European literature during the Middle Ages. In Italy it attained a towering monument of perfection in Boccaccio's *Il Decamerone* (The Decameron, 1348–1353), later making noteworthy appearances in France in the *Cent nouvelles nouvelles* (One Hundred New Novellas, 1462–1486) and in Marguerite de Navarre's *L'heptameron des nouvelles* (The Heptameron, 1559). Subsequently, it left its particular mark on Spanish literature with Cervantes's *Novelas ejemplares* (Exemplary Novellas, 1613). It experienced an astonishing rebirth in Germany in the late eighteenth century, most conspicuously with Goethe's *Unterhaltungen deutscher Ausgewanderten* (Entertainments of German Emigrés, 1795). Now, in Møller's able hands, the novella made its sensational entry into Danish literature.

In 1805 a Danish translation of *Il Decamerone* appeared in Copenhagen,[29] certainly causing a stir in Danish literary circles, for the Danes had not seen a new translation of Boccaccio's masterpiece in more than two hundred years. Although this was an exceptional literary event, Møller set

---

[28] Mogens Brøndsted og Sven Møller Kristensen, *Danmarks litteratur*, 8th ed. (Copenhagen: Gyldendal, 1982), 136.

[29] *Boccazes Fortællinger. Fra det Italienske. Af Odin Wolff* (Copenhagen: Christensen, 1805).

up a milestone of even greater importance in Danish letters when the quicksilver of this landmark translation stimulated him to adapt Boccaccio's model to a Danish setting and compose *En dansk Students Eventyr*. That marked the end of the age of mythological drama championed so strongly by Oehlenschläger, ushering in a new age of Danish realistic prose.

Møller made the historic decision to invoke Boccaccio's model to replace mythological drama with a genre more congenial to the literary movement he wished to inaugurate. He knew that the lavish stage settings, picturesque tableaus, opulent costumes, glittering lighting effects, and ingenious theatricality of colorful drama so cherished by Oehlenschläger and his Romantic imitators[30] were out of tune with rugged realities. Post-Napoleonic Denmark demanded a more trenchant, a much stricter, and certainly a far less grandiloquent mode of presentation than the one offered in the gilded arena of Copenhagen's Royal Theater. The responsibility of the writer, Møller believed, lay in focusing attention sharply on the crucial problems of everyday reality. That was what Denmark's sad hour of trial and tribulation demanded. The strict prosaic form of the novella curbed the Romantic bent for luxuriant fancy and rambling construction and excluded everything lustrous or superfluous (as opposed to the extravagances of the drama and the long, necessarily episodic format of the novel). For Møller the ideal poetic medium of the moment, it organized itself around a specific concern of everyday living in an extraordinarily concise poetic fashion. Within the smallest imaginable compass, it enjoyed the distinct advantage over both the drama and the novel of concentrating far more succinctly on a particularly relevant problem of contemporary life.

Møller's adaption of Boccaccio's model opened up an ideal vista for the spread of Poetic Realism; the novella form became Poetic Realism's most celebrated vehicle. In the novella Poetic Realism would find its most characteristic stamp and supreme glory. The authors of Poetic Realism would use no other genre so often or so intensely. Despite the gems of lyric poetry and the occasional novels these writers produced, the reception of the oeuvres of most Poetic Realists recognizes them first and foremost as great masters of the novella. Conversely, too, the ancient genre of the novella achieved in Poetic Realism its finest flowering. In Poetic Realism, as the Princeton New Critic Walter Silz (1894–1980) has rightly said,

---

[30] Frederick J. Marker and Lise-Lone Marker, *The Scandinavian Theatre: A Short History* (Oxford: Blackwell & Totowa, N.J.: Rowman & Littlefield, 1975), 102 ff.

the art of novella-writing attained heights it had never known before and has never seen since.[31]

Møller's transfer of Boccaccio's formal pattern to Danish artistic exigencies might not so successfully have heralded in a new age of Poetic Realism had he not used another technical characteristic of Boccaccio's style: the legendary framelike structure of *Il Decamerone*. Its sharply-drawn double optic had reminded audiences again and again through centuries how the twin spheres of art and reality could be reconciled in a single meta-literary act.

In that monument of European novella-writing, several young Florentines take flight from the plague that laid waste to Florence in 1348, finding shelter and safety in a country house where they while away their time entertaining one another with a series of highly amusing stories. After fifteen utopian days together in this marginal state of aestheticism, the group separates, and they all return to Florence, resuming the reality of the workaday worlds from which they earlier disengaged themselves.

Similarly, Møller's novella is articulated in two distinct but closely related framing and framed spheres. We are confronted with the framing world of Møller's contemporary Copenhagen and its environs at the beginning and end of the narrative. In between, a number of ingeniously concocted stories abound in rare buoyancy and humorous satire, imaginatively contrived to represent the arena of sterile fiction divorced from the truer social and political activity of war-torn Copenhagen and its environs.

"On a beautiful afternoon in the month of June a large company of students marched out of the city through Copenhagen's east gate." So opens *En dansk Students Eventyr*.[32] Immediately we find ourselves transported to Copenhagen in the Napoleonic era. When the main building of Copenhagen's university was destroyed in the bombardment of the city in 1807, leaving many of the houses in which the students lived also lying in ruins, Danish authorities suddenly deemed it necessary to release the students from the bonds of the semi-cloistered life that for centuries had re-

---

[31] Walter Silz, "The Achievement of the German Novelle," *Schoolmen's Week Proceedings* 46 (1960): 131-32, 137.

[32] There is no study of this novella in English and only one in German: by Bernd Henningsen in *Poul Martin Møller oder Die dänische Erziehung des Søren Kierkegaard*, 23-37. The Danish analyses of this novella include those by 1) Vilhelm Andersen in his biography *Poul Møller, Hans Liv og Skrifter*, 187-272; 2) Hans Brix in *Analyser og Problemer* 2 (1935): 275-93; 3) Helge Toldberg, "Bemærkninger til En dansk Students Eventyr," *Danske Studier* 44 (1944): 65-77. There is also a good modern introduction to the novella in Brørson Fich's edition of the work (Copenhagen: Gyldendal, 6th ed., 1956), 9-25. Useful though all these studies are, they suffer from not viewing this novella in the tradition established by Boccaccio.

stricted their movement outside the confines of the university. The lifting of the ancient restrictions left the students at liberty to join large segments of the rest of Copenhagen's hapless population in the search for refreshment, solace, and shelter beyond the walls of the ravaged city. Hence, with the opening sentence not only do we know where and approximately when in Denmark's history the story begins, but more importantly we can assume Møller's acute awareness of the sordid events that gave rise to the students' exodus from the city.

From this beginning the subsequent passages of the novella gain their meaning. Like the plague panic of Boccaccio's Florence that prompted the group of young Florentines to establish a temporary mode of communal living outside of the institutionalized life of their city, so, too, the dissolution of traditional social order in Møller's Copenhagen in the Napoleonic era offers the student population the chance to withdraw to a safe distance in the countryside, where time-honored customs and institutions can be ignored and even openly flouted. Quitting the arena of daily living in contemporary Copenhagen, the students voluntarily retreat to an anti-world, lapsing into a seemingly atemporal aesthetic reverie. The author gives us ample opportunity to eavesdrop on the plethora of ludicrous tales with which the members of the group entertain one another in their blissful exile, undisturbed by the pressures of everyday living.

We hear of a mayor beguiled into locking himself up in a cow stall, of a poor farmhand leaving home absurdly convinced he will return someday as a knight in shining armor. We hear, too, what happens to an irresponsible youth participating in a duck-shooting competition with experienced hunters, although he has never before held a rifle; we learn of a mischievous lad's hilarious descent down a chimney one night to catch a glimpse of a nocturnally-clad girl spending the night in his sister's chamber, etc. These anecdotes appear so thoroughly contrived we feel them more a part of the world of comic fiction than of any recognizable reality. Noticeably lacking any unity of continuous action, only the strain of laughter holds them together. The provisional retreat from the city seems depicted only to mock this world outside with satire. Hence, the world of fiction untouched by any considerations of time, place, or environment gives rise to an acute awareness of literature as an aesthetic snare.

At the end of the novella, the main character disengages himself from the trap of this sterile, imaginative act by reentering the world of Napoleonic Denmark introduced in the opening passages. The utopian impulse to escape into the arena of silly laughter connects that escape dialectically with the real world. Although Møller never concluded the final part of his novella, we have enough to realize that the end is colored by a far more optimistic apprehension of contemporary Danish institutions than was the beginning. Napoleonic Denmark is no longer a world from which one flees, but a world to which one willingly returns. Since everything narrated on the final pages points to the fulfillment of natural passion with the prospect of a happy marriage for the novella's hero, the Danish present no longer seems something from which one must escape.

Møller's juxtaposition of a commonplace contemporary Denmark with the poetic satire of an atemporal world of escape serves two purposes. It exposes the folly of fiction divorced from the world of everyday living. (Is Møller obliquely satirizing the distanced dreams of Oehlenschläger's alien Nordic mythology?) In addition, it inspires a vitally renewed faith in the institutions of contemporary reality, for, after laughter and satire have thoroughly exposed the silliness of the detached fictional world, we are convinced that, like the hero, we, too, must turn again to life in the present, equipped with a better understanding of its structures than before.

Danish audiences probably never before felt the lash of satire as sharply as when reading of the ludicrous, contrived world of escape in *En dansk Students Eventyr* nor ever witnessed such a powerful, if subtle, argument for the value of everyday life as that implied by the sturdy frame of this novella. Little wonder that Møller made such an extraordinary impact on his listeners when he read this novella to them, and little wonder, too, that it so greatly helped him in advancing his doctrine of Poetic Realism at that hour. The sting of satire and the dynamic vision of present possibility contained in this Danish adaptation of Boccaccio's famed literary genre contributed immensely to the propagation of the new attitude Møller was preaching. Indeed, with this novella Møller's early training as an evangelist apparently combined effectively with his campaign for a new realism in literature. In *En dansk Students Eventyr* Møller engaged obviously and directly with an artistic form as novel as it was trailblazing in Danish letters. No listener could fail to be profoundly stirred by the message Møller sought to convey. The flood of novellas that followed in the wake of this experiment with Boccaccio's model retroactively confirms the crucial role this novella played in precipitating the remarkable literary reorientation for which Møller had so zealously fought.

Dropping the torch

The torch with which Møller had ignited a new literary movement in Denmark suddenly dropped from his hands when in 1826 Christiana's (Oslo's) university called him to a teaching position in philosophy. He was not well equipped for this professorship; his earlier academic training had been in theology rather than philosophy. As a consequence of this deficiency, he had to spend an inordinate amount of time preparing lectures, trying to obtain the philosophical knowledge he should have acquired beforehand. But the more he strove to close his educational gaps the more he realized, to his chagrin, how large they actually were. His students reported he seemed unsure of himself delivering lectures; no longer did his face light up as it had back in Copenhagen.[33] The prodigious amount of reading he did still was not enough to give him mastery over the subject. He always had to read more.

All of this naturally left him less and less time for his efforts in Poetic Realism. To make matters worse, a whole series of difficult and pressing family matters also began to compete for his time and energy. These new demands of both family and occupation quickly made it obvious that he could no longer remain the leading articulator of the fledgling literary movement. He had to withdraw to the sidelines. (In effect, of course, he had already done so at the very moment he took up residence in Norway, far removed from the Danish literary scene.) Fortunately for his cause, however, other talents appeared on the horizon to pick up the torch he had relinquished. These successors not only carried on where he left off but brought the movement to new heights, spreading it in ever-widening ripples beyond the narrow confines of the little Danish state to other parts of Scandinavia and south of the Danish frontier to the vast German-speaking world.

Møller did not live to see how the seed he sowed came to fruition abroad. He died young in 1838, only forty-three years old. Yet he did live long enough to observe that the blow he dealt Danish Romanticism in the 1820s proved fatal. As W. Glyn Jones aptly says in his highly readable account of modern Danish history, the "escapist aspect of the Romantic age had gradually been replaced in the 1830s by what is known as poetical realism."[34]

3. The second apostle: Steen Steensen Blicher

Of all the Danish writers who tamed the Romantic bragging and baying of Nordic heroism with a new poetic realism, none has been more closely associated with Poul Martin Møller's literary crusade than Steen Steensen Blicher (1782–1848). Indeed, the handbooks of Danish literature almost uniformly treat both authors in conjunction, often in a single sentence, on the same page, or at the very least on two consecutive pages.

---

[33] Henningsen, 61.

[34] W. Glyn Jones, *Denmark, A Modern History* (London: Croon Helm, 1986), 53.

The two names have been linked as much as Corneille and Racine in French classical drama, Goethe and Schiller in German letters, or Tolstoy and Dostoyevsky in Russian prose fiction. In many variations one can read again and again what the noted Cambridge Scandinavianist Elias Bredsdorff once succinctly and simply said: "During the first quarter of the 19th century the early Romantic movement was unchallenged. Then appeared two men who brought a new element of reason and realism into Danish literature. Their names are Poul Møller and Steen Steensen Blicher."[35] The historical story is always the same: not only contemporaries and preachers who had turned to poetry, Møller and Blicher also — and more importantly — together and with equal passion hoped to kill the sense of the all too divine mission of Danish literature that had flowered in the heady days of Denmark's extravagant overseas empire.

It is easy to see why Blicher rushed in to take up the banner that the father of *Poetisk Realisme* let fall. While studying at the University of Copenhagen he eye-witnessed the shelling that leveled one third of the Danish metropolis. He fought hard on the ramparts with the defenders of the city against the army of invaders and saw, too, the defense crumble in the face of overwhelming odds. Following the city's surrender, he was allowed to return to his student lodgings, only to discover them gone, along with all his earthly possessions, casualties of the inferno that destroyed so much of Copenhagen. Badly shaken, he necessarily joined the exodus of hapless multitudes fleeing the capital to seek refuge in the rural parts of the kingdom. Obtaining passage on one of the crowded boats leaving Sjælland, the island on which Copenhagen stands, he sailed to the Jutland peninsula. Upon landing he set out for his father's obscure vicarage in the interior of the land. He had barely arrived there when Napoleon sent an army of Spanish mercenaries into Jutland to launch from there a well-calculated attack on Sweden. Swarms of marauding soldiers marched up and down the Jutland countryside, requisitioning lodgings, confiscating all the food and supplies they could obtain, making life not only oppressive but almost intolerable for a local populace already shackled by the burden of wartime taxation.

Doubtless, the Napoleonic typhoon over Denmark hit Blicher as hard as it had its worst victims. No Dane felt more painfully how Napoleon had reduced the nation to rubble and poverty; no Danish writer understood more clearly the urgency of Møller's call for a new literature that would not turn its back on the disappointments and sorrows pressing hard from all sides.

---

[35] Elias Bredsdorff, Brita Mortensen, Ronald Popperwell, *An Introduction to Scandinavian Literature* (Copenhagen: Munksgaard, 1951), 89.

Møller had been busily preaching his new gospel of *Poetisk Realisme* ever since his return to Denmark in the summer of 1821. His influence as an inspiring friend of new writers grew from month to month, reaching its pinnacle in late 1823 and early 1824 when "Glæde over Danmark" was published and the fame of *En dansk Students Eventyr* began to spread. The new trend of aesthetic protest quickly infected Blicher. Before the year 1824 could advance far, he sustained the enterprise Møller had conceived, producing another distinguished novella of *Poetisk Realisme*.

En Landsbydegns Dagbog

The new novella's title was *En Landsbydegns Dagbog* (The Diary of a Parish Clerk). Many additional novellas by Blicher followed his debut in the arena of *Poetisk Realisme*, but none were more widely read, more often translated, or more unreservedly acclaimed than this first masterpiece. One of the reasons for its wide acclaim is its extraordinary appeal to realistic candor. No less than Møller, Blicher in this novella seems fanatically bent on a complete break with the literary Romanticism of Denmark's yesteryear. Even the place he chose to publish gives an air of revolutionary defiance to the novella, initially printed neither under the aegis of a reputable literary publishing house in the capital city Copenhagen, nor in any elitist literary journal noted and esteemed for the publication of belles lettres. Instead, Blicher chose an obscure provincial magazine, the *Læsefrugter* (Fruits of Reading), of the Aarhus bookseller Adolph Frederik Elmquist (1788-1868) — a forum where essays of literary merit were interspersed with all sorts of articles addressed to economic and political issues. Conspicuous among these, significantly, were popular articles telling about the tyranny of Napoleon.[36] Blicher's novella meant, therefore, to appeal to readers who took an avid interest in the plight of Denmark at the hands of the epoch's despot. Blicher could have thought of no more ostentatious display of his and Møller's belief that Danish literature had to connect intimately with the pressing political and economic problems facing the Danish populace in the wake of the French dictator.

If the place Blicher chose to publish his inaugural novella seemed as startling as it was revealing for the new anti-Romantic trend in Danish letters, then the setting in the novella itself suggested an even greater break with the irrelevant sallies of earlier Danish literature. The action happens almost exclusively on the peninsula of Jutland, in the most back-

---

[36] The novella was printed in vol. 23, pp. 145-87, of Elmquist's *Læsefrugter*. In the same year (1824) this magazine published five different articles addressed to the tyranny of Napoleon. This has escaped the attention of Blicher critics.

ward region of the Danish nation, far removed from the idyllic embellishments of Copenhagen's high society. In Jutland poverty had always stalked the countryside: the murky landscape contained little more than gale-swept stretches of open heath or other desolate spaces that hardly seemed habitable except to gypsies, tramps, and the poorest of peasants. Country squires owned scattered tracts of barely productive land and generally contributed to the region's further misery by being more often bankrupt than solvent. A widespread chronic alcoholism amongst the population also brought its share of hardship and grief to the area. In short, the Jutland peninsula was the obverse side of the civilization surrounding the court life in the kingdom's capital city — a world totally bereft of any of the illusions of national grandeur lingering amongst those still living in the palatial residences of Copenhagen's upper-class elegance.

This gloomy and unattractive Jutland peninsula had never, in Danish literary history, claimed any artistic attention. The Danish countryside beyond Copenhagen had hardly ever existed on the literary map of Denmark. All intellectual life took place within the protective embankments of the royal capital. But the Jutland moors were considered even a further step removed from the countryside beyond Copenhagen; indeed, the characters flitting across the sandy soil of Jutland's forlorn peninsula were thought to live outside the borderline of ordered society.

Blicher set his novella in this depressed and depressing area of the nation. Nothing could have been more sensational, nothing could have seemed more revolutionary to the traditionally inclined literary hierarchy of Denmark's capital city. Yet nothing could have been more consistent with Møller's demand that literature face up to the truth of the dismal new age than this appeal to rural poverty and the depressive tragedy of the most impoverished segment of Denmark's citizenry, with its corresponding repudiation of both upper-class elitism and the glamour of Nordic heroes. Like Møller, Blicher wanted to be a realist, not a writer who idolized his characters and literary landscapes. Being a realist meant striking the note of sorrow and resignation so widespread in a Denmark that had suffered the calamity of defeat and humiliation at the hands of Napoleon. What could have better preached the realistic gospel of Danish disillusionment than calling attention to life in the most doleful part of the country? In Jutland there were few delights to enjoy. A peaceful haven of escape would have been difficult to find. Little glamour was perceptible — certainly nothing worth poeticizing about in elevated rhetoric.

Moreover, to assure no reader would ever find in this appeal to rural obscurity any comfort away from the sorrows of daily life, Blicher sedulously avoids giving any stroke of pastoral charm to his landscape. The novella begins with a horrible winter scene. A snowstorm rages furiously, and the narrator's father is discovered frozen stiff in a snowdrift. In the spring all references to colorful blossoms are noticeably absent. In the descriptions of summer even the reader acquainted with the doleful monotony of Jutland will find it strange that Blicher makes no mention of the stately poplar trees or the graceful windmills dotting the landscape. Neither is there any mention of the vegetation of wild plants, the merry trills of skylarks, the changing light, blue horizon and soft clouds drifting across the countryside, or the apricot twilight of the long northern summer days. In autumn the bright purple and rose colors of heather in bloom are nowhere to be seen. Neither can the laughter of the children on the farms or the happy songs of the gypsy population be heard. In vain the reader of *En Landsbydegns Dagbog* looks for any scene of country bliss at which to take pleasure in lingering, if only for the shortest of time.[37] Particularly strange, especially in a work written by a clergyman and in which the narrator assumes the persona of a parish clerk, a church deacon, the novella contains no stabilizing influence such as that reflected in the depiction of ageless village churches dominating Jutland's landscape. Indeed, the picturesque white towers of the numerous Danish Lutheran churches, so typical of Jutland's countryside, are conspicuously missing from Blicher's fictional canvas. What remains in *En Landsbydegns Dagbog*, from the beginning to the end, are only the grey and somber shades of human life, serving as eerie reminders of the tombstones of civilization.

Perhaps more indicative of Blicher's intent to attune us to life's dismal aspects is his use of historical dates. The action of the novella occurs between 1708 and 1753, in Denmark's pre-Napoleonic "golden age," a time

---

[37] It is unfortunate for German students of Poetic Realism that the most comprehensive book in German about Blicher distorts the meaning of his fictional portraits of the Jutland landscape by viewing them as designed to convey to the reader a sense of rustic beauty: "Gleich groß in der Menschen- wie in der Naturschilderung führt Blicher seinem Volk darin in ähnlicher Weise Jütlands herbe Reize vor Augen wie Chr. Winther dies mit Seelands Schönheiten getan hat." Paul Elsner, *Steen Steensen Blicher, Der Heidedichter und Heidepfarrer, Ein Lebensbild* (Copenhagen: Lehmann & Stage, 1917), 52. Nothing could be further from the truth than this statement by Elsner. German students of Poetic Realism badly need a more modern, less idealized biography of Blicher. English-speaking readers are more fortunate, for they have easy access to the splendid introduction to Blicher provided by Sigrid Undset in *Twelve Stories* by Steen Steensen Blicher, trans. Hanna Astrup Larsen (Princeton: University Press, 1945). After reading Undset's essay, we know that Blicher's landscape painting was meant to be sordid, rather than blissful; monotonous, rather than charming. But if Undset's essay constitutes a more accurate introduction to Blicher than Elsner's biography, a *comprehensive* modern study of Blicher in English remains nevertheless as much a desideratum of scholarship as does a new biography of him in German. The most solid source of information on Blicher is, of course, in Danish: Johs. Nørvig, *Steen Steensen Blicher, Hans Liv og Værker* (Copenhagen: Munksgaard, 1943).

when the Danish nation enjoyed peace and unprecedented prosperity, when conditions were notably better than those of Blicher's own time. The reader of this novella can draw, however, no inspiration from that historically ideal time, for Blicher sedulously avoids giving any glimpse of the opulence of that age. Instead, he goes out of his way to acquaint us with the sordid occurrences of an apparently ideal society. For instance, at the manor house — the place in the novella where we tarry longest — we get no opportunity to admire any of the ornate furnishings which normally decorate such a mansion. We see none of the rich tapestries or gilt-framed portraits of noble ancestors which usually adorn the high walls of such squirearchal residences. Neither does the reader catch sight of any of the family heirlooms or objets d'art on which members of the Danish gentry in the eighteenth century prided themselves. Passing over the items which would normally impress any visitor to such a manor house, the narrator concentrates instead on the moral corruption of the inhabitants living inside this imposing edifice. As Denmark's greatest literary critic, Georg Brandes (1842–1927), once astutely observed, most of the characters portrayed here are "absolutely repellant."[38] The insight into the seemingly ideal society of 1708–1753 is, therefore, not only as shattering as any picture Blicher could offer us of his own desolate age half a century later, but even more so, for it concerns a period in history supposed to have given cause for pleasure, not abhorrence.

Following the example of Møller, Blicher chose the genre of the novella to present a gloomy but accurate reflection of the despair of a nation convulsing in the wake of a calamitous flirtation with Napoleon. Like Møller, the second apostle of *Poetisk Realisme* needed this stringent vehicle of prosaic expression to rivet attention all the more acutely on the plight of everyday life. He discarded, however, the framed structure of the genre which Møller had adapted from Boccaccio and replaced it with a new form of the novella resembling a diary. The story unfolds within the garb of a quotidian record. Such a *journal-intime* of an actual life was a far cry from the impersonal flights of the imagination to the aureate mythological kingdoms so cherished by Oehlenschläger and his consorts. Instead of escaping from real time, as with Oehlenschläger, we become, with Blicher's diurnal novella, trapped within the well-marked chronology of the calendar, which only underscores the realistic candor called for by Møller. Yet such a diary is also private, confiding the innermost thoughts of the writer, usually only intended for the eyes of its author. It gives another reader a peculiar feeling of intimacy with the daily life therein described.

---

[38] Georg Brandes, *Creative Spirits of the Nineteenth Century* (New York: Crowell, 1923), 88.

The reader, eavesdropping on the guarded secrets of Blicher's diarist, associates more intensely with the reality of everyday existence than with Møller's novella.

But what are the earmarks of the reality that Blicher's diarist confides so intimately to us? Most noticeable is its diurnal presentation: the calendar dates of the frequent entries assume altogether amazing prominence. Indeed, the intricate web of references to calendar time makes the individual characters and, especially, the action of the story pale by comparison. As the sharp-eyed critic Georg Brandes once noticed, "the action is of but little moment."[39] The reader must look hard to discover the story, which, of course, is not only present but also far from uninteresting, since it revolves around sensual inclination, unrequited love, carnal adventure, seduction, and even a triangular affair in which problems become compounded when two of the characters mistakenly — à la Boccaccio — find themselves in bed with an unexpected lover. Yet, even though the narrator pretends to give us glimpses of individuals whose hearts beat and, more often, seem to bleed from trying circumstances, the principal character of this novella is actually none of these living figures, but rather *time*. Felix Nørgaard, the president of the Blicher Society, has pointed this out clearly and emphatically.[40] Time puts in its appearance as early as the first diary entry, "den 1ste Jannuar 1708," at the top of the opening page. And time intrudes again and again with the mention of every further diary entry on the succeeding pages, often as frequently as two or three times on every page. There are no fewer than sixty-four dated entries in this brief diary! At the end, time appears perhaps in its most obtrusive form: the reader senses that time has crushed all the dreams and aspirations of a lifetime, so much so that one must sadly say, on looking back at a life ex-

---

[39] Ibid.

[40] Felix Nørgaard in the preface to Steen Steensen Blicher, *Diary of a Parish Clerk*, trans. A. Fenton (Herning: Kristensen, 1976), 7. Despite the brevity of Nørgaard's introduction, his observations (as well as the brief commentary by Brandes) are more illuminating than what has been written in the secondary literature on this novella. The most extensive interpretations are by 1) Hans Brix, *Blicher Studier*, 2nd ed. (Copenhagen: Gyldendal, 1967), 9-30; and 2) Søren Baggesen, *Den blicherske novelle*, 2nd ed. (Copenhagen: Gyldendal, 1967), 254-71. The first of these is a reprint of an analysis originally published in 1916. One of the strengths of Baggesen's study is its attempt to relate Blicher's novella to both Boccaccio (14-20) and the German novella of the nineteenth century (21-40). Oddly, however, Baggesen makes no mention of Blicher's immediate Danish predecessor, Poul Martin Møller. As a result, the reader gathers the wrong impression that Blicher (not Møller) was the first to adapt Boccaccio's model to a Danish setting. A gold mine of background material and statistical data has been provided by Peter Brask, *Om En Landsbydegns Dagbog*, 2 vols. (Copenhagen: Gyldendal, 1983).

tended over many decades: "Alas, how changed" (the title of another of Blicher's novellas).

Only forty-two years old, Blicher wrote this novella in such a way that it reads like a story of an old man weeping over the missed opportunities of a life now approaching its appointed end. The selectivity of the diary form and the compressed form of the novella genre give the narrator the freedom to omit, it seems, the joys of life to dwell more heavily on its frustrations and, in particular, on the chilliest frustration of all: death, that sure and certain product, we are constantly reminded, of the reality of time. Again and again there are jumps in time: intervals in the narrator's lifespan about which we learn nothing except that forces shaping his fate are slowly and covertly at work. These jumps in time assimilate death within life. Time asserts itself as a dimension of transience, heading whatever joys life may hold toward destruction. It is from this perspective that all errands in the novella are surveyed, bound as they are to a diarist-narrator who has been through it all.

The narrator mentions death in the diary's opening entries as well as in the closing ones, and throughout the rest of the diary all sorts of references to death's uncanny imminence abound. He tells us about nine human deaths and a large number of animal deaths, some described in seemingly excessive morbid detail. He is also obsessed with his own impending death, perhaps nowhere more so than in the final entry, when we realize his final moment is drawing near. After we close the book, the chilling sting of death, like a harrowing echo, tarries long in our emotions.

In completing this novella, Blicher carried to fulfillment, for the first time in Danish literary history, the genre which Møller with his unfinished novella had established on Danish soil. By endowing it with a diurnal form foregrounding the crushing effects of passing time on human life, he also transformed this genre into a document that proved anything but a peaceful haven for personal meditation. Indeed, it would be hard to imagine a writer of fiction preaching a gospel to the Danish readership of the post-Napoleonic age as honestly, effectively, and convincingly as the one now offered by the clergyman-poet Blicher.

Immediately before this novella appeared, some serious-minded Danes perhaps still had a certain reluctance to face up to the truth of the nation's new dismal reality. Maybe they deceived themselves into thinking conditions were not as bad as they seemed, or perhaps they duped themselves into thinking prosperity was just around the corner. Perhaps they preferred to take solace in nostalgic dreams of a better yesteryear. Whatever the case, such modes of thinking now lost their viability in the light of the "gospel of disillusion and disappointment"[41] that Blicher was preaching. No less a thinker than Søren Kierkegaard has referred to this second apostle of Poetic Realism (in a pointed allusion to the biblical John the Baptist) as "the voice of one crying out in the wilderness."[42] No stronger voice than Blicher's could have been found to awaken Danish sensibilities to the fact there could be neither a turning away nor any escape from the somber truth facing the Danish populace at the time. If Blicher's funereal novella more forcefully awakened a new Danish consciousness of reality than did the satirical novella of Møller, it was not only because Møller had already well prepared the ground for Blicher's message (whereas nobody made ready the path for Møller), but because the chilling diurnal novella Blicher held up to the Danes with *En Landsbydegns Dagbog* turned a private grief into a profound meditation every reader could intimately share. Human transience and death were grim emotional realities every reader could identify with, sad truths of life comprehended not only by those with a sense of the actualities of the present but also by those willingly or unwillingly remaining indifferent to the political and economic malaise of the day.

As a result, the novella struck its readers with equal force everywhere in Denmark. It stirred the emotions of Jutland's despairing peasantry, for whom the story was intended and for whom Blicher later produced a whole series of further compelling novellas published in Elmquist's *Læsefrugter*. But it made no less an impact on readers in Copenhagen's snobbish society. The novella was on the lips of so many citizens of the nation's capital in such a short time that an enterprising publishing house in Copenhagen's Pilestræde, the C. Steens Forlag, quickly saw the opportunity to capitalize on its popularity by circulating an invitation to subscribe to a book edition.[43]

The line forward to Theodor Storm

More astonishingly, the work also travelled with unusual speed across Denmark's language frontier to the northern outposts of German-speaking Europe. A publisher in Lübeck in northern Germany commis-

[41] Bredsdorff et al., 92.

[42] *Søren Kierkegaards Samlede Værker*, ed. A. B. Drachmann et al., 2nd ed., XXX (Copenhagen: Gyldendal, 1930), 765. See also, because of the splendid commentary, the modern German translation: Søren Kierkegaard, *Gesammelte Werke*, trans. Emanuel Hirsch, XXX (Düsseldorf/Cologne: Diederich, 1960), 54.

[43] *Blicher Bibliografi*, udarbejdet af Jørgen Kaj Bertelsen (Copenhagen: Hassing, 1933), 12.

sioned a translation almost immediately after the initial Danish publication, appearing in 1827.[44] In 1829 it was reprinted by another German publisher, in Hamburg, reaching an even larger German audience.[45] This publication, too, must have quickly found many readers, for the same publisher in Hamburg hurried to reprint the novella again in 1833.[46]

When the German translation first appeared in Lübeck, doubtless it was as much talked about there as in Denmark. What affected Denmark also affected this port city at the southeastern tip of the Jutland peninsula, with its strong commercial ties to the island nation in such close geographic proximity. And Lübeck, too, had become a cultural and intellectual center of northern Germany with a renowned university preparatory academy, the *Katharineum*, and several literary salons where the latest trends in literature were heatedly debated. Discussions and reading of this novella, it must be assumed, had a particular impact on the future German Poetic Realist Theodor Storm, who, only seven years after the publication of the German translation in Lübeck, joined the *Katharineum* as a pupil and quickly became an intimate friend of the important participants of the city's literary colloquia. No doubt because of such an introduction to Blicher's novella at Lübeck, Storm's own art of novella-writing came to have a closer resemblance to Blicher's story of transience and death than to the stories of any other writer of Poetic Realism.

Curiously, but perhaps not surprisingly, the striking similarity between Storm and Blicher has been noticed by only a few critics: Kierkegaard's German translator, Emanuel Hirsch; the circumspect critic of Danish literature at the University of Heidelberg, Victor A. Schmitz; the Storm biographer Franz Stuckert; and the British Germanist Roger Paulin, who rightly insists that we must now begin to read German nineteenth-century prose fiction in its European context.[47] Other critics, the individual special-

---

[44] *Bruchstücke aus dem Tagebuche eines Dorfküsters, aufgefunden, durchgesehen und herausgegeben von S. S. Blicher*, trans. L. Kruse, in *Hemera, Taschenbuch auf das Jahr 1827*, ed. Heinrich Asmus, I (Lübeck: Schmidt, 1827), 5-104.

[45] *Das Wiedersehen, Bruchstücke aus dem Tagebuche eines Küsters, Die Prinzessin mit den Rosen und die Kunstreiter-Familie*, trans. L. Kruse (Hamburg: Herold, 1829), 41-100.

[46] In L. Kruse's *Ausländische Romane und Erzählungen*, VI (Hamburg: Herold, 1833), 41-100.

[47] See Hirsch's commentary in Søren Kierkegaard, *Gesammelte Werke*, XXX, 181. See also Schmitz's references in 1) *Dänische Dichter in ihrer Begegnung mit deutscher Klassik und Romantik* (Frankfurt am Main: Klostermann, 1974), 142, and in 2) *Dänische und norwegische Dichtungen* (Heidelberg: Kerle, 1949), 78. Referring to Blicher's *En Landsbydegns Dagbog*, Schmitz, in the last-mentioned book, 78, says: "In einer uns an Theodor Storm erinnernden Tagebuchchronik werden darin Vorgänge gespiegelt, in denen das Ewig-Menschliche sich im Gewand einer vergänglichen Zeit verbirgt...." Franz Stuckert

ists on Blicher or on Storm, except for Stuckert, have not found time to look across the narrow language frontier that separates these two Poetic Realists, born only approximately 120 miles from one another on the same heather-covered flatlands of the Jutland peninsula. Despite the neglect, however, no reader, having read, for instance, both Blicher's *En Landsbydegns Dagbog* and Storm's *Zur Chronik von Grieshuus* (A Chapter in the History of Grieshuus), could miss the thematic congruence of the two novellas. The chilling dirge on time and death lingering in our emotions after we finish reading Blicher's tale flares up again and haunts us anew when we turn to Storm's novellas, in particular to *Zur Chronik von Grieshuus*. It seems as if Blicher's harrowing ending to *En Landsbydegns Dagbog* were being recreated when the poet Storm, at the conclusion of *Zur Chronik von Grieshuus*, cries out:

> Auf Erden stehet nichts, es muß vorüberfliegen;
> Es kommt der Tod daher, du kannst ihn nicht besiegen;
> Ein Weilchen weiß vielleicht noch wer, was du gewesen;
> Dann wird das weggekehrt, und weiter fegt der Besen.[48]

> (Nothing lasts on earth, for all is fleeting;
> Death comes to all, of that there's no defeating;
> A while perhaps but one knows what you have been;
> Then that is cleared away. Time's brush sweeps clean.)
>   *Translated by Lewis Jillings*

We shall return to Storm and his debt to Danish *Poetisk Realisme*, but there is more to say still about the dawn of the literary movement in Denmark.

---

in his biography *Theodor Storm, Sein Leben und seine Welt* (Bremen: Schünemann, 1955), 447, is apparently the only Storm critic to have noticed the connection: "Die Erzählung 'Aus dem Tagebuch eines Dorfküsters' ... mutet den Stormleser völlig vertraut an." The most recent, and most powerful, plea to start reading Storm from the vantage point of Blicher's prose fiction comes from the pen of one of the most eminent British Germanists of our time, Roger Paulin: "There is no reason to suppose," Paulin shrewdly observes, "that Storm's attitude to Denmark excluded his knowledge of one of its great prose writers." R. Paulin, *The Brief Compass, The Nineteenth-Century German Novelle* (Oxford: Clarendon, 1985), 118.

[48] Theodor Storm, *Sämtliche Werke*, eds. K. E. Laage & D. Lohmeier, III (Frankfurt am Main: Deutscher Klassiker Verlag, 1988), 293.

4. The golden touch: Thomasine Gyllembourg

A German critic at the beginning of this century remarked that Blicher had found his most immediate Danish successor in the Countess Gyllembourg-Ehrensvärd (1773–1856),[49] commonly known as Thomasine Gyllembourg or (most frequently) simply Fru Gyllembourg, Denmark's most famous female author. In Danish literary history her name has come to be as closely associated with Blicher's as his with Møller's. Mentioning the fictional accomplishments of Blicher and Fru Gyllembourg on the same page in a history of literature[50] seems as natural as referring in one breath to Blicher and Møller as the twin fathers of *Poetisk Realisme*. Other critics have linked her more closely to Møller than to Blicher. Indeed, the claim has even been made that Møller may have actually written the novellas we ascribe to her.[51]

Yet no matter how closely her literary legacy may be related to either Blicher or Møller, no matter how much she continued their strains of fiction, we cannot miss the independent, golden touch she bestowed upon the Danish novella of Poetic Realism. She brought to flower most profusely the genre begun by Møller and then firmly established with Blicher's first completed masterpiece. Kierkegaard clearly recognized this. He praised Møller lavishly and found equally generous words for Blicher, but he reserved the highest laurels of all for the novellas of Fru Gyllembourg.[52]

Taking up her pen to compose the first of her many renowned works of Poetic Realism at fifty-four years old, she brought to the craft of fiction a wealth of experience only a few writers could boast of. She had grown up in the pre-Napoleonic imperialistic epoch of Danish literature. At seventeen she had married Peter Andreas Heiberg (1758–1841), a prominent writer of comic fiction. Through him she had come into contact with all the important men of Danish letters in the age of the powdered wig and three-cornered hat. Oehlenschläger, in particular, had frequently visited her hospitable home in Copenhagen's fashionable Bredgade. Later, she experienced, as painfully as anyone, the nightmare that rocked the royal capital as a result of Denmark's disastrous flirtation with Napoleon. She learned what it meant to live under oppressive economic conditions when

---

[49] Heinrich von Lenk in his introduction to Thomasine Gyllembourg, *Eine Alltagsgeschichte* (Leipzig: Reclam, 1901), 4.

[50] Perhaps most strikingly visible in Traustedt's new *Dansk Litteratur Historie*, III, 145.

[51] Henning Fenger, *Kierkegaard, The Myths and their Origins,* Studies in the Kierkegaardian Papers and Letters, trans. G. C. Schoolfield (New Haven & London: Yale University Press, 1980), 3-4.

[52] Fenger, 88, 129.

the wealth, wit, superfluity, elegance, and refinement she once had known could no longer be taken for granted. This chilling experience, no less than her divorce and a dubious remarriage, had severely tried her strength. Subsequently, in 1822, she accompanied her son, the illustrious critic Johan Ludvig Heiberg (1791–1860), on a mission to the German-speaking parts of the kingdom, aiming to foster there, at royal request, a patriotic interest in the literature of gods and heroes, in which the formerly glorious empire of Denmark had basked, but which she, as a result of her recent anguishing experiences, found difficult to defend. All these things combined to awaken in her a sensibility for the new form of literature Møller was preaching. Returning to Copenhagen in 1825, she soon became an avid disciple of Møller, and the two embraced a bond of lasting literary kinship. If, in the happier days of the Danish world empire, it was Oehlenschläger who seemed to have been the most welcome guest in Fru Gyllembourg's home, now Poul Martin Møller, when he was in Copenhagen, regularly occupied the prominent place at her dinner table.

Encouraged, or even prodded by Møller, she decided to follow in his and Blicher's footsteps by fictionally presenting, with the form of the novella, the plight of everyday existence, as she perceived it. Blicher had achieved his success in the new novella of Poetic Realism by rejecting the cultured setting of royal Copenhagen in favor of the provincial wilds of Jutland; in contrast, Fru Gyllembourg transported her novellas back to the Paris of the North and into the mainstream of Danish society. Blicher had thought he could more movingly portray the crippled actuality of the present by taking fiction to the back roads of Danish life on the desolate moors of Jutland, where contemporary Danish poverty and despair could be seen at its worst. He made his point, however, at the cost of removing fiction from the hub of Danish intellectual activity in Copenhagen and by becoming a regional writer. Fru Gyllembourg, by rooting her novellas in the actuality of Copenhagen, returned fiction again to the center of all Danish activity. Yet since far less despair was on parade in the royal capital than in the wasteland of Jutland, her novellas turned out somewhat less bleak than Blicher's. Her characters were not the poorest of the poor in the nation but, rather, those of the middle classes, who comprised the bulk of Copenhagen's citizenry. These, primarily, were men and women torn between, on the one hand, the Romantic yearnings for the grandeur of yesteryear — still lingering in the furnishings of their homes and in their memories — and, on the other hand, a concern for the new economic and political urgencies of the war-shattered contemporary scene. As with so many of the members of Copenhagen's civilized society, her vigorous appetite for experiencing life to its fullest had given her a taste for both lifestyles. She had been elated by Oehlenschläger, and she had been sobered by Møller. She had enjoyed the fruits of a marriage to a comic artist and, after she remarried, she knew the advantages of being wedded to a man rooted in the politico-economic world. She had felt the pleasures of a Romantic gaze to the heavens, and she had learned the usefulness of keeping one's eyes on earthly events. Most importantly, she learned what it was like to be caught in the schism of two disparate worlds. While married to the writer of comic fiction, she carried on a relationship with a man of practical affairs; and later, after divorcing the artist to find more comfort in a union with a man of fewer lofty ideals, she sought to escape the tedium of this more down-to-earth life by renewing again, in the form of an uplifting spiritual correspondence, the relationship with her former artist-husband. But which marriage was her real one? Which the artificial one? It seemed her misfortune never to find out in the world of reality. Only in the realism of fiction did she succeed in comprehending.

Similarly, which life in Copenhagen became the truer one for her: the rich life of the literary salon in her cultured home where the hallmarks of good literature could be discussed in plush isolation from the problems of a nation choking in bankruptcy, or the life she encountered on Copenhagen's public thoroughfares, where the nation's chronic shortage of money seemed to make the pleasures of the arts an irresponsible luxury? The dilemma between illusion and truth was, she saw, the most fundamental predicament in the world around her. And nowhere to her did this dramatic tension strike more acutely than in human love, where the heart beats loudest. She filled her fiction with stories of real and imagined love. In these fictional portraits of couples falling in love, becoming engaged, and marrying, in the happy as well as unhappy unions of the rightly and wrongly matched partners, Fru Gyllembourg unfolds one of the quintessential problems of human destiny.

Searching for a theory of the novella

Before we turn to Fru Gyllembourg's art of novella-writing, we note another way she advanced the novella of *Poetisk Realisme:* searching for a new theory of the novella. Møller, despite his pioneering initiative in introducing this genre to Danish literature, had imitated Boccaccio too slavishly to have added anything new to the genre's theory. Blicher, however successful a novella-writer, had shunned theory: his novellas were the products of his unsophisticated natural gifts, of "a deep, poetic mood, veiled in the mists of spontaneity," as Kierkegaard informs us.[53] Fru

---

[53] Fenger, 129.

Gyllembourg, in contrast, worked with a clear and new idea of the novella genre. One of her distinct contributions to *Poetisk Realisme* was the specific theory of the novella she developed, from which her practice of that theory cannot be separated.

Fru Gyllembourg did not present, however, her theoretical reflections in an organized treatise or set of treatises, from which we can easily cull the essentials of her theory. She left only a number of scattered references indicating she had developed such a theory.

Her search for, and development of, this theory resulted from the remarkable literary relationship she enjoyed with her ingenious son, Johan Ludvig Heiberg. It is fascinating to learn how the time, place, and circumstance of this mother-son collaboration combined to reveal how she arrived at a theory of the novella of Poetic Realism.

Its beginnings were in April 1825. Heiberg had just returned to Copenhagen from Kiel in the duchy of Holstein. The royal favor he had gained championing Danish culture in the German-speaking parts of the monarchy quickly got him the Court backing so essential for assuming leadership on the Danish Parnassus. Someone had to fill the vacancy left by the discredited Oehlenschläger, and Heiberg, with his enviable Court connections, had no trouble filling Oehlenschläger's vacated seat at the center of Danish cultural life. Royal patronage, important as it was in Denmark at the time, was not Heiberg's sole advantage toward securing such a prominent position. He also had an unusually acute mind, immeasurably sharpened by personal contact in Berlin with Hegel, doubtless the greatest European thinker of the day. Moreover, by teaching at the University of Kiel he had also learned to explain his ideas about literature, and Danish literature in particular, cogently and persuasively. Perhaps his greatest asset, however, was his brilliant, eminently sensible, and enormously sociable mother; in their fashionable Copenhagen home, the charming hostess and he entertained the Danish intellectual elite. For six crucial years, from 1825 until his marriage in 1831, mother and son were the central figures of Copenhagen's cultural life. Rarely has literature owed so much to a relationship between mother and son. Her role in Danish literature is scarcely conceivable without him, and his is hardly imaginable without her.

What is of most interest to us at this point are the clues to the theory of the novella that developed out of this unique literary collaboration. When Heiberg assumed his position of leadership on the Danish Parnassus in 1825, succeeding Oehlenschläger, he had, of course, to turn his attention first to the Royal Theater. Long the main cultural showplace of the nation, Oehlenschläger had achieved his triumphs there, and it was there that he had convincingly reminded the Court and the public of the nation's historical grandeur. Clearly, then, that institution was particularly close to the king's heart. With Oehlenschläger's fall from grace, the Royal Theater ran aground. The heroic tragedies that had filled the national theater night after night during the heyday of the glorious Danish empire now, in Denmark's age of despair, proved uninspiring. The meager revenue from tickets to the now almost empty Royal Theater hardly sufficed for the building's essential repairs. Heiberg, as the new moderator of Danish culture, knew he had to do something. To retain royal patronage, he would have to attract audiences again to the Royal Theater. He acted quickly and deftly. Before 1825 drew to a close, he launched his offensive with the birth of a new comic theater. For the heroic tragedy of Oehlenschläger he substituted a form of hilarious comedy, breathing new life into the royal stage, filling once more the coffers of the box office, to the undisguised delight of its most important patron, King Frederick VI. Of course, Heiberg had almost immediately to defend the Royal Theater's comic renaissance against the grumblings of the more conservative and serious-minded members of Copenhagen's intellectual elite. In this defense he developed an aesthetic program: he outlined, defined, and justified a plethora of genres, including, most especially, the various forms of comedy. To make his theories better known, properly understood, and widely accepted, he organized a school of criticism that met regularly in his home. He routinely invited all the important arbiters of taste in literature living in Copenhagen. Fru Gyllembourg, always the unwavering ally of her idolized son, took an integral and essential part in these gatherings. In many ways she was even the school's mainstay. With her great practical knowledge she provided the sense of balance, the amendment, and the refinement necessary to keep the group together and insure that others would continue to listen to her son as an authority. When he, because of his administrative affiliation with the Royal Theater, overemphasized drama and comedy in the hierarchy of literature, she invariably stepped in to make certain that non-dramatic forms were not sidelined. Above all, she successfully championed the novella. The more her son propagated, defended, and defined dramatic genres, the more she, for balance, called attention to the virtues of the epic. And if her son placed comedy at the apex of his theory of drama, she, influenced by her good friend Poul Martin Møller, gave the novella the towering role on the epic side. Thus, comic theater and the novella became the two genres most discussed in the so-called Heiberg school of criticism. True to the dialectics Heiberg had learned from Hegel, he prodded his mother to offer a harmonious opposition to his new theory of comedy — a theory of the rival genre, the novella.

She scattered her pronouncements throughout the large body of critical commentary in the periodical Heiberg edited from 1827 to 1830 with her assistance, *Kjøbenhavns flyvende Post* (Copenhagen's Flying Mail), and in the prefaces to her many novellas published under her son's aegis. Also, much of her thought on the novella appears in various parts of her "literary testament," published posthumously on several occasions.[54]

This wide dispersal of Fru Gyllembourg's ideas has prevented scholars of the novella from taking sufficient note of her attempt to postulate a theory. Indeed, in the many historical accounts of this genre published in the English- and German-speaking worlds, Fru Gyllembourg's search for a theory of the novella has never once been mentioned, regrettably yet understandably. But Fru Gyllembourg's historic contribution to the theory of this genre should remain unknown no longer, for Elisabeth Hude has made an exhaustive exposition of it in a lengthy monograph (available, alas, only in Danish).[55] (A brief summary by the Danish critic Henning Fenger has been translated into English by Frederick J. Marker.)[56]

In the following we shall rely, to a great extent, on the account of Elisabeth Hude. She clarifies the key feature of Fru Gyllembourg's theory: the demand that this genre be pregnant with characteristics of drama — in Danish literary history, an entirely new claim, one Møller, in imitating Boccaccio, had not known, and one Blicher, the theoretically disinclined writer from Denmark's back roads, never considered. Fru Gyllembourg's demand, however, resulted most naturally from her wish to elevate the novella in the esteem of her drama-loving son as well as the patrons of drama who flocked around him, much to the delight of his mother. Wishing to widen her son's following and to elevate the novella, she insisted on that genre's inherent kinship with drama. Like the drama, she pointed out, the dramatically inclined novella is filled with powerfully charged action,[57] "the strong effects" of this action,[58] in her opinion, "altogether analogous to the crass effects of plays."[59] The novella is capable of

---

[54] The latest is *Fru Gyllembourgs litterære Testamente* (Copenhagen: Reitzel, 1884).

[55] Elisabeth Hude, *Thomasine Gyllembourg og Hverdagshistorierne* (Copenhagen: Rosenkilde & Bagger, 1951), esp. 266 ff. Hude's book is the most comprehensive study available on Fru Gyllembourg. Klaus P. Mortensen's study, *Thomasines oprør* (Copenhagen: Gad, 1986), is more modern but contains far less information.

[56] Henning Fenger, *The Heibergs*, trans. F. J. Marker (New York: Twayne, 1971), 142-53.

[57] Hude, *Thomasine Gyllembourg og Hverdagshistorierne*, 272.

[58] Ibid., 273.

[59] Ibid., 283.

"exciting" its readers[60] much as drama excites an audience, primarily because of its sharply delineated or "mathematically constructed" plot around which every detail "strictly revolves."[61] Another important attribute of the novella lending to its theatrical excitement, she felt, is its "limited scope," permitting it to "jump right into the middle of life" (*in medias res*) without forcing the reader "to become acquainted with the lives of the main characters in their entire chronological development all the way from the cradle to the grave."[62] As a consequence of all this, Fru Gyllembourg, in her search for a definition of the novella, came to stress "the art of omission" and dramatically "arresting events."[63]

But if Fru Gyllembourg sought to make the novella acceptable to her son and other drama-loving critics, she knew full well that despite the dramatic qualities she assigned to it, it remained something quite distinct from the drama he and his followers championed. The awareness of this difference prompted her to emphasize the advantages of her favorite genre.

Her son had thought to make literature respond to the problems of post-Napoleonic Denmark by giving the theater public a release from daily cares. He created hilarious entertainment, a steady stream of intoxicating musical comedies, night after night. They would provide the laughter and refreshment needed to combat anew the ills of the nation the next morning. That was Heiberg's way of assigning to literature a valuable function in Danish life at the time. His mother agreed fully that literature had an important role in coping with the anguish in contemporary Danish life, but, in addition to the refreshment of Royal Theater comedy, the public, she believed, needed a form of fiction that would be neither amusing nor remote from everyday existence. Rather, it would lead directly into reality and the salient problems and conflicts haunting Copenhagen's daily life.[64] Thus, Fru Gyllembourg's "dramatic novella" (Heiberg's term for his mother's tales)[65] addressed the urgent present reality no less than did his theatrical comedy, but she could also chuckle in triumph that the rival genre she contemplated seemed far more acutely attuned to real life than the plays he and his cohorts were feverishly designing.

---

[60] Ibid., 280.

[61] Ibid., 273.

[62] Ibid., 281.

[63] Ibid., 284.

[64] Ibid., 270.

[65] See the essay "Thomasine Gyllembourg," in Paul V. Rubow, *Betragtninger* (Copenhagen: Munksgaard, 1947), 85.

En Hverdags-Historie

Of all the many novellas with which Fru Gyllembourg put her theory into practice, none hit Danish readers harder than *En Hverdags-Historie* (An Everyday Story), which appeared first in 1828.[66] The title informs us, before the novella even begins, that we are about to encounter everyday reality, but after a few pages we recognize a stringent artistry presiding over realistic depiction. Garbed as a densely constructed portrait of reality, the story is truly fiction. Seemingly describing contemporary Danish life and middle-class society in Fru Gyllembourg's Copenhagen but omitting much scene painting, the artist noticeably excerpts, regulates, and manipulates contemporary life for a specific fictional purpose. Fru Gyllembourg forces everything into a highly controlled novella to concentrate, excluding all else, on the essential drama she sees haunting her fellow men and women: the clash between reality and illusion. Her one driving purpose is to ask the question: "What is reality?" She achieves this by constantly juggling reality and appearance, confronting them, juxtaposing them, interchanging them, and mixing them, until, frustrated, we scarcely know which is which. Fru Gyllembourg succeeds so well in devastating us with this realization because she lets truth and illusion struggle and tangle in the shadow of our most central human experience: the taste of love. What could be more vital in understanding reality than the love experience?

Fru Gyllembourg, adapting her idea of the illusive nature of reality to the succinct, pithy form of the novella, soon absorbs us completely with her disquieting thesis. The narrative hardly gets under way when its narrator (he seems to have no real name: did he really exist or is he the product of artistic imagination?) tells us of his first taste of love. It is love at first sight. Vacationing in northern Germany, he becomes infatuated with a Danish girl, Jetta, also vacationing there. He finds her exceptionally pretty, particularly in comparison to the local German girls, and quickly becomes formally engaged to her. Soon, however, Jetta dramatically reveals her true character. Her talents prove without essence or soul, and her earlier kind-hearted openness now seems to her fiancé a false familiarity bordering on rudeness. He gradually realizes that her coquettish manners signify not cuteness, as he first imagined, but indicate, rather, severe deficiencies in her knowledge and education. Under the veneer of her captivating beauty

---

[66] The best analysis of this novella is by Steffen Auring et al., "Thomasine Gyllembourg: En Hverdags-Historie, 1827," *Litteratur & Samfund* 31 (1980): 30-58. Elisabeth Hude's monograph refers to the novella frequently in passing: 70, 122-24, 177, 224, 229, 234, 273-74. Although the novella has been translated several times into German, nothing of a critical nature has been written about it in German. For the English-speaking world Fru Gyllembourg's tale has remained, alas, terra incognita.

and middle-class respectability, almost everything seems shallow, mediocre, or deceptive. Thus, he spends thoroughly disagreeable hours with the girl he once thought so charming. Indeed, she seems incapable of reciprocating his love: she and her mother preoccupy themselves with dressmaking and idle gossip in the evenings, leaving him looking on in lonely boredom. As Jetta's youth and beauty prove deceptive, so does her domestic occupation, for Jetta and her mother, despite their pretense of always keeping busy, demonstrate a total incompetence in domestic affairs. In reality, she and her mother, whom she resembles so closely and who thus reinforces doubly their trivial lifestyle, live in a fantasy world where they only create the illusion of being busy and productive. Numerous scenes reveal the household in great disorder, if not utter chaos. The artificial, inessential external trappings of everyday life emblematize Jetta's feelings for the man she is supposed to marry: her heart hardly beats with emotion; she seems more content imagining love than actually experiencing it. Were the German girls the narrator earlier perceived as deficient in feminine beauty next to Jetta perhaps more capable of love than the more attractive Danish girl?

This dichotomy of real and unreal comes into even sharper relief when Maya, Jetta's half-sister, arrives on the scene, precisely as the reader concludes that the engagement has soured. Related by blood and similar in age to Jetta, Maya — in classic contrast to her half-sister — lacks external beauty but is capable of a deep and abiding love. In her the narrator finds everything missing in Jetta. The moment he sees her, she seems like her namesake goddess, catching him under her spell with her soulful demeanor, her devotion of spirit, and her mysterious expression. Her lack of outer beauty fails to excite him, but her inner beauty shines the more brilliantly; and the reader, too, finds the plain sister radiant, a beautiful soul. Even the order she brings to the household — without making her stepmother lose face — reflects her inner beauty. Naturally, the narrator, despairing at his fiancée's superficial appearances, falls in love with this girl. The two are now drawn together by profound emotions and the promise of true love. When they encounter one another, the reader feels every heartbeat. The anxiety both Maya and the narrator feel particularly indicates the genuineness of this love, all the more genuine because of the contrast with the shallow, insincere expressions characterizing the relationship of the engaged. Yet the engagement of Jetta and the narrator seems such a commitment that the two new lovers conclude they are carrying on an illicit affair and take steps to end it. They agree that they should separate and forget one another. He embarks on a set of travels. Of course, the more they are separated by geographic distance, the more both yearn for one another; thus, finally, the actual separation is no separation, for it only brings them closer. The real engagement between Jetta and her fiancé is then unmasked as false and accordingly dissolved, while the other relationship, before thought illicit, gains, from church and state, official license with the marriage bond.

But is the relationship between Maya and the narrator, apparently the truer and certainly the more enduring, a real love match? Can the relationship between a man and a woman *sans* physical attraction be a genuine love affair? Or does it only seem genuine because the married couple has so much in common spiritually? The reader wonders whether the physical passion the narrator felt for Jetta might have more the spark of genuine love than the spiritually uplifting marriage to Maya. The narrator and Maya may have consented to join as husband and wife, but the reader feels the husband hardly loves his wife as a man would a woman. Sensual attraction is altogether absent. There is something unnatural, something unreal, about this marriage and the love affair that led up to it. If the narrator's love for Jetta never rose above sexual longings, his attachment to Maya never has any spontaneous vitality. Does a relationship so totally devoid of *eros* constitute a real love affair between a man and a woman? Which of the two interrelated love affairs is, then, the real one? The perplexed reader never quite knows. To make things even more confusing, Fru Gyllembourg compounds this tantalizing composition of her invented narrator's true and superficial love with references to other love affairs which echo further the bewilderment over what is real and what is artificial, what appears real but is not genuine, what is genuine but appears unreal.

The story of the half-sisters Jetta and Maya interrelates with the two marriages of their father, Herr H. After the untimely death of his first wife, Maya's mother, his still youthful impetuosity leads him into a marriage with a woman he does not seem to love, by whom he has another daughter, Jetta. The second marriage is little more than a charade compared with the more passionate love that apparently bound him to his first wife and which supposedly continues after her death, so much so that he appears to love the dead wife more than the living one. But the reader must guess whether imagined love for a phantom could be more genuine than the actual love for a wife sharing his life in the present. Isn't the love for a person no longer living actually a fictitious love? Similarly, the reader wonders whether the supposedly deep love for the first wife was as genuine during her lifetime as he later seems to imagine after her death. Did he really love the first wife more than he now does the second? Or does the first love only now appear, colored by his sentimental memory, more authentic than the other he fancies, in comparison, less fulfilling? We never glimpse Herr H. during his marriage to his first wife, never really know whether that love actually ran deep or only seems so to him now looking back.

Another character, Henning F., Maya's cousin, loves two different women as well. After her mother's death and her father's remarriage, Maya goes to live with her wealthy uncle in Sweden. The uncle wants her to marry his son, Henning F., and eventually they become engaged, despite loving each other more like brother and sister than as man and woman. Shortly afterwards Henning travels to Italy and falls madly in love with a ravishing Florentine beauty named Beatrice. Feeling the fire of a consuming love he had never known for Maya, he sends a letter to Sweden asking release from his engagement, which Maya then grants. But his new passion in Italy quickly proves seriously lacking in commitment, floundering because of an external religious reason: she will only marry a Catholic, and he cannot convert for fear of the reaction of the soldiers in the brigade he commands. Lacking enduring commitment, only the product of a momentary sensual urge, was the love for Beatrice a true love? The reader doubts it. After Henning returns from his passionate sojourn in sunny Italy to the cooling climate of Scandinavia, he seeks to renew his engagement to Maya and settle down with her in marriage. This relationship lacks all the passion we sensed in his affection for Beatrice and will lead merely to a marriage of convenience, perhaps to satisfy his guilty conscience for having broken the original engagement. Might this be nothing more than a weak substitute for the love he felt for the Italian girl he did not succeed in marrying? Which of the two relationships is more genuine? Of course, when he later proposes to a third girl, Jetta, who, as we learned earlier, is poor at reciprocating affection, we question his sincerity in all his declarations. Did he ever know what true love meant? Or did he only imagine he knew because one woman seemed to offer him an escape from another?

We would imagine the latter if not for Henning, in his wooing of Maya, having a rival, Anton B. For in comparison with Anton, who appears anything but the real lover he strenuously tries to be, Henning seems so very natural. Anton's artificiality surfaces almost as soon as we meet him. He wishes to marry Maya but lacks the courage to confront her in person to ask her. He uses the narrator as an emissary bearing the message of love. Would he resort to this indirection if truly in love?

Apparently Maya, too, doubts his conviction, for she declines such a bloodless offer of marriage, whereupon Anton reveals his real motives for asking for her hand in marriage: he never expected to be loved by her but wanted to honor her as a sister if only she would grace him with her presence and bear his name. By this time we feel he probably does not love her, but we are hardly convinced. We begin to have second thoughts when

Anton B. challenges his rival Henning to a duel over Maya. Would he be willing to risk his life for her hand if he did not love her intensely?

Our heads spin as we watch this panoply of everyday men and women, genuinely in love but appearing not in love at all, or appearing not in love but actually very much in love. But if at the end we remain unclear about who really loves whom, we nevertheless know for certain that Fru Gyllembourg tried to deal with the real as it was available to her in the elusive amorous relationships of her time and place. Moreover, the novella leaves us unwaveringly convinced that Thomasine Gyllembourg tried, harder than the other Danish Poetic Realists perhaps, to insure that fiction could serve as the means to acquire the most adequate knowledge of reality.

Pressing a parallel to Gottfried Keller

At the end of our discussion of Steen Steensen Blicher, Fru Gyllembourg's immediate predecessor in the novella of *Poetisk Realisme*, we noted that four critics have viewed his novella as anticipating the Poetic Realism of the German author Theodor Storm. No claim has ever been made about Fru Gyllembourg's novella foreshadowing anything in the German current of the literary movement. But this does not deter us from opening another door in the cross-national history of Poetic Realism. As with the line forward from Blicher to Storm, a case can be made for Fru Gyllembourg as a forerunner of Gottfried Keller.

Keller, too, as we shall later observe, parades before us artless and yet artful samplings of genuine and apparent love. In *Romeo und Julia auf dem Dorfe* (A Village Romeo and Juliet), for example, a man and woman, supposedly from a fictional town named Seldwyla but actually from a real place in Switzerland, find themselves truly in love and decide to marry. The reader wonders, however, whether this occurs in a carnivalistic betrothal too fantastic to be real, or whether the two actually join together within a very real context fundamentally at odds with the pretended beliefs of a society too ridiculous to be taken seriously.

Similarly, in Keller's *Der grüne Heinrich* (Green Henry), the reader continually loses track of which of the two women in the protagonist's life offers the real love, and which the love of his dream world. To Anna he feels drawn for idealistic reasons rather than because of any sensual inclination; Judith awakens in him the itch for carnal relations. Heinrich flits so often between these two in his quest for feminine affection that we never find out whether his apparently abiding love for Anna is more genuine than his briefer flirtation with Judith, whether his apparently passionate involvement with Judith is not a more real love than his spiritual attachment to Anna. Heinrich never seems to know himself which of the two women he really or only apparently loves. As in Fru Gyllembourg's work, Keller's ingeniously contrived love scenes so thoroughly compound appearance and reality that we are unable at any moment to say which we actually see.

Those who would care to press further the parallel between Fru Gyllembourg and Keller — a genuine desideratum of literary scholarship — should note that her novellas were widely read in German translations when Keller was developing his well-known prose style. Fru Gyllembourg's novellas began to hit the German-speaking world in the 1830s. Few critics, if any, today in either Denmark or German-speaking Europe seem aware of this. In the early 1830s two competing publishing firms in Leipzig, the center of the German book trade at the time, commissioned translations of anthologies of her novellas, and when they were published, virtually simultaneously, *En Hverdags-Historie* became, each time, the collection's showpiece.[67] It was chosen for the opening pages and singled out in the prefatory comments as particularly suitable to awaken German interest in the new trail of Poetic Realism Fru Gyllembourg had helped to blaze in Danish literature. "It must be considered a fact," the Dano-German translator Laurids Kruse (1762–1839) told his German readers, "that it was one novella in particular, *En Hverdags-Historie*, which, because of its apparent artlessness, clarity of thought, poetic style, and other praiseworthy fictional qualities, had aroused the universal attention [of the Danes]."[68]

The fame of this subtly composed symphony of real and imagined love spread to all parts of the German-speaking world when translations of other tales by Fru Gyllembourg appeared in major cities of Germany, advertised each time as novellas "by the author of the *Alltagsgeschichte*."[69] Its popularity circulated also when one of the leading forums of literary criticism in Germany at the time, the *Allgemeine Literatur-Zeitung* of Jena, published a glowing review.[70] The publicity and institutional respect this novella now received must then have influenced countless lending libraries in towns and cities all across central Europe to add to their shelves of

---

[67] *Erzählungen aus der Copenhagener fliegenden Post*, trans. L. Kruse, 5 vols. (Leipzig: Kollmann, 1834-1836); *Novellen vom Verfasser einer "Alltagsgeschichte,"* trans. W. C. Christiani (Leipzig: Kummer, 1835).

[68] *Erzählungen aus der Copenhagener fliegenden Post*, I, iv.

[69] *Zwei Zeitalter. Novelle vom Verfasser der Erzählung: "Eine Alltagsgeschichte,"* trans. Gottfried von Leinberg (Frankfurt am Main: Brönner, 1848); *Die Novellen des Verfassers der "Alltagsgeschichte,"* trans. Edmond Zoller, 17 vols. (Stuttgart: Franckh'sche Verlagsbuchhandlung, 1852).

[70] *Allgemeine Literatur-Zeitung*, Ergänzungsblätter, 60 (Jena, 1836). Cited by Gottfried von Leinberg in his preface to the translation *Zwei Zeitalter*, xiii.

belles lettres volumes of the *Alltagsgeschichte* and other novellas by the famous Danish authoress.

Keller, we know, was always hurrying to the lending libraries in his native Zurich to devour the latest literature acquired. There is no end to the latest acquisitions he consulted in lending libraries. We do not know whether he read *En Hverdags-Historie*, but we can imagine that if he had read this novella, his heart would have gone out to it. One can think of no other work that could more confirm for Keller his concept of fiction than the kindred spirit he could discover in Fru Gyllembourg's concentrated vignette of real and unreal love. The parallel with his own creative production suggests that Keller read one of the many German translations of *En Hverdags-Historie* fresh on the shelves of new books in the lending libraries he visited. This Danish melody of fact mistaken for fiction or of fiction mistaken for fact, as a German contemporary of Keller had called it in 1848,[71] probably entered his experience when he was an ambitious young writer groping for originality and grateful for influences he could put to creative use.

5. Further momentum: Carl Bernhard

Encouraged by the astonishing success which *En Hverdags-Historie* encountered from the reading public, Fru Gyllembourg continued the tradition of the novella of *Poetisk Realisme* and wrote a series of other absorbing "everyday tales." No fewer than thirty such works of prose fiction came from her prolific pen. Up until the middle of the 1850s "the author of *An Everyday Story*," as she became known to so many readers, remained in Denmark one of the most widely-read writers of her time. She still is Denmark's most prominent woman writer, occupying a position on the Danish Parnassus similar to the one held by Annette von Droste-Hülshoff (1797–1848) on the German literary scene. (Both are the only women writers of their nations in honor of whom bank notes are in circulation today.)

Fru Gyllembourg's adoring son greatly aided, of course, her extraordinary popularity, as well as the cause of *Poetisk Realisme* she sought to further. After returning from Kiel to Copenhagen in 1825, he assumed the role of a *pontifex maximus* in Denmark's literary world. Because of his position, he understood the mechanics of publishing literature so it would come to the attention of the largest possible audience, and no author ever found a better promoter than had Fru Gyllembourg in her influential son.

---

[71] Gottfried von Leinberg in the preface to *Zwei Zeitalter*, xvi.

The interest in Fru Gyllembourg's fiction also grew, however, when another family member, her cousin's son, Andreas Nicolai de Saint-Aubain (1798–1865), commonly known by his pen name Carl Bernhard, started to publish novellas that took their inspiration from hers.[72] The more Danish readers became acquainted with his everyday tales, the more the aunt he was successfully imitating captured public attention. Conversely, the more the Danes eagerly read one tale after the other from her pen, the more they desired to acquire the tales of the nephew following in her footsteps.

With her active encouragement, he published his first novella, *Nummer Syv* (Number Seven), in the pages of his cousin Heiberg's *Kjøbenhavns flyvende Post* (1828), before the ink of *En Hverdags-Historie* (1828) had barely dried. He had listened in awe to his aunt reading her story in the circle of family and friends before it found its way into print. Inspired, he quickly brought all his youthful energy to bear, composing his own everyday novella of life in Copenhagen. Many other such novellas then followed in rapid succession. Indeed, Bernhard seemed bent on rivaling his aunt in the number of everyday novellas published. His novellas were also translated into German practically as quickly as were his aunt's. For the Danish reading public, as well as for the many readers in Germany quickly devouring the novellas of aunt and nephew, it soon became difficult to distinguish, or even to remember, which novella was written by whom. To what extent were the novellas of aunt and nephew similar? How did they differ? Which of the two authors had earned the greatest laurels? With these puzzling questions on their lips, many men and women in Denmark and Germany (and presumably Sweden as well) were learning of the compelling force of *Poetisk Realisme*.[73]

Of all Bernhard's novellas, few have attracted more attention both in Denmark and abroad than *Tante Franciska* (Aunt Francisca), which appeared first in Copenhagen in 1836.[74] Particularly in Germany it captivated many imaginations, for it was printed frequently in German translations. One of the more prominent appeared in the pages of Paul Heyse's widely circulated *Novellenschatz des Auslandes* (A Treasury of Foreign Novellas), published in Munich beginning in 1872. These German translations could scarcely have been without consequence for the encouragement which

---

[72] The most detailed study of Bernhard is still the old-fashioned biography by H. Schwanenflügel, *Carl Bernhard, Hans Liv og Forfattervirksomhed* (Copenhagen: Schuboth, 1895).

[73] See the introduction in Carl Bernhard, *Lebensbilder aus Dänemark in Novellen und Erzählungen*, I (Leipzig: Weber, 1840), xxv-xxviii.

[74] There seems to be no modern interpretation of this novella in any language.

German readers and writers gave to the growth of their own linguistic branch of Poetic Realism.

As in *En Hverdags-Historie,* so, too, in *Tante Franciska* we discover the author constantly juggling the phenomena of reality and appearance in everyday life. What we imagine real emerges as illusion; conversely, what seems illusion proves actually real. This novella so densely compounds the tantalizing dichotomy of the real and the unreal that we never seem to know which is which.

Clearly visible in the novella are two strands of narrative: Aunt Francisca's romantic love life and the other life she leads performing charitable works. On the face of it, her romantic involvement with Theodore seems a life more real to her and to us, for she truly loves him with all her emotions. Her commitment to charitable love lacks any emotional fervor, seeming insufferably dull, indeed even lifeless — at best but a weak substitute for the deep love between a man and a woman. Yet the actual love experience between Francisca and Theodore remains unfulfilled. Although she was officially engaged to him, with a ring, he felt drawn to another woman, Aurora. That relationship, not the one between Francisca and Theodore, is crowned with the marriage bond. To complicate matters further, Theodore's marriage to the woman he loved more than he did Francisca is, in reality, no love match after all, for Aurora has affairs with other men and does not reciprocate Theodore's love. The match, hence, is devoid of real love; Theodore had only imagined they loved each other. One's head spins even more when one discovers this complicated puzzle of real and unreal romantic attachment woven together in the narrative fabric with another story that revolves around an old maid's charitable love for her fellow men instead of around the genuine passion felt by a woman or a man in love. At first, the old maid's love for mankind appears, compared with the romantic attachment, rather sterile, but soon we realize that this love for humanity is actually more fulfilling than the earlier romantic one. It appears, moreover, more real, for it occurs in the reality of present time, whereas the sexual love story only comes to us indirectly, through the disguise of a narrated account told many years after the fictional events had supposedly happened.

Climaxing all in a sort of grand finale, the narrator adds another element of confusion about what is real and not real: Francisca's gifts of charitable love are distributed just opposite the way we would imagine. Two couples receive proceeds from Francisca's will: Louise and Rudolph, Flora and Arnold. From the flow of the narrative the reader knows that Francisca loved Louise and Rudolph but shared no affection with Flora and Arnold. Yet to our great surprise, we learn at the end that Francisca left Flora and Arnold a sum of money three times the amount bequeathed to Louise and Rudolph. We discover the reason for this almost unbelievable act: Flora and Arnold, because of this inheritance, could marry immediately and enjoy a full life of real love, something that would have been impossible without this financial help. Louise and Rudolph, on the other hand, already had the financial means to have a genuinely happy married life. The benefactress, Francisca, appears here more of a fairy-tale angel than a real human being, a role diametrically opposed to her role as a person experiencing the joys and pains of real love, as we saw her in the earlier strand of the narrative. But we also take leave of this novella knowing that the two couples in love in the present, Louise and Rudolf, Flora and Arnold, can both enjoy a genuinely permanent love in marriage, whereas the other two couples from the fictionally narrated past, Francisca and Theodore, Aurora and Theodore, failed in becoming truly happily married. The apparently passionate love affairs of the narrated past thus seem, at the end of the novella, to have been actually loveless, while the seemingly loveless present, dominated more by concerns of money than by the tears and emotions of romance, becomes the setting for lasting, genuine marital bliss.

The tale thus ends on an apparently happy note. Or does it only seem to do so? The novella's heroine, Aunt Francisca, whose charitable bequests have made it possible for love to triumph at the end, dies as an old maid; we are left weeping for her. She endured sorrow, disappointment, and loneliness almost all her life because the only man she had ever loved broke his engagement to her and married another woman. Is this a happy or a sad conclusion to the story? We never really know.

6. *Poetisk Realisme* finds an extension in pictorial art: Christen Købke

Danish literary critics have frequently alluded to Fru Gyllembourg's influence on Carl Bernhard. But Elisabeth Hude, Fru Gyllembourg's principal biographer, has also called the art of Denmark's most famous woman writer not unlike the art of the greatest painter of the time in Denmark: Christen Købke (1810–1848).[75] This lone reference relating the painting of the younger Købke to the novellas of Fru Gyllembourg merits attention, and all the more so because Danish art historians today speak of

---

[75] Hude, *Thomasine Gyllembourg og Hverdagshistorierne*, 326-27.

Købke as an artist of Poetic Realism.[76] If Fru Gyllembourg is often recognized as the leading spirit in the school of literary *Poetisk Realisme* at Copenhagen in the late 1820s and 1830s, the younger Købke has come to be regarded as the outstanding genius of pictorial *Poetisk Realisme* flourishing in Copenhagen during virtually the identical time span.[77]

Like Fru Gyllembourg in literature, Købke in painting rejected the monumental art stressing the glory of ancient Nordic mythology, the art in vogue during the pre-Napoleonic Danish empire. Like Fru Gyllembourg, he shunned heroic themes and focused instead on what he could actually observe in everyday life in and around Copenhagen. Moreover, just as she had rejected grandiose dramas or expansive novels in favor of more compact, tightly constructed novellas, he felt uncomfortable, as a painter of *Poetisk Realisme*, with huge canvases, preferring to cram his details into smaller, highly organized compositions. If Fru Gyllembourg's novellas stood out for their strongly delineated, almost mathematically designed plots, Købke's realistic paintings, correspondingly, beg notice for their strict "linear perspective," around which every detail is rigidly coordinated.[78] Both Fru Gyllembourg and Købke, furthermore, had a strong penchant for dramatic structure, to which they likewise subordinated their familiar subject: matter taken from everyday life.

Consequently, Købke's paintings in the 1830s constituted visual complements to Fru Gyllembourg's novellas, imparting, as her works did, to Copenhagen's citizenry truths — as the Keeper of Exhibitions and Education at the National Gallery in London, Alistair Smith, has said — "on the essential, eternal aspects of life."[79]

Parti af Østerbrogade i morgenbelysning

Of the many paintings that have made Købke famous in Denmark and abroad, few have been acclaimed more than *Parti af Østerbrogade i morgenbelysning* (A View of a Street in Copenhagen, Morning Light), completed in 1836. On permanent display in the State Museum of Art in Copenhagen, in recent years it has also been a showpiece of Danish art at loan exhibitions in Berlin, London, and Paris.

---

[76] See the essay by the art critic Henrik Bramsen in *Danish Painting: The Golden Age*, Exhibition Catalogue (London: The National Gallery, 1984), 11-41, esp. 36.

[77] *Danish Painting: The Golden Age*, 187.

[78] Hans Edvard Nørregård-Nielsen, "The Lyricism of Christen Købke," *Apollo* 113 (1981): 372.

[79] *Danish Painting: The Golden Age*, 48.

In the informative catalogue of the exhibition in London from September 5 to November 20, 1984, Kasper Monrad, Curator at the State Museum of Art, gives the following description of the picture:

> In this tightly constructed composition the painter shows events typical of an early morning. Fishwives rest on the embankment on their walk to town; peasants in their Sunday best are coming to town by horsecart; cows plod on their own familiar way to the common; other citizens promenade in the shade alongside the houses. The rays of the morning sun pick out the road, the poplars between the houses, and the water pump in the foreground. The sky, with its variety of clouds, may be seen as an attempt at describing weather typical of Copenhagen.[80]

Reading this description, we might easily conclude that a mood of delightful charm permeates the painting; indeed, when we pause on our tour of the museum to observe it closely, much of its detail supports such an impression. We see a quaint Danish landscape in the summertime, bright and early in the morning. We enjoy the pleasing greenery of the poplar trees. We share in the merry laughter of the peasants on the way to discover the amenities in the big and enchanting city. We chuckle as we try to eavesdrop on what we imagine to be the trivial but not uninteresting conversation of the fishwives, all dressed in picturesque, billowing green skirts. We rejoice with them for the money they will receive later during the morning, selling their catch of fish at the city's marketplace. We smile when we notice the curious cows ambling unpretentiously along or skidding with fear in front of an oncoming horsecart. Last but not least, we feel pleasantly relaxed at the sight of the well-dressed ladies and gentlemen promenading in the cooling shade alongside the houses. All in all, Købke seems to have succeeded quite well, with this painting of an early summer morning, in uplifting our spirits.

Yet when we tarry to study the picture longer, or when we return to look at it again after having visited a number of adjacent chambers in the State Museum of Art at Copenhagen, we begin to have our gnawing doubts as to whether Købke really intended the painting to exude the calm and joyful feeling we sensed when we at first stood still to admire his talent. After a more protracted viewing, we notice that the cheerful street scene is set off against a background created by a proportionately larger aerial perspective. Indeed, the vanishing point marked by the perspective of the street scene, separating it from the aerial space, is remarkably low in the picture, and quite intentionally so, for in Købke's earliest preliminary

---

[80] Ibid., 214.

sketch for the painting the aerial space was not as vast.[81] Once we become aware of this perspective, the sky assumes unusual significance, demanding our special attention. We see here not a clear, blue northern European summer sky but, rather, a variety of clouds in all sorts of strange shapes and drab hues. Købke, we begin to realize, must have invested as much technical virtuosity in painting these unusual clouds as he did in drawing the people, animals, trees, and houses on the lower part of the canvas. The vast, beclouded sky above tends to overwhelm and reduce the figures of the people below to insignificant size; it also effectively shuts out any lavish rays of the sun and lets everything in the picture appear in an ominous, grey light.

Should we now, after viewing the painting for a considerable amount of time, take pleasure at the apparent charm of this Copenhagen street scene, or are we to be frightened by the mass of threatening clouds, which seem to be pushing downwards and possibly portending catastrophe? Has Købke given us a picture of the joys of everyday life in Copenhagen, or has he deceived us by creating only an illusion of such a joyous scene? Since we feel compelled to come to this latter conclusion, we must ask how we could at first have believed that Købke had actually portrayed a scene of idyllic bliss.

Eventually, we sense that for Købke things are not either reality or illusion but both of these in a perplexing dramatic interplay. To make this belief understandable, as well as acceptable, must have been the driving purpose that impelled him to paint this two-dimensional picture, which has never ceased to intrigue its many viewers.

Efterårsmorgen ved Sortedamssøen

We become all the more convinced of the message of *Parti af Østerbrogade i morgenbelysning* when we observe a number of other pictures Købke painted around the same time. Particularly telling is the complemental *Efterårsmorgen ved Sortedamssøen* (Autumn Morning on Lake Sortedam), which he began in the autumn of 1837 and completed in early 1838. It can be seen today in Copenhagen's Ny Carlsberg Glyptotek; it is described in great detail (in Danish and French) in a publication issued by that museum in 1971.[82]

---

[81] Erik Fischer, "Bemærkninger om kompositionsudkastene til Østerbrobilledet," in *Købke på Blegdammen og ved Sortedamssøen* (Copenhagen: Statens Museum for Kunst, 1981), 24-27.

[82] Arne Brenna, "Et Efterårslandskap av Christen Købke," *Meddelelser fra Ny Carlsberg Glyptotek* 28 (1971): 25-50.

A rather well-dressed man is taking a stroll along a lake just outside the ramparts of Copenhagen. At first sight, this seems a rather idyllic scene. A man of some means, at least according to his attire, and with apparent leisure at his disposal, is enjoying the refreshment of natural beauty. Yet when we pause longer to observe this picture, we begin to notice that the lonely character seems terribly insignificant: the vast landscape surrounding him is not in bloom and is desolate, downright depressing. To make matters even more chilly, the solitary human being is dressed in ominous black clothing. We almost fear for him. It is as if he were threatened by a huge, hostile, melancholic environment.[83] After a prolonged viewing, we hardly gather the impression that we would relish trading places with this figure, although that was precisely the initial impression we received catching sight of the painting. We realize now that the interplay of an idyllic everyday reality with the illusion of such a scene, which had become so clear to us with Købke's *Parti af Østerbrogade i morgenbelysning*, echoes in this complemental picture completed two years later.

7. *Poetisk Realisme* becomes overshadowed by newer forms of Danish art

Political and economic conditions

In the course of the 1830s the wounds of the Napoleonic War began to heal in Denmark. The Danish *daler*, which had continued its precipitous decline until the year 1827, finally reversed its downward spiral and started once more to climb, by 1838 reaching its par value again. With the advent of fiscal stability came a return to economic prosperity. Prices for agricultural products, the mainstay of the Danish economy, rose; land values increased. Between 1830 and 1845 prices advanced by as much as 160% in some agricultural districts. In the same time span exports more than doubled. A new generation of Danes had also entered the job market, as a result of which new ideas, new tastemakers, and new leaders emerged.

All of these things combined to diminish the feeling of pessimistic resignation that had for so long stalked the streets of Denmark's cities, towns, and villages. Life in the nation could once again begin to look

---

[83] For a description of the melancholic atmosphere in this painting see the informative introduction to Købke's art by Hans Edvard Nørregård-Nielsen, *Guldaldermaleren Christen Købke* (Roskilde: Umbra, 1980), 39.

bright and merry. As self-confidence was restored, the Danes quickly embraced a delirious optimism only too understandable when one remembers the long period of time they had to wait and suffer until prosperity could once again return. Outwardly, this optimism found easily recognizable expression in the frenzy of railway building and in the sudden proliferation of luxurious cafés all across the map of Denmark. No later than the accession of a new king in 1839, Christian VIII, the Götterdämmerung of the Napoleonic era was all but forgotten. The entire nation seemed suddenly caught up in the upsurge of a new and jubilant nationalism, actively racing almost blindly to the second Danish Armageddon of the century: the humiliating defeat at the hand of Bismarck in the Dano-German War of 1864.

Yet before the Danes could recognize, alas too late, the broad delusions underlying their blind assent to a new era of prosperity, irrational nationalism, and unbridled optimism, *Poetisk Realisme*, nourished by the anguishing realism of the Danish tragedy in the Napoleonic era, had run its course and been superseded by a series of adventurous forms of art more in line with the increasingly affluent tastes of the late 1830s.

Hans Christian Andersen

Most conspicuous among the new generation of innovative Danish artists to adapt to the changing tastes of the revitalized Danish nation (as well as to contribute to the changing of these tastes) was the ingenious Hans Christian Andersen (1805–1875). The first collections of his immensely entertaining fairy tales began to appear in 1835 — just as the Danish *daler* was approaching par value again. They constituted the antithesis of everything the Poetic Realists had stood for. If these writers had insisted upon unabashed portraits of everyday life in art and upon a pensive reflection on the fundamental realities of an age darkened by Napoleon, Andersen now turned to a new and exciting world of ebullient fantasy, emphasizing laughter in literature. He delighted his readers with purposely improbable tales with unlikely plots. He raised the genre of the fairy tale to a position of prestige utterly unthinkable in the age of *Poetisk Realisme* but now nevertheless all too representative of the delirious optimism ever increasingly infecting Danish sensibilities.

Further to counteract Poetic Realism, Andersen produced plays emulating Johan Ludvig Heiberg's comedies of escapism, though in contrast to Heiberg's comedies, Andersen's plays provided the Danes with more than just brief nocturnal releases from the cares of daily life. Andersen added a particularly strong dose of entertaining melody to his comedies, their operatic quality exceeding that of Heiberg's shows. After the cares of the Napoleonic era had mostly subsided, such dramas of intoxicating music could only abet further (and mirror) the spreading feeling of jubilant nationalism. The more the Danes took to Andersen's buoyant plays of musical intoxication (thirteen of them witnessed many performances at the Royal Theater in the decade 1836-1846),[84] the more, naturally, they lost sight of the sobering concerns of Poetic Realism.

Curbing Poetic Realism no less, Andersen produced buoyant musical poetry. As with his plays, the strength of his verse lies in its intoxicating melody. Indeed, Andersen's poetry constituted exhilarating tonal painting to such an extent that the eminent Danish critic Georg Brandes, who could only appreciate literature when it focused on reality, had nothing but contempt for it.[85] But the disdain of the critic with no use for a poetry estranged from the realities of everyday life only makes us the more aware that Andersen's verse comes alive almost exclusively because of its lilting, polyphonic scores. The most telling example, "Gurre" (written in 1842), a poem meant to be sung,[86] makes audible with fastidious orchestral skill a chorus of cooing doves. The bird-like melody, echoing the song of the doves, seems all-pervading, completely intoxicating the listener with the musical qualities of language. Adolf Strodtmann (1829–1879), a forgotten spokesman of German Poetic Realism and a critic with a knowledge of Danish letters probably never equalled by a non-Dane,[87] once referred to this poem as a piece not only most representative of Andersen but of its entire literary age.[88] A literary intoxication had now surfaced in Denmark to displace *Poetisk Realisme*. What counted now was the outburst of a jubilant melody — a momentarily uplifting emotional experience with little or no regard for comprehension of values inherent in actual existence.

Andersen's energetic initiative had created a new literature of emotional ecstasy congenial to the tastes of a new generation of overly self-confident Danes; it also prompted other men of Danish letters to experiment with modes of literary form that would deviate from the stringent norms of Poetic Realism. Around Andersen regularly gathered a congregation of the most prominent minds of Copenhagen, meeting to apply its collective intelligence to the criticism of literature. In session after session

---

[84] Frederick J. Marker, *Hans Christian Andersen and the Romantic Theatre* (Toronto: University Press, 1971), 208-9.

[85] Bo Grønbech, *Hans Christian Andersen* (Boston: Twayne, 1980), 78.

[86] *H. C. Andersens Dagbøger 1825-1875*, eds. K. Olsen & H. Topsøe-Jensen (Copenhagen: Gad, 1971-1976), II, 295; V, 426; VI, 30, 54, 64; IX, 159; X, 393.

[87] Alken Bruns, *Übersetzung als Rezeption, Deutsche Übersetzer skandinavischer Literatur von 1860 bis 1900* (Neumünster: Wachholtz, 1977), 106-49, esp. 115-16.

[88] Adolf Strodtmann, *Das geistige Leben in Dänemark* (Berlin: Paetel, 1873), 90-91.

Andersen could read from one of his latest works and watch the members of the group taking pleasure in his successes. Or he could listen to a fellow author reading from a recent work. He could contribute to the heated give-and-take of debate on how a rival was meeting the literary demands of the age. Whether reading from his own works or discussing the accomplishments and blunders of his rivals, Andersen's fertile intellect and engaging personality — the king vied with Denmark's greatest patron of the arts at the time, the Duke of Augustenburg, for Andersen's company at the dinner table — quickly challenged others to experiment with forms of artifice which could reflect and give assent to the buoyant spirit of the new age.

N. F. S. Grundtvig

Another towering Danish author, whose writing echoed the essence of the optimistic revival of the 1830s, was Nikolaj Frederik Severin Grundtvig (1783–1872). If Andersen had ingeniously composed a dazzling array of ebulliently fantastic fairy tales, plays, and musical lyrics in order to carry the delirious Danes of the late 1830s off to a new harbor of beguiling optimism, Grundtvig chose the ecclesiastical lyric for the purpose of seeking a joyful haven where the Danes could wipe away the tears of yesteryear. He wrote some 1,400 religious songs with an uplifting melodious swing of an intensity altogether unknown in Danish music until he came along.

By the time the first volume of his monumental *Sang-Værk til den danske Kirke* (Hymnal for the Danish Church) appeared in 1837, it was clear to everyone in Denmark that Grundtvig's uncommonly stirring verses were as much a call for a new day in Danish literature as a mirror of the new day that had already dawned in Danish life. His eloquent sermons in rhyme sought to inspire his countrymen to push aside the last remnants of gloom still lurking in the corners of the nation and to embrace a new sense of hope based on a victorious belief: a benevolent God would right all wrongs and bring everlasting happiness to everyone.

Naturally, the more the Danes took to Grundtvig's uplifting poems of hope, and the more they sang them in their churches and homes, the more they also directed their gazes heavenward and away from the realities of everyday life. The preciousness of eternity overshadowed the worthlessness of time, necessarily furthering the eclipse of the message and form of literature so characteristic of the Poetic Realists. Indeed, the attempt to awaken men and women from the prison of everyday life to prophetic visions of a more blissful afterlife constituted nothing less than the most radical departure possible from *Poetisk Realisme*'s call for an intense preoccupation with everyday reality in an age of national sorrow.

To this jubilant poetry of idealism the Danish populace responded tumultuously, their response even surpassing the impact of Andersen's more original fantastic fiction. Not surprisingly, the pervasive influence exerted by this poetic evangel of a form of literature devoid of realism incurred the particular ire of the father of *Poetisk Realisme*, Poul Martin Møller. Møller felt obliged to step forward and express his dismay over the rousing welcome the Danes were giving this poetry. With biting satire he attacked his rival bard,[89] so vehemently that the assault might have proven fatal for the further reception of the rival's work, were the rival any lesser genius than Grundtvig. Despite its vehemence, and despite the eminence of the critic (himself a clergyman!), Møller's satire could not prevent Grundtvig from piloting, with this new poetry, an ever-increasing number of Danes away from the reality of everyday life and into an imaginary — though biblically anchored — harbor of grace. Worse yet for Møller, the more the Danes found comfort and joy in these sonorous verses, the less, naturally, they let themselves be wooed by the quietness of *Poetisk Realisme*'s search for a clearer understanding of the workings of the everyday world.

Meïr Goldschmidt

A third powerful voice in Danish letters contributing markedly to the dislodging of *Poetisk Realisme* from its position of preeminence was that of Meïr Goldschmidt (1819–1887). Although he came somewhat later to the literary scene than did Andersen and Grundtvig, his achievement helped no less to hasten the recession of *Poetisk Realisme*.

Like so many of the growing number of optimists in Denmark, Goldschmidt believed a new millennium had finally arrived for his nation; and he wished to do his part in advancing it by sweeping up the remnants of older thinking overlooked in the making of the new society. People could be moved best by what they read, his clever instinct told him, giving him the itch to seek a vocation in letters.

His first important chance to influence public opinion with his pen came when he wrote journalistic articles in support of a patriotism that left little or no room for any anti-Danish sentiment among the German-speaking populace in the southern districts of the Danish kingdom, though he was equally outspoken against an oppressive Danish rule over the German minority. The Danish and German citizens of the kingdom should join hands, he optimistically urged, to bring about a new and glorious (and ideal) nation: both should live together in a peace and harmony

---

[89] Møller, *Efterladte Skrifter*, II, 217-22.

that would increase the wealth and prosperity of Greater Denmark and of every individual citizen in it.

Goldschmidt's idea of how the ideal Danish nation should look politically, and the journalistic initiative he took to arouse the nation's compassion in favor of his idea, soon made him feel the remaining problems in Denmark were remediable if he were to describe the faults vividly enough to his compatriots. There were no limits to what progress could achieve, he realized, if the imaginative medium of fiction and, more particularly, the *limitless* genre of the novel (rather than the *limited* canvas of the novella) brought before the public, with all possible gripping description, the flaws of the civilization the Danes needed to correct. Goldschmidt's optimistic vision of literature as an ally of progress inspired him, therefore, to write not only journalistic articles but expansive and colorful novels. He became the first important novelist in the history of Danish literature. The novel *En Jøde* (A Jew, 1845) turned out to be his best, dealing with prejudices lingering on from the past. In the ideal Danish society, Goldschmidt felt, hateful prejudices should have no place; so with *En Jøde* he incited his fellow Danes to rid their society of this blight. The most deeply ingrained of all prejudices in Denmark were, he knew, those that had perpetuated religious bigotry. Because of the restrictions maintained by a rigidly structured state Lutheran Church, the gates of religious freedom had remained solidly shut in Danish society. No amount of social progress in Goldschmidt's time had been able to open them. A stodgy episcopate presided over by an old and reactionary primate, Bishop Jakob Mynster (1775–1854), had sought to preserve the ancient privileges of the established Lutheran Church and had succeeded well — not least of all because of the intense collaboration of throne and altar — in stifling everything that breathed of freedom or tolerance in religious matters. Danish society had little place for Jews, Catholics, dissenting Protestant sects, or even for any renewal of or departure from ancient creeds within the established church. The youthful Meïr Goldschmidt found this snobbish attitude on the part of Lutheran orthodoxy thoroughly at odds with the new progressive age. In *En Jøde* he took his plea for the abolition of religious prejudice directly to the people, optimistically believing they could do their part as responsible citizens to eliminate the national vice that stood in the way of achieving an ideal society. He also implied a patriotic belief that the Danish nation was very much worth preserving, if only the lack of religious freedom could be corrected.

But the overt fictional utilization of the mechanisms of prejudice caused a departure from realistic art, distorting reality in favor of an imagined concept of a more ideal society. Goldschmidt in this novel exaggerated the need for religious tolerance and exploited the religious issue so much that the work conforms more to the prescriptions of wishful thinking than to historical accuracy. Goldschmidt showed his readers the benefits of religious tolerance in a nonexistent ideal Danish state. His descriptions seem to manipulate the reader's sympathy to cause an improvement in religious conditions. In particular, the character portrayals are too black or too white to make them realistically convincing. The main female character, a Christian, is an utterly unsympathetic, faithless adulteress; the horrible Christian mob in the novel stops at virtually nothing in its merciless persecution of Jews. The incessantly taunted Jewish character, conversely, so elicits our sympathies that we feel he triumphs in defeat and death; we overlook his human faults and prefer to think of him more as a saint, hallowed by God with the crown of martyrdom. All in all, we sense here a fictional enterprise that is not a mirror of reality but, rather, a contrivance to sway public opinion. Its idealized intention, rousing the imaginations of men and women to a vision of a better society, no less than the emotional impact its noble message made on the Danish public, inevitably diminished the appeal of Poetic Realism: the more the Danes bought *En Jøde* (and other novels by Goldschmidt), the more they felt that the ambitious desire to raise people higher — rather than the sobering understanding of themselves as they actually existed — should now become the major guiding force of Danish literature.

The visual arts: Thorvaldsen and Købke

A glance aside at the visual arts further confirms the impression that the concerns of *Poetisk Realisme* had lost their appeal in Denmark after the mid-1830s. The increasing wealth in Denmark in the 1830s had given rise to a craving for a new monumentalism in the visual arts. Painting, in particular, became overtly larger and more stately. The more grandiose the canvases became, the greater the pride the Danes could take in the upsurge of this new feeling of national self-assurance. Monumentalism, a logical outcome of the growing national confidence, in turn helped spread that confidence.

The greatest artist of monumentalism at the time in Europe was the Danish sculptor Bertel Thorvaldsen (1770–1844). To him now all Danish eyes suddenly turned. He had been living in the Eternal City for forty years; more of a Danish Roman than a Dane, he had developed an extravagant style inspired by the monuments and statues he saw in Rome. Essentially, he had reinterpreted the gladiators and themes of antiquity, idealized in a colossally proportioned world of marble. Far removed from contemporary life, this art bore little or no resemblance to anything measurable on a realistic scale. Yet, Thorvaldsen's spectacular accomplishments had gained him an international fame and even a papal patronage more lavish than anything given to any artist since the time of Michelangelo in the Italian Renaissance.

That this renowned champion of the art form now so seemingly congenial to the new national pride in Denmark should himself be a Dane, and yet living in Rome instead of Copenhagen, made almost everyone in the Danish nation eager to press for his return to his native land. The concerted effort of many in the kingdom, with royal support, succeeded. On September 17, 1838, Thorvaldsen sailed into Copenhagen's harbor. It was a national occasion — the entire population of the (now madly populated) city went out to greet him. The implicit faith in the nation's destiny, which the Danes found confirmed when their national hero again took up residence in their capital city, led, of course, to an enormous popularization of his art of unrealistic monumentalism. This confirmation helped further to fade from sight the despair from which the Danes were now hurrying to free themselves. Significantly, one of the most popular sculptures Thorvaldsen completed soon after his triumphal return was a self-portrait in which he is seen leaning on a statue of "Hope" (1839).

Accompanying Thorvaldsen's return and the preceding much publicized preparation, the mania for a monumental art of unrealistic proportions awakened even in a prominent realist like Christen Købke an interest in the grand style of the ancients. In the spring of 1838, when Danes everywhere could read daily accounts of the anticipated return of Thorvaldsen, and Danish enthusiasm for the classical grandeur of the Eternal City reached a high point, Købke applied for and received a fellowship for a study trip to Italy. With undisguised joy he set out for the land that had suddenly received so much publicity in Denmark because of Thorvaldsen, arriving there on perhaps the same day his great artistic relative's many gigantic marble pieces were being unloaded at Copenhagen's docks. Almost immediately, one of Købke's biographers informs us, the Poetic Realist came out of his gloomy mood to become one of "the merriest of the merry."[90] And as he quickly adapted the cheerfulness of his new Italian surroundings, so, too, did his painting. For the hazy light of the North on his canvases he now substituted the sunny brightness of the South. For concentrated realistic portrayals of daily life in Copenhagen he now substituted monumental compositions exhibiting imposing conceptions of Italian subject matter.

The most important work he completed in Italy is his *Castel dell' Uovo* (1839–1840) — now on permanent display at the State Museum of Art in

---

[90] Emil Hannover, *Maleren Christen Købke, En Studie i dansk Kunsthistorie* (Copenhagen: Kunstforeningen i København, 1893), 106.

Copenhagen — a picture of the famous fortress at the entrance to the harbor of Naples. Clearly not intended to be a tourist or topographical picture, the canvas conspicuously lacks all the modern life around the ancient edifice that would catch the eye of the tourist (today and in Købke's day): no indication of any busy seaport life, none of the commercial vessels, fishing or sailing boats plying in and out of the harbor daily, anywhere in sight. In the sky we observe none of the seagulls ceaselessly fluttering about. On the ground we find, strangely, no sight of any of the colorful street hawkers who always hurry about peddling their wares. We have only a huge, closed building resembling a massive sculpture, bathed in such a strong sunlight its volume seems virtually suspended.

The picture impresses, therefore, not because of its recognizable reality, but because of its monumental effect, its sunny peace, and the serene beauty of a setting that appears so ageless we sense it to be practically lifted out of actual time. In short, the painting evokes an image of sublime grandeur, but not one of real life — a far cry from anything Poetic Realism wanted to convey.

Yet, if this painting is not at all representative of Poetic Realism, it is, nevertheless, enormously significant for the history of that artistic movement. When Købke, the quintessential painter of *Poetisk Realisme*, left Denmark in late 1838 and then pressed his brush into the service of an art concerned more with the ideal than the real, he delivered *Poetisk Realisme* a staggering blow.

8. *Poetisk Realisme* exhausts its creative vigor on Danish soil

The lengthening of the shadows

The blow the movement received with Købke's defection in 1838 — coupled with the fast rise of newer forms of art resulting from the vastly changed social and political situation in Denmark, and the new ground broken by such literary luminaries as Andersen, Grundtvig, and Goldschmidt — might have proven fatal for the movement in that year. To make matters worse for Poetic Realism in Denmark in 1838, Copenhagen's citizens had turned out en masse to extend a rousing welcome to Thorvaldsen and to hail a new dawn for an artistic monumentalism that represented, after all, the virtual antithesis of everything *Poetisk Realisme* represented. Climaxing all the blows *Poetisk Realisme* received in 1838 came the death of its illustrious founder, Poul Martin Møller. He died saddened, knowing full well that the movement in Danish literature he had inaugurated was being replaced by a form of literature alien to his way of thinking. Everything he had lived and worked for now seemed to be collapsing. "Much of Danish literature," he lamented in one of his last public statements, is now being "written without a view of life as its basis."[91]

But if hopes for the continuation of Poetic Realism in Denmark could hardly have looked bleaker than they did in 1838, the movement was not yet thrown into a state of total deliquescence. For one thing, Blicher, Fru Gyllembourg, and Bernhard, still living, continued to champion the cause of Poetic Realism, even though their creative powers had visibly declined because of the changed attitudes in the nation.

The light before the final eclipse: Bernhard Ingemann's conversion to *Poetisk Realisme*

More important for the prevention of the total eclipse of Poetic Realism by the end of 1838, however, was the sudden surge of strength the movement acquired when another towering giant of Danish letters entered its camp, just as the shadows hovering over it were rapidly lengthening. This latecomer to *Poetisk Realisme* was Bernhard Severin Ingemann (1789–1862). Early in his long and distinguished literary career an accomplished poet of Danish Romanticism, he had come very close to rivaling Oehlenschläger for the primacy in that literary movement. Successful as he had been as a Romantic writer, however, he possessed too much versatility to remain all his life solely in the tent of Romanticism. Later, he entered the poetic camp of Grundtvig and gained no less popularity for the poetry he wrote in competition with that eloquent poet. As a result, Ingemann became, as P. M. Mitchell (concisely summarizing the general opinion held by Danish literary historians) has said, "something of a combination of Oehlenschläger and Grundtvig."[92]

An additional dimension to Ingemann's versatile literary creativity also deserves note: his gravitation, quite late in his career of belles lettres, toward Poetic Realism. This opinion has jelled largely in defiance of traditional Danish criticism. Karl Mortensen (1867–1942), a Danish schoolmaster who had assumed the headship of a German Gymnasium at Haderslev in Schleswig-Holstein when it came under Danish rule in 1920,

---

[91] English translation by W. Glyn Jones in "Søren Kierkegaard and Poul Martin Møller," 81.

[92] Mitchell, *A History of Danish Literature*, 118.

first specifically called attention, it seems, to Ingemann's "ultimate drifting into the camp of Poetic Realism."[93] (Had Mortensen's sense of Ingemann's Poetic Realism been conditioned by an awareness of German Poetic Realism, which the critic could have acquired at a school where Theodor Storm's works belonged to the canon of the literary curriculum?) More recently, Fritz Paul, the prominent German Scandinavianist of our day, has also spoken of Ingemann's "conversion to Poetic Realism."[94] But it has remained essentially for the scholarly acumen of a contemporary Danish Germanist, Leif Ludwig Albertsen, finally to offer the proof for the belated glow Ingemann had bestowed on *Poetisk Realisme*.[95]

Varners Sommer-Vandringer

Ingemann added his considerable artistic weight to the movement of Poetic Realism, Albertsen informs us, when, in 1845, he refashioned one of his earlier well-known Romantic compositions into a new and brilliantly representative piece of Poetic Realism. In the earlier version from 1813, *Varners pöetiske Vandringer, Et romantisk Digt* (Varner's Poetic Wanderings, A Romantic Composition), readers saw Varner, the wandering hero of the novel, happily singing on his pilgrimage through life. When readers took leave of the novel, they felt as certain as did Varner that, at the end of his life, he would be richly rewarded by God. The novel of 1813 forced all poetic description into the perspective of an individual sustained by the joyous hope of salvation within a divinely ordained order. In the revised version of 1845, *Varners Sommer-Vandringer, En Sangkreds i Brevfragmenter* (Varner's Summer Wanderings, A Series of Songs in Fragmentary Letters), Ingemann joins forces with the writers of *Poetisk Realisme*, adopts an avowed anti-Romantic purpose, and purges his earlier novel not only of its elaborate metaphorical structure but of its uplifting music as well. The original novel is now scarcely recognizable and greatly shortened, approximating more the size of a concise novella of Poetic Realism than a cumbersome novel of Romanticism. Gone, in particular, are all the superimposed trappings of Christian imagery and angelic music that the

---

[93] Karl Mortensen, "Spredte Betragtninger fra konservativt Stade," *Det Nya Sverige* 19 (1925): 352.

[94] Fritz Paul, "Romantik und Poetischer Realismus," in *Grundzüge der neueren skandinavischen Literaturen* (Darmstadt: Wissenschaftliche Buchgesellschaft, 1982), 99.

[95] Leif Ludwig Albertsen, "Die neuen Tabus des poetischen Realismus: Ingemanns Änderungen am eigenen romantischen Frühwerk," in *In Search of the Poetic Real, Essays in Honor of Clifford Albrecht Bernd on the Occasion of his Sixtieth Birthday*, eds. John F. Fetzer, Roland Hoermann, Winder McConnell (Stuttgart: Heinz, 1989), 1-10.

pious Romantic narrator of the first version had so obviously fancied. If, in the first (Romantic) version, Varner was ever journeying on the ageless pilgrim's pathway leading to a sure and certain redemption in a world beyond the grave, in the revised (Poetic Realistic) text, Varner's main task as a traveler is to discover the validity of the visible world to which he belongs. The culmination of this succinct version thus asserts, in marked contrast to the earlier one, the vitality of the everyday world and makes the wandering hero, even in his brief eccentric course, a figure from reality searching for a self-awareness and an identity in it.

Ingemann, in recasting his Romantic *Varner* in the mold of *Poetisk Realisme*, captured a fading literary mood, and by virtue of his achievement, Poetic Realism experienced something of a belated renewal of vitality. Yet, in spite of Ingemann's ability to emulate successfully the contributions of other outstanding Poetic Realists, tragically he embraced the movement too late. *Varners Sommer-Vandringer*, despite its artistic merits, never became popular. Nor did any of the subsequent, weaker pieces of Poetic Realism he wrote. The sobering style of Poetic Realism simply did not impress Danish audiences in 1845 and thereafter. A new generation of writers had already achieved another working aesthetic and had infected the tastes of the reading public to accommodate it.

Significantly, the lack of enthusiasm in Denmark for Ingemann's late contribution to Poetic Realism was compensated by the recognition he received at the time in Sweden, and by none other than the critic who had assumed the position of moderator of Poetic Realism in Sweden: Per Daniel Amadeus Atterbom. During the identical years the interest in Poetic Realism most visibly declined in Denmark, between 1838 and 1845, the friendship between Ingemann and Atterbom grew in warmth and intensity,[96] and Poetic Realism acquired — not least of all because of Atterbom's critical efforts — a new vitality in Sweden and Swedish-speaking Finland.

Poetisk Realisme suspends its functions in Denmark and strikes out in different directions abroad

By 1845, hence, Poetic Realism had all but exhausted its creative vigor on Danish soil. Soon it would suspend its functions altogether in the land of its birth. But this was only a pause in the lengthy course of Poetic Realism, for even before the movement could come to a halt in Denmark, it

---

[96] See the correspondence of Ingemann and Atterbom edited by Kjeld Galster, *Ingemann og Atterbom, En Brevveksling* (Copenhagen: Hagerup, 1924).

had already struck out in different directions, crossing the Danish frontiers and making its way across adjacent Swedish- and German-speaking territories. There, after initial periods of adaptation to differing tongues and other historical circumstances, its streams would rise again — as we shall see in the following pages — to new and spectacular heights.

Poul Martin Møller
Courtesy of *Det Kongelige Bibliotek*, Copenhagen

Steen Steensen Blicher
Courtesy of *Det Kongelige Bibliotek*, Copenhagen

Thomasine Gyllembourg
Courtesy of *Det Kongelige Bibliotek*, Copenhagen

Carl Bernhard
Courtesy of *Det Kongelige Bibliotek*, Copenhagen

Christen Købke
Courtesy of *Det Kongelige Bibliotek*, Copenhagen

Bernhard Ingemann
Courtesy of *Det Kongelige Bibliotek*, Copenhagen

SWEDISH *POETISK REALISM*

1. The Danish movement spreads to other parts of Scandinavia

Readers have always assumed a close literary interaction between the various parts of the Scandinavian world. It has seemed particularly logical to critics outside of Scandinavia to look at the literatures of Denmark, Norway, and Sweden in conjunction with one another. Instead of studying Danish, Norwegian, or Swedish literature in isolation, these critics have preferred to address themselves to "Scandinavian literature," and with good reason. The circumstances of a common Old Norse heritage, close geographic proximity, related language, and shared religious beliefs often enough combined, wholly or partially, to make a literary movement in one Scandinavian nation wash over onto the shores of another.

2. *Poetisk Realisme*'s failure to reach Norway

One would expect that the first foreign shore any Danish literary movement would reach would be Norway's. Denmark and Norway had been joined politically under a common sovereign as early as the year 955, and the two nations remained together as a united kingdom until 1814. For more than eight and a half centuries Norwegian and Danish cultural elements had generously intermingled. Yet, since Copenhagen was the home of the monarch, the seat of government, and, above all, the center of culture in the Dano-Norwegian kingdom, Danish culture invariably flooded Norway, rather than the other way around. James McFarlane, the eminent interpreter of Norwegian literature in our day, summed up the situation clearly when he said: "However one may care to define what had been 'Norwegian' in the life and letters of the twin kingdoms of Denmark-

Norway before 1814, there was certainly very little that did not in some way or other bear the stamp of Copenhagen."[97]

In looking for reverberations of Danish *Poetisk Realisme* in Norway, one must take the great watershed of 1814 seriously. After so many centuries of political and cultural union with Denmark, Norway, in that year, finally freed itself from domination by Copenhagen and became, according to the constitution adopted at Eidsvoll on May 17, "a free, independent, indivisible, and inalienable kingdom." This is not the place to argue over the accuracy of such a proclamation in view of the new political union with Sweden, which immediately followed, but Norwegians everywhere rejoiced so much in their new feeling of liberation from Denmark that they suddenly looked back at the centuries of cultural union with Denmark as a humiliating period of subservience. Voices claimed to adduce "evidence enough that Norway, having suffered the insult of Denmark through the course of generations, had gained nothing and lost all ... lost its kings, its freedom, its courts, its fleet, its flag, its language, its territories, its resources and its name in the political and literary world."[98]

With such anti-Danish sentiment running rampant, it could hardly be expected that Norwegians at that moment in their history would willingly embrace yet another literary movement arising in Denmark. The new patriotic fervor of the Norwegians mandated that they now shun, rather than welcome, further cultural influences originating in Denmark. No one could have sensed this more acutely than the father of Poetic Realism himself, Poul Martin Møller. He had joined the faculty at the newly established University of Christiana (Oslo) in 1826, receiving his appointment because the first university in Norway had in its beginning years little choice but to recruit faculty from abroad, and Danish scholars, because least hampered by language difficulties, were the best pool of candidates to which Norwegian authorities could turn. Owing to the icy Dano-Norwegian tensions, however, Møller felt isolated in Norway from the very start and was remarkably unsuccessful as a teacher. According to biographical statements, neither he nor the Norwegians understood one another, nor did either side apparently have much inclination to do so — the political climate at the time was simply too hostile. Consequently, Møller leaped at the chance to leave Norway and return to Denmark as soon as an occasion presented itself, four years later in 1830.[99]

---

[97] James Walter McFarlane, *Ibsen and the Temper of Norwegian Literature* (London: Oxford University Press, 1960), 28.

[98] Ibid.

[99] Bernd Henningsen, *Poul Martin Møller oder Die dänische Erziehung des Søren Kierkegaard* (Frankfurt am Main: Akademische Verlagsgesellschaft, 1973), 58-64.

Thus, notwithstanding Møller's presence in Christiana (Oslo), *Poetisk Realisme* did not gain a foothold on Norwegian territory. It would have been too much to expect that precisely when Norway was striving to cut its apron strings to Denmark, the awakening national consciousness of the new nation could tolerate any apparent continuation of the Danish cultural yoke. Later in Norwegian history this overblown, but understandable, hostility toward Danish culture would diminish, but too late to allow the import of *Poetisk Realisme*. By then other literary modes were in vogue.

3. Swedish foreign policy favors the travel of Danish culture to Sweden

While Norway was shutting its ports of entry to Danish influence — just when *Poetisk Realisme* had matured enough to flow across the Skagerrak Strait that separates the two — the passage for literary culture from Denmark to Sweden opened wider than it had for centuries. The Swedish defeat in the Russo-Swedish War of 1807–1809, and the accompanying rise of Russia as a greater power than ever before in northern Europe, forced Sweden suddenly to abandon many long-established channels of cultural communication to the lands of the eastern Baltic. Following the shakeup of the Napoleonic era, Sweden also lost its important bridgeheads in Germany, Swedish Pommerania with the Isle of Rügen, held for some two hundred years, and the port of Wismar in Mecklenburg, through which the flow of culture between Sweden and Germany had passed so naturally for longer than anyone could remember. Ousted for the first time in centuries from traditional spheres of influence on its entire eastern flank, stretching in a huge semicircle from northern Finland to the southern shores of the Baltic, Sweden now sought to design a new foreign policy, featuring closer links to its twin Scandinavian sister-nations to the west. This outlook gave birth to a "Pan-Scandinavianism": the idea that Sweden, Denmark, and Norway could form a single cultural unit and possibly even a political one. The latter seemed especially within reach in the early 1830s, when war appeared imminent between the rival great powers in northern Europe, England and Russia. Sweden's king, Charles XIV, then felt it wise to establish a joint policy of political neutrality with Denmark in order to keep the Scandinavian countries out of the conflict. Further close contact between Denmark and Sweden came with the inauguration of regular steamboat service between Helsingör (Denmark) and Hälsingborg (Sweden) in 1836, and with the beginning of daily passenger service between Copenhagen and Malmö in 1838. In short, Danish culture began, in the 1820s and 1830s, to have unprecedented access to Sweden. It was a situation ideal for the travel of a Danish literary movement to Sweden.

4. Conditions retarding the travel of *Poetisk Realisme* to Sweden

Under these circumstances Danish *Poetisk Realisme* might have enjoyed a speedy, triumphant march across Sweden. Two things, however, prevented this from happening. Unlike in Denmark, life in Sweden in the 1820s was not caught in the throes of economic chaos and rampant poverty. After the fall of Napoleon, Sweden had lost its empire in Finland and northern Germany but had also acquired Norway; the losses to the east and the south were thus sweetened by the huge gain on the western frontier. If Denmark had grown poorer by forfeiting Norway, Sweden grew richer by receiving it. Sweden had come out of the Napoleonic era infinitely better off than had Denmark. Sweden lacked the sense of shock on which *Poetisk Realisme* had fed in Denmark, to nourish the rise of a similar literary movement.

Concomitantly, Romanticism, as firmly entrenched in Sweden as in Denmark, could not be dislodged from its enviable position as easily as in Denmark. Quite to the contrary, the new Pan-Scandinavianism developing out of Sweden's post-Napoleonic foreign policy seemed even to strengthen the Romantic notion of a literature emphasizing the common Scandinavian heritage of the Viking gods — an idea thoroughly alien to Møller, Blicher, Fru Gyllembourg, and other Danish Poetic Realists. It stood for everything they opposed. How, then, could they appeal to a nation casting its sights on something they rejected? On the other hand, the Swedish situation seemed almost made to order for Oehlenschläger. What sort of literature could be more consonant with Swedish foreign policy at the time than the one championed by Oehlenschläger, centered on the common Scandinavian heritage of the Viking gods? Thus, when the gates of Sweden opened wide to welcome Danish culture, it was Oehlenschläger's brand of Romanticism, rather than Poetic Realism, which made the quickest entry. Fritz Paul has noted that Oehlenschläger's Pan-Scandinavian Romanticism, debunked in Denmark by the Poetic Realists, received a welcome constituting a curious anachronism in literary history.[100] Nevertheless, under the existing historical-

---

[100] Fritz Paul, "Romantik und Poetischer Realismus," in *Grundzüge der neueren skandinavischen Literaturen* (Darmstadt: Wissenschaftliche Buchgesellschaft, 1982), 87.

political circumstances, it was neither astonishing nor incomprehensible. Of course, Oehlenschläger rejoiced as much as any writer could have. If the loss of his prestige in Denmark had saddened him, now the upsurge in the Swedish interest in his work gladdened him. To compensate for the humiliating chagrin he had felt at being toppled from his position of literary primacy in his native land by the new Poetic Realists, with all the energy at his command he asserted himself in the company of Swedish men of letters. The high point came in 1829. In his memoirs Oehlenschläger describes the important moment: the mighty bells of the ancient cathedral of Lund rang out across the Swedish countryside. Together with the bishop of Wexiö, representing the crown prince of Sweden, and the *Rector magnificus* of Lund's university, Oehlenschläger entered the cathedral in solemn procession and proceeded to the high altar. There with trumpets resounding the bishop crowned him "Nordic Poet Laureate."[101] Could Sweden have bestowed a higher honor upon a foreign writer? The degree of intellectual contact between Denmark and Sweden had reached remarkable heights. Yet the Poetic Realists in Denmark, seeing the author they had dethroned now receiving the laurel wreath of Sweden, could not help being embarrassed. The more Romanticism in Sweden grew stronger, the harder it became for Poetic Realism to take root there.

This setback, however, was only temporary. Ideal conditions prevailed for the flow of Danish culture to Sweden; the Swedes sooner or later had to note such a powerful Danish literary current as *Poetisk Realisme*, and it, too, would then hit Sweden. The preoccupation with the past so characteristic of Oehlenschläger's Romanticism had to lead in Sweden no less than in Denmark to a literary conservatism (if not to a cultural stagnation) crying out for reform — for a newer, fresher breeze. Where could the Swedes more easily discover such a fresh breeze but in the literary movement that had already reinvigorated Danish literature, precisely when its vigor, too, had been impaired by Oehlenschläger's stubborn attempts to escape into poetic dreams of an ancient Viking world?

5. Thomasine Gyllembourg finds a Swedish successor in Fredrika Bremer

In the earliest Swedish attempt to embrace Poetic Realism, Fredrika Bremer (1801–1865) wrote in the 1830s a series of short prose works entitled *Teckningar utur hvardagslifvet* (Sketches from Everyday Life). It

---

[101] Adam Oehlenschläger, *Meine Lebens-Erinnerungen*, IV (Leipzig: Lorck, 1850), 69-71.

has been observed that they bear a remarkable resemblance to the *Hverdags-Historier* (Everyday Stories), the set of tales that Fru Gyllembourg published continuing (and including) *En Hverdags-Historie.*[102] This similarity suggests that Fredrika Bremer wanted to emulate her older Danish sister-authoress. At the time Bremer wrote these stories, Sweden's ports of entry for the importation of Danish literature were wide open, more so than ever before. How could Fru Gyllembourg's popular Danish novellas fail to reach Sweden's shores? And how could Fredrika Bremer fail to be impressed with Gyllembourg's accomplishment? Can we interpret the striking similarity between the tales of the two writers otherwise than that the younger imitated the older sister?

Yet, however much we may wish to regard Fredrika Bremer as a successor of Thomasine Gyllembourg, however much we can view Fredrika Bremer's literary legacy as a milestone in the spread of Poetic Realism beyond the Danish frontiers, we must also recognize that the *Teckningar utur hvardagslifvet* did not rise above the level of a weak offshoot of the literary form Fru Gyllembourg advocated. Fredrika Bremer may have been a successor to Thomasine Gyllembourg, but she was not a particularly distinguished one. The history of the reception of her work in Germany offers the most telling evidence for her weak position within the ranks of the Poetic Realists. Widely and enthusiastically received in Germany in the 1830s, Bremer's works rapidly lost appeal in the German-speaking world once publications by Danish and German Poetic Realists flooded the German booktrade (after 1848).[103] The German reading public did not find her works nearly as good as those of other Poetic Realists and simply turned to better works. Fritz Paul said it all when he stated that although Bremer's prose fiction possessed some "tendencies toward Poetic Realism," she cannot be considered "a great representative writer" of that literary movement.[104]

6. Johan Erik Rydqvist's manifesto for *Poetisk Realism*

Of more far-reaching consequences for the advance of Poetic Realism in Sweden than Bremer's pale imitation of Fru Gyllembourg's fiction was the critical debate that the *Teckningar utur hvardagslifvet* had sparked.

---

[102] Mogens Brøndsted, ed., *Nordische Literaturgeschichte*, trans. H. K. Mueller, I (Munich: Fink, 1982), 354.

[103] Karin Carsten Monten, *Fredrika Bremer in Deutschland, Aufnahme und Kritik* (Neumünster: Wachholtz, 1981), 73, 103, 159-61.

[104] Paul, "Romantik und Poetischer Realismus," 141.

Quickly men of letters in Sweden sensed that with the publication of Fredrika Bremer's tales the steady and complacent stream of Swedish Romantic literature had received an unexpected jolt. Was the Romanticism that had been the main staple of Swedish literature for so long now drying up? Facts seemed to belie this, for the commanding figures of Swedish literature continued to write in the Romantic vein just as before, and to the uninterrupted delight of Swedish readers.

Still, an authoress had now appeared on the Swedish literary scene for whom neither metaphysical flights to the Nordic Middle Ages nor the floating imagery of the Romantics seemed important. What was she trying to achieve? The sages on the Swedish Parnassus had received fresh food for thought, and it seemed only natural that they should debate the impact and meaning of Bremer's abrupt departure from the established course of Swedish literature.

This new critical debate centered in the ancient university town of Uppsala. One of the foremost participants in the discussions was the university librarian Johan Erik Rydqvist (1800–1877). It is to the credit of a circumspect Swedish literary critic of modern times, Kurt Aspelin (1929–1977), that he called attention to Rydqvist's seminal role in helping Poetic Realism take root in Sweden. In vain one searches through the standard histories of Swedish literature for Rydqvist, but undeterred we should recognize with Aspelin that Rydqvist was a fountainhead for Swedish Poetic Realism.[105] Nor should we deny to Rydqvist any longer the credit of historical importance for writing what Aspelin rightly calls "a manifesto for Poetic Realism."[106]

More than anyone else in Sweden at the time, Rydqvist, in the quiet of his library study, fruitfully reflected on what Bremer had contributed to Swedish literature. His analysis of the third part of the *Teckningar utur hvardagslifvet* gave him the excuse to indicate to his fellow Swedes a theoretical incentive to conquer an entirely new area of literary expression. The analysis appeared in the form of a review published in 1831 in the critical journal *Heimdall;* from this analysis he derived the scheme to set up a guideline for a new form of Swedish literature. As a timid librarian he had, in the words of Aspelin, a "dislike of general cocksureness and minted stereotypes." He had a basic unwillingness to formulate a literary theory in any bold or categorical manner, and therefore he found it more congenial

---

[105] Kurt Aspelin, *Poesi och verklighet*, I (Göteborg: Akademiförlaget, 1967), 26.
[106] Ibid., 30.

to his temperament to enunciate his literary position by critically analyzing the novelty of Bremer's experiment.[107]

What most informs these reflections on Bremer — this manifesto for Poetic Realism — is the way Rydqvist, in the course of his analysis, constantly oscillates between the "real" on the one hand and the "poetic" on the other. He says, for instance, that just as Fredrika Bremer visualizes realistically convincing pictures originating in fantasy, so, too, she recaptures engagingly the minutiae of everyday life, events ignored and changes unobserved.[108] She portrays reality with unflinching candor, he writes, yet she also endows that reality with poetic interest. To a genuine poetic eye, Rydqvist continues, our everyday reality becomes neither lifeless nor indistinct nor boring; it only appears so to an uninspired mind, a blunted intellect, or languid powers of observation. A well-equipped imagination, however, breathes spirit into what is inanimate, beautifies what looks ugly, imparts grace to what is rigid or repulsive, and offers comfort to the whole. Such an imagination does not change reality; it only lets another component of that reality surface. If one has an eye for what is characteristic for every situation, and if one can mirror this so the soul actively recognizes what it once observed in reality, Rydqvist adds, then the most insignificant detail of reality often acquires a heightened value.

Never in this programmatic statement does Rydqvist lose his grip on the set of principles that constitutes for him a germinal theory of Poetic Realism. As circuitous as his manifesto may be, as uncategorical as his declaration of a new Swedish aesthetic may sound, he insists that in literature reality not be copied in any "soulless" manner, but neither may it be "beautified," illuminated with some false romanticized halo. Rather, Rydqvist believes, reality must be presented as a poetic discovery of something forgotten or unobserved. The regulating idea of Rydqvist's thought is thus always a dogged determination to interweave the poetic with the real. The divorce of the two, so typical of Scandinavian Romanticism, must not be a cardinal feature of the literature Swedish writers should now aspire to and embrace.

Closing our discussion of Rydqvist's salutary role promoting a Danish-born literary movement in Sweden, it is appropriate to mention, as we learn from Carl Santesson's biography of this Uppsala librarian, that he was a regular reader of *Kjøbenhavns flyvende Post*, the periodical in which so much of Thomasine Gyllembourg's critical commentary on Poetic Real-

---

[107] Ibid., 31.

[108] Ibid., 30. This account is based on Aspelin's quotations of particular relevant passages from Rydqvist's manifesto.

ism first saw the light.[109] Not only Rydqvist's remarkable manifesto but also the Danish literary influence to which he, in the great reading room of Uppsala's university library, was regularly exposed helped to mark a change in the intellectual atmosphere of Sweden.

7. Per Daniel Atterbom introduces the term *Poetisk Realist*

The spread of Poetic Realism to Sweden took another giant step forward when Rydqvist's most important contemporary in Uppsala, Per Daniel Amadeus Atterbom (1790–1855), turned his attention toward it. In histories of Swedish literature Atterbom has come to be associated almost exclusively with the Romantic movement in literature. Typically, the literary historian Ingemar Algulin introduces Atterbom to non-Swedish readers as "the clear leader of a high Romantic Phalanx that had its seat in Uppsala."[110] But this Romantic label affixed to Atterbom, passed on from one history of literature to another, fails to consider how profoundly he had been affected by the changing tides of Danish literature during his lifetime. Atterbom was in no sense the parochial Swedish poet-critic that his modern countrymen label him. His knowledge of the Danish literary scene, for instance, was as vast as his familiarity with Swedish letters.[111] If early in his career he joined the Romantic movement, this was largely due to the strong influence of Oehlenschläger, whom he knew personally. But Atterbom had also known other members of the Danish literary elite — it would be preposterous to think that he could have limited himself to championing in Sweden solely the sort of Danish literature represented by Oehlenschläger. Later in life Atterbom's literary inclinations were, as the German Scandinavianist Fritz Paul (correcting prevailing Swedish critical opinion) has said, far more closely aligned to Poetic Realism than to Romanticism.[112] In particular, Atterbom's correspondence with the last of the Danish converts to Poetic Realism, Bernhard Ingemann, bears this out. Fritz Paul has not referred to this correspondence, and Swedish critics ap-

---

[109] Carl Santesson, *Johan Erik Rydqvist, Kritikern och Publicisten* (Stockholm: Geber, 1944), 71, 72, 120.

[110] Ingemar Algulin, *A History of Swedish Literature* (Stockholm: Swedish Institute, 1989), 74.

[111] This vast knowledge is amply documented throughout Elisabeth Tykesson's biographical study *Atterbom, En Lernadsteckning* (Stockholm: Norstedt, 1954).

[112] Paul, "Romantik und Poetischer Realismus," 127.

parently have not noticed it (perhaps because the letters were published in Denmark, thus not easily accessible to Swedish scholars). But if Swedish sages had read, for instance, the letters of August 23, 1842, and December 19, 1843, it would have been clear to them the extent to which Atterbom had learned from his Danish friend that Romanticism had been superseded by Poetic Realism.[113]

So assiduously, indeed, did Atterbom preoccupy himself with the phenomenon of Poetic Realism that to him must go the credit for being the first person anywhere in Europe to give this literary movement its name. No one today outside of Sweden seems aware of this naming, and it is high time all modern critics concerned with Poetic Realism in its various national voices should recognize Atterbom's coining the formula.

Atterbom, a professor of aesthetics at the University of Uppsala, used his academic position, his erudition, and his literary perceptiveness to make himself the central figure in the critical debate in Uppsala over the blow Fredrika Bremer dealt Swedish Romanticism. As a close personal friend of Rydqvist, moreover, he had a familiarity with the latter's critical principles as thorough as anyone living in Uppsala at the time could have had.[114] He could easily recognize Rydqvist's attempt to give Swedish literature new theoretical impulses, but just as readily he could observe that the librarian's manifesto for a new literature linking fiction with reality remained at best an awkward statement, a far cry from the great literary-critical treatises of the various centuries he customarily introduced to his students from the podium of his university lecture hall. For all the initiative Rydqvist took, the manifesto only circumscribed with long and vague thoughts what the shy librarian was trying to say. Atterbom, the academic teacher and historian of literary theories, could see that Rydqvist's proposal to link fiction with reality in a new form of literature lacked, in its critical language, a fixed term for this desire. The need for a term or concept as a reference frame for the debate over Rydqvist's manifesto only became more acute for Atterbom when he heard from the Uppsala coterie of literary critics the bewildering set of possible terms invented to describe the new post-Romantic literature proposed by Rydqvist. Kurt Aspelin gives us an entertaining survey of some of these various terms circulated in

---

[113] Kjeld Galster, ed., *Ingemann og Atterbom, En Brevveksling* (Copenhagen: Hagerup, 1924), 34, 39.

[114] Concerning the Atterbom-Rydqvist literary friendship see Tykesson, 166, 212, 220, 223, 226-28, 265, 273, 288, 293-95. Further references can be found in Jacob Kulling, *Atterboms "Svenska siare och skalder," En undersökning av hans litteraturhistoriska forskning* (Stockholm: Norstedt, 1931), 76-149, esp. 83, 109, 123. Atterbom's letters to Rydqvist can be read in *P. D. A. Atterboms Brev till J. E. Rydqvist*, ed. T. Höjer (Stockholm: Norstedt, 1945). Rydqvist's letters to Atterbom have not been published.

Uppsala. First came "ideal realism," soon discarded as not well chosen and suffering from a philosophical connotation thoroughly alien to Rydqvist's thought. Then followed "late romanticism," "liberalism" (meaning liberated from Romanticism), and "beginning realism," all rejected almost as soon as they emerged, since they risked being too broad or vague.[115]

In this confusing state of affairs Atterbom made use of his position of leadership in the Uppsala school of critics and propagated the most ingenious term of all those put forward and the one, moreover, which has maintained itself most persistently to the present day: "Poetic Realism" or, in the Swedish version, *Poetisk Realism*.[116]

Although critics have not pointed this out, there can be little question about how Atterbom had first become acquainted with this term. Quite early in his academic career he had come under the spell of the German philosopher Friedrich Wilhelm Joseph Schelling (1775–1854). He visited Schelling often in the latter's home in Munich. Their shared interest in aesthetics led to an abiding friendship, which even included various members of their families.[117] We know Atterbom had been profoundly influenced by Schelling's terminology.[118] Schelling had coined the German formula *Poetischer Realismus* in 1802 to refer to Plato's polemic against those trying to achieve a synthesis of the real and the ideal in poetry.[119] Amid the Uppsala debate over Rydqvist's manifesto, searching for a precise, easily handled term of reference, how could it be otherwise than that Atterbom, who never tired of referring to Schelling as his "great," "inspiring," and "beloved" teacher,[120] should not then remember Schelling's formula and apply it to the new demand for a literature of realism in Sweden?

---

[115] Aspelin, 20.

[116] For the enduring importance of the term *Poetisk Realism* for Swedish literary historiography see the recent studies by 1) Oskar Bandle, "Periodiseringen i nyare nordisk litteraturhistoria," *Samlaren* 105 (1984): 65, 72; and 2) Christer Westling, *Idealismens estetik* (Stockholm: Westling, 1985), 236.

[117] *Aufzeichnungen des schwedischen Dichters P. D. A. Atterbom über berühmte deutsche Männer und Frauen nebst Reiseerinnerungen aus Deutschland und Italien aus den Jahren 1817-1819*, trans. Franz Maurer (Berlin: Heymann, 1867), 115, 129-33, 148-49, 166-69.

[118] Elias Bredsdorff, Brita Mortensen, Ronald Popperwell, *An Introduction to Scandinavian Literature* (Copenhagen: Munksgaard, 1951), 112.

[119] *Schellings Werke*. Nach der Originalausgabe in neuer Anordnung herausgegeben von Manfred Schröter, III (Munich: Beck, 1927), 368-69. See, too, the commentary by Heinrich Reinhardt, *Die Dichtungstheorie der sogenannten Poetischen Realisten* (Würzburg: Triltsch, 1939), 17.

[120] "Atterboms bref till Schelling," Meddelade af Ruben G:son Berg, *Samlaren* 39 (1918): 72, 87, 91, 92, 97, 101, 107, 110.

In Uppsala, where literary criticism had become an institutionalized part of daily life, the term doubtless spread from mouth to mouth among pupils and literary friends gathered around Atterbom. It became an enduring fixture of criticism, however, when Atterbom used it in an essay addressed to "Runebergs Dikter" (Runeberg's Poetry) published in volume 6 (1838) of the *Swenska Litteratur-Föreningens Tidning* (Journal of the Swedish Literary Society), the leading forum for literary criticism in Uppsala after the *Heimdall* had ceased publication in 1832.

This "great critical essay," as it has been called,[121] appeared in the issue of February 28, 1838. Right at the beginning Atterbom refers to the much talked of contemporary Swedish-language poet of Finland, Johan Ludvig Runeberg, as "afgjordt en poetisk realist" (decidedly a Poetic Realist).[122] Atterbom then explains what he means calling Runeberg a "Poetic Realist." In the first place, he says, Runeberg is an "objective" writer, in contrast to most contemporary Swedish authors, who are "subjective." Runeberg begins, when writing fiction, with the realistic object rather than the subjective reflection about it.[123] Yet, even though the subjective reflection may not be of primary importance in Runeberg's "objective" or realistic art, Atterbom continues, this does not mean that a subjective personality is absent in his fictional enterprises. For if such a subjective personality were absent in any poetic construct, such a work of art would be insufferably arid and more dead than alive.[124] Such is not the case in Runeberg's poetry, we read, for he is a poet of the first order;[125] hence, the objective reality we find in Runeberg's poetry does not lack a personality behind the scenes.[126] This subjective or poetic personality (who selects, shapes, and arranges the objective reality) makes use of his manipulating power, Atterbom concludes, to "transfigure" (*förklara*, a term already heavily used in the Atterbom-Rydqvist correspondence)[127] the observed reality so that it becomes a commentary with "timeless and universal validity."[128]

Atterbom's usage of Schelling's formula "Poetic Realism," describing the new Swedish style of writing practiced by Runeberg, had, of course,

---

[121] Aspelin, 102.

[122] *Swenska Litteratur-Föreningens Tidning* 6 (1838): 130.

[123] Ibid., 131.

[124] Ibid., 132-33.

[125] Ibid., 129.

[126] Ibid., 134.

[127] *P. D. A. Atterboms Brev till J. E. Rydqvist*, 82.

[128] *Swenska Litteratur-Föreningens Tidning* 6 (1838): 137-38.

little in common with Schelling's understanding of Plato. The only thing Atterbom and Schelling shared was the formula itself. Endowing it with a different meaning than Schelling's, Atterbom, in effect, coined a new term in literary criticism. Moreover, with the formula and his explanation of it, Atterbom also "succeeded," as Kurt Aspelin has said, "in formulating a program for a [Swedish] Poetic Realism"[129] — a theoretical program that other Swedish writers could put into practice.[130]

8. The triumph of theory over practice in Sweden

Atterbom's theoretical program for a *Poetisk Realism* in Sweden added another building stone to the new tower of literary theory being erected then at Uppsala. Like Rydqvist's manifesto, it furthered the critical debate at the university about the new form of literature which should supersede Swedish Romanticism. Yet, the more scholars at Uppsala discussed, debated, and defined a theory of Poetic Realism, the more the evolving theory resembled an academic exercise with little impact on the Swedish world beyond Uppsala's ivory tower. The more attention paid to a theory of Poetic Realism, the less, it seemed, the practice of Poetic Realism could get off the ground.

The best the theorists at Uppsala could do, aside from fostering their own academic debate, was to inspire several students at the university to press their pens into the service of a new art of Poetic Realism. These budding talents in fiction, known as the *Signatur-poeterna* (Signature Poets), gave the developing theory of Poetic Realism some additional momentum. When their student days ended, however, they adapted to their practical professions in various towns and cities of Sweden. Their youthful poetic forays soon petered out, into hardly more than timid trickles of Poetic Realism.

Other, greater literary talents who could have put Poetic Realism into practice in Sweden were lacking.[131] Atterbom, a poet of the first magnitude according to the historians of Swedish literature, would doubtless have been the most ideal person to show the way in practically applying his theoretical program, but so strongly oriented to theoretical apostleship

---

[129] Aspelin, 102.

[130] See Aspelin's further references to Atterbom's "program om en poetisk realism": 101, 105, 106.

[131] Paul, "Romantik und Poetischer Realismus," 141.

was he that he had neither time nor energy left to practice what he preached.

In sum, therefore, Poetic Realism's emergence in Sweden must be described as the triumph of its theory over its practice.

9. The blaze of glory in Finland: Johan Ludvig Runeberg

When Atterbom formulated his program for *Poetisk Realism* in Sweden, he explained Poetic Realism by calling attention to an exemplary contemporary poet living and writing across the Gulf of Bothnia among the Swedish-speaking minority population in Finland: Johan Ludvig Runeberg (1804–1877). He appeared to Atterbom as the model Swedish-language writer of the day, a "Prince of Swedish Poets"[132] — high praise already, and, since Runeberg was not a Swede but a Finn by birth and domicile, the highest praise. Rydqvist, too, singled out Runeberg's talent for special praise,[133] and the commentary greatly impressed Atterbom, as could only be expected.[134] Another member of the Uppsala school of criticism, also writing in the pages of the school's leading forum, the *Swenska Litteratur-Föreningens Tidning*, even called Runeberg "the greatest poet of the century writing in the Swedish language" and "the only poetic genius of the age."[135] Hence, everything the theorists of Poetic Realism in Uppsala had hoped to see materialize in the literature of Sweden they now discovered in actual practice across the sea in Finland. Ever since the sages at Uppsala recognized that this Swedish-speaking Finnish writer represented the "breakthrough" of Poetic Realism in Swedish literature,[136] he has repeatedly across national frontiers been recognized as the brightest star of the movement's Swedish-language current, the epitome of Poetic Realism in its Swedish expression.[137]

---

[132] *Swenska Litteratur-Föreningens Tidning* 6 (1838): 129.

[133] Ibid., 2 (1834): 1-6, esp. 3. Runeberg is referred to as "en lofwärd talent" (a commendable talent).

[134] *P. D. A. Atterboms Brev till J. E. Rydqvist*, 40.

[135] *Swenska Litteratur-Föreningens Tidning* 5 (1837): 502.

[136] Algulin, 104.

[137] See, for instance, Bredsdorff et al., 124; Paul, "Romantik und Poetischer Realismus," 143; Brøndsted, ed., *Nordische Literaturgeschichte*, I, 353; Alrik Gustafson, *A History of Swedish Literature*, 3rd printing (Minneapolis: University of Minnesota Press, 1971), 224; Brøndsted, "Der skandinavische Beitrag zum europäischen Realismus," in *Europäischer Realismus*, ed. R. Lauer (Wiesbaden: Athenaion, 1980), 185.

The conditioning factors enabling Runeberg to become a *Poetisk Realist*

How did it happen that *Poetisk Realism* in its practice showed most brightly in the geographic area of the Swedish-speaking world furthest from the seat of its theory at Uppsala in Sweden's heartland? One might expect the practice of *Poetisk Realism* to have flowered more profusely nearer to the site of its invigorating theoretical development. The answer lies in the fact that the political-economic climate of Finland at the time was far more congenial for the establishment and growth of *Poetisk Realism* than in Sweden proper. Sweden had come out of the Napoleonic conflagrations rather well off. Political stability and the steadily increasing prosperity of Sweden during the uneventful years after 1830 encouraged a general apathy for the arts and gave the Swedes little cause to revolt against Romanticism.[138] Consequently, that movement lingered on in Sweden, despite the preaching of the Uppsala theorists, whose influence did not extend far beyond the walls of academia. Romanticism, thus, continued to mingle its currents of idea and form into the new literature of *Poetisk Realism* that was struggling for recognition, and that prevented the tides of the newer movement from rising to any appreciable heights.

In Finland the situation was completely different. If in Sweden the political-economic climate hindered any radical departure from Romanticism, in Finland historic events thoroughly precluded any continuation of a complacent faith in the mythological gods of Nordic Romanticism.

In the middle of the icy winter of 1808 Russian armies, instigated by Napoleon, invaded Finland to wrestle it away from Sweden, to which it had been attached for seven centuries. The war went badly for the Finns and the Swedes from the start but especially for the Finns, since practically all the fighting and bloodshed occurred, for almost two years, on Finnish soil. The pages of history recording this war are blotched with treachery, gory battles, chaotic flights of the ever-dwindling number of Finnish soldiers relentlessly pursued by immensely superior Russian forces, and by innumerable other horrible atrocities — mutilating the wounded, flogging innocent peasants to death, hanging them head down over a slow fire, or tying them to wild horses.[139] An occasional victory of the Finns

---

[138] Bredsdorff et al., 124.

[139] See Hanna Astrup Larsen's vivid account of the "Historical Background" in the edition of Runeberg's *The Tales of Ensign Stål*, trans. C. W. Stork, C. B. Shaw, and C. D. Broad (Helsinki: Söderström, 1952), ix. Additional information of a more general nature on the historical context of Runeberg's place in literature is available in the panoramic survey (written in Swedish) by the Finnish scholar Matti Klinge, *Runebergs två fosterland* (Helsinki: Söderström, 1983).

gave them the courage to continue the hopeless struggle longer, but the prolonged war also let Finland choke longer in the convulsion of death, destruction, and defeat. The Finns finally had no choice but to acquiesce to the occupation of their land by the nation which for centuries they dreaded as the perennial enemy.

Runeberg was four years old when the Russian armies broke into Finland. He grew up seeing the wounded trailing exhausted from battle; almost from the beginning of his life he had been an eyewitness to the poverty the vanquished Finns endured. He listened to an unending series of horror stories about the lost war. He knew, too, what it meant to be poor and what it was like to suffer from deprivation. Most of the boys growing up in Finland at the time were poor, but few had a harder struggle than Runeberg.[140]

Runeberg learned early, therefore, "to take up the bitter struggle against economic cares and a thousand other adverse circumstances," as he himself said.[141] The struggle only grew harder when Finland, annexed to Russia following the war, felt increasingly the chilling winds of Russification blowing across the land. The menace seemed all the more frightening for the Finns when they realized that the czar, the personification of autocracy, demanded blind obedience of his subjects.[142] The Finns had never felt that fear when Finland was part of the Swedish kingdom and her inhabitants participated as Swedish subjects in all administrative affairs.[143] Runeberg's fear of the Russian whip found perhaps its most vivid expression when he openly professed his sympathy for the Poles in their 1830 uprising against the Russian occupational forces in their country. This profession immediately put him on a collision course with the Russian forces in Finland, and they, in turn, threatened compulsory conscription into the Russian army, as well as censorship of his publications.[144]

---

[140] Tore Wretö, *J. L. Runeberg* (Boston: Twayne, 1980), 15-16. This book is the first one written in English on Runeberg. It offers an unusually excellent introduction to the writer. George C. Schoolfield, in an exemplary review of the book, has referred to it as "valuable to beginners and *conoscenti* alike" (*Scandinavian Studies* 53 [1981]: 246). Another reviewer has called the volume "learned and at the same time imaginative, presenting a solid synthesis of existing Runeberg scholarship through the discerning eyes of an accomplished Runeberg scholar" (Virpi Zuck in *Germanic Review* 57 [1982]: 45). A third reviewer, Randolph Bufano, considered it to be "without rival" (*Scandinavian Review* 69, no. 3 [1981]: 82).

[141] Ibid., 22.

[142] Eino Jutikkala with Kauko Pirinen, *A History of Finland*, new and revised ed. (London: Heinemann, 1979), 168.

[143] Ibid., 161.

[144] Wretö, 23.

Such were the dire political and economic conditions in Finland that agitated Runeberg's boyhood and early manhood. Neither he nor other Finns with literary leanings could have been expected to take flight from this bitter reality and escape into an enchanted land, florid with Viking Romanticism. The past was now of little significance, the present all-important. "Finland is an impoverished mother who needs all her sons," Runeberg said.[145] He knew he would not serve his country well if he did not make use of his literary talent to help his fellow Finns think more boldly about the vexing reality of the present. "The greatest charge of art," he said, "is to *förklara*."[146] That means, in the sense in which he uses the Swedish word here, both to "explain" and to "transfigure." To artistically explain the reality of his day, to poetically transfigure that reality into a timeless message about the reality of mankind, or, in other words, to interpret the essence of that reality, is the calling to which he — as a clergyman turned poet — felt himself ordained. The parallel of this personal calling resembles the artistic ministries embraced by the two important clergymen-poets of Danish Poetic Realism, Møller and Blicher.

This mission put Runeberg immediately at odds with the main body of Swedish writers across the Gulf in Sweden proper. No one knew this better than Runeberg himself. As a member of Helsinki's Swedish *Lördagssällskapet* (Saturday Society) for literature, he had become thoroughly conversant with the fiction appearing in Sweden at the time.[147] He took issue extensively with it, most negatively in his essay "En blick på Sveriges nu gällande poetiska litteratur" (A Look at the Current Poetic Literature in Sweden, 1832). In that essay he goes particularly out of his way to chastise his literary colleagues in Sweden for being feeble, colorless, and insignificant. They are all still singing, he said, in some sort of lofty Romantic chorus,[148] having, he clearly implies, little to do with the harsh reality he knew in Finland.[149] Only one year later, in 1833, he felt this even more acutely, for a horrible famine spread across Finland, bringing such destruction and misery that he forfeited his own meager income from royalties for the relief of the starving.[150]

Of course, he knew not all of contemporary Swedish literature was involved in a remote and out-of-date Romanticism. He appreciated, for in-

---

[145] Ibid., 22.
[146] Johan Ludvig Runeberg, *Samlade Arbeten*, VI (Helsinki: Edlund, 1900), 192.
[147] Wretö, 22.
[148] Runeberg, 65-66.
[149] Wretö, 30.
[150] Ibid., 97.

stance, the realistic novellas of Fredrika Bremer and sought to make them known to a wider circle of readers in Finland.[151] Condemning the Swedish Romanticists and endorsing Bremer's move toward Poetic Realism, Runeberg pointed out the direction he wanted the literature of his time and place to go. When he then took up his pen to write fiction in Swedish, he became, as Atterbom and other members of Uppsala's school of critical theory observed, the model *Poetisk Realist* of the Swedish language.[152]

The masterpiece: *Fänrik Ståls sägner*

Runeberg's creative flame burned with its most sustained and brilliant glow when he wrote *Fänrik Ståls sägner* (The Tales of Ensign Stål). Especially with this work, Scandinavianists tell us, Runeberg succeeded in setting up "new standards of Poetic Realism."[153] It was published in two parts, the first appearing in 1848 and the second in 1860.

The author offers us a series of poetic tales about Finland's struggle against the Russian forces in the War of 1808–1809.[154] From the start the reader is introduced to the interweaving of poetry and reality. Fact and fiction are compounded here in an account which repeatedly feigns truth and then implicitly disclaims it. Claiming to relay events from the disastrous War of 1808–1809, the speaker assumes the historian's mantle and mission, but his many glaring departures from historical accuracy belie this

---

[151] Lauri Viljanen, *Runeberg och hans diktning: 1804-1837* (Lund: Gleerup, 1947), 267.

[152] *Swenska Litteratur-Föreningens Tidning* 2 (1834): 3; 5 (1837): 502; 6 (1838): 129-30.

[153] Bredsdorff et al., 124.

[154] The secondary literature on *Fänrik Ståls sägner* is vast, and interpretations differ widely depending on whether the particular critic is Finnish or Swedish. Rarely in literary criticism has the feud of exegetes been as acrimonious as the one existing between Finnish and Swedish interpreters of this work. In general, it can be said that Swedish critics have tended to focus their attention on aesthetic form, whereas Finnish critics have preferred to concentrate on historical content. A most penetrating commentary (from a Swedish viewpoint) is included in Tore Wretö's modern book in English, *J. L. Runeberg*, 112-41. The seasoned American Scandinavianist George C. Schoolfield called it "first-rate" (*Scandinavian Studies* 53 [1981]: 245). Recent Finnish studies are by Johan Wrede, *Jag såg ett folk ... : Runeberg, Fänrik Stål och nationen* (Helsinki: Söderström, 1988) and "Runeberg's *Fänrik Ståls sägner:* On the Life and Significance of a Patriotic Work," in *Studies in German and Scandinavian Literature after 1500, A Festschrift for George C. Schoolfield*, eds. J. E. Parente & R. E. Schade (Columbia, S.C.: Camden House, 1993), 155-65.

project,[155] no less than does his choice to reproduce the historical accounts in the fictional environment of metrical and rhyming discourse.

The most compelling parts of the collection, for instance the poems addressed to "Sandels," "Döbeln vid Jutas," and "Adlercreutz," relate the historic exploits of specific military commanders during the war. At the same time, however, the tales distort the actual facts so the reader must conclude that fantasy presides here over truth. On the other hand, the thoroughly invented characters seem so real that no reader would believe they had no counterparts in actual history. There is Sven Duva, the well-meaning but doltish soldier who comes through in the test of fire, and Lotta Svärd, who always gives the weary soldier credit at her bar, unless he has failed to act bravely. The reader finds these products of the poetic imagination more genuine, more natural than the portraits of the exalted generals who actually lived. Which set of characters represents truth? Which one resembles more the world of fiction?

By the time we reach the last page of this work, we know that the intellectual potency of Runeberg's art rests firmly on this double perspective. From beginning to end of the huge realistic canvas fact and fiction become compounded increasingly in an almost baffling array of ingeniously contrived literary strokes.

The first signs of this Poetic Realist project appear in the collection's incantatory opening poem "Vårt land" (Our Land):

> Vårt land, vårt land, vårt fosterland,
> Ljud högt o dyra ord!
> Ej lyfts en höjd mot himlens rand.
> Ej sänks en dal, ej sköljs en strand,
> Mer älskad än vår bygd i nord,
> Än våra fäders jord.
>
> Vårt land är fattigt, skall så bli
> För den, som guld begär,
> En främling far oss stolt förbi;
> Men detta landet älska vi,
> För oss med moar, fjäll och skär

---

[155] For a detailed account of the many instances in which Runeberg took liberties with historical accuracy see Eirik Hornborg, *Fänrik Ståls sägner och verkligheten* (Helsinki: Svenska Litteratursällskapet i Finland, 1954). In Germany, no lesser person than the Grand Duke of Baden, Frederick I, called attention to Runeberg's use of poetic license in the portrayal of Swedish history. See Wolrad Eigenbrodt, "Runeberg in Deutschland, Erinnerungen," in *Johan Ludvig Runebergs hundraåsminne* (Helsinki: Svenska Litteratursällskapet i Finland, 1904), 118.

Ett guldland dock det är.[156]

(Our land, our land, our fatherland,
Let the dear words ring forth!
No hills to heaven their heights expand,
No valley dips, seas wash no strand,
More cherished than our home far north,
Than this our native earth.

Our land is poor, it has no hold
On those who lust for gain,
And strangers pass it proud and cold,
But we, we treasure every grain,
For us, with moor and fell and main,
It is a land of gold.)

Translated by C. D. Broad[157]

These two stanzas mark out an already familiar notion in Poetic Realism. One wonders at the similarity between this doughty commitment to a "poor land" and the lines from Møller's "Glæde over Danmark" with its antiphonal refrain: "Denmark is a little, beggar land." The Poetic Realist in both cases seeks poetic material not in lavish Viking escapism but in the hard terrain of austere, everyday reality. "Vårt land" (Our Land) explicitly rejects the enticements of an easier place:

Och fördes vi att bo i glans
Bland guldmoln i det blå,
Och blef vårt lif in stjernedans,
Der tår ej gjöts, der suck ej fanns.
Till detta arma land ändå
Vår längtan skulle stå.

(And were we wafted to the skies,
Their golden fields to till,
Should life become a paradise
With no more tears and no more sighs,
Yet this poor land of ours would still

---

[156] The Swedish text is cited according to the definitive scholarly edition: *Johan Ludvig Runeberg, Samlade Skrifter*, V, eds. G. Tideström and C. E. Thors (Helsinki: Svenska Litteratursällskapet i Finland, 1974).

[157] All English translations of this work are taken from Runeberg, *The Tales of Ensign Stål*.

Our hearts with longing fill.)

Translated by C. D. Broad

This poem is a fitting overture to the tales that follow, for it sounds the broad themes of the whole, suggesting the intermingling of truth and fiction by focusing on the everyday through the rhapsodic tone of a hymn more characteristic of poetic artifice than of the world of reality.

Following immediately upon "Vårt land," the poem "Fänrik Stål" tells of the speaker's encounter with an old ensign, a veteran from the War of 1808–1809. Considering the medley of historic fact and poetic fiction reverberating throughout this work, the encounter transpires appropriately midway between the war, our ground of fact, and the publication date of the poetically realized *Fänrik Ståls sägner* in 1848. This character is modeled on Runeberg, who spent time in the 1820s as a tutor at a country estate where he met an old ensign.

The young speaker here, full of "college lore" and the arrogance of youth, at first mocks and teases the old ensign, only to grow bored eventually with this and all his activities. His relief from a life of idle waste comes after he discovers, looking absently one day through a bookshelf, a battered history book with enthralling tales of the war. The historically savvy reader will recognize this much as pure fiction, for as Tore Wretö observes, a book dealing with the war was nonexistent at this time.[158] Our historical account lies to us already, we conclude, and we must wonder from this point on where truth leaves off and fiction begins.

The opening stanza of this second poem in the realistic narrative clearly suggests that what follows is deeply colored by the sepia tint of an individual's nostalgic perspective.

> Till flydda tider återgår
> Min tanke än så gerna,
> Mig vinkar från förflutna år
> Så mången vänlig stjerna.
> Välan, hvem följer nu mitt tåg
> Till Näsijärvis dunkla våg?
>
> (What joy it is, alone at night,
> To feel my thoughts returning
> To youthful years, wherein the light
> Of friendly stars is burning!
> Who'll join me on the road I take

---

[158] Wretö, 119.

To Näsijärvi's dusky lake?)
Translated by Charles Wharton Stork

The speaker summons up remembrances of things past and clarifies the collection's governing narratorial situation. An older speaker recalls his younger self, who listens to the tales of an old ensign, who, in turn, tells not his own stories but stories about others of whom he has heard. This multiplicity of perspective drives home again the overriding vision of the *Fänrik Stål* poems, presenting the interrelatedness of fact and fiction by showing that not only does a historic reality tie a people together but so do the fictionally expanded and abbreviated stories they tell one another about the actual occurrences.

In another interweaving of reality and fiction, the shabby ensign parallels the very history volume the young tutor idly stumbles upon on the bookshelf, which much like the ignored ensign, "... stood unbound and out of place / Amid the rest, as in disgrace." Runeberg provides dual catalysts for the speaker's narrating purpose: the real ensign and the imaginary book of history together engage the imagination of the young man and reveal his susceptibility to the lingual magic of real story.

This fictionally drawn, yet seemingly authentic speaker claims that a good deal of the *Fänrik Stål* volume represents a straightforward retelling of the ensign's stories. This leads into the curious point central to Runeberg's Poetic Realism: the retelling is patently *not* straightforward. As noted, Runeberg's use of verse instead of prose alerts the reader from the beginning that something more is afoot than a simple transmission of historical fact. Moreover, as one reads further in the tales, a marked degree of fabrication and modification of the actual event occurs: people in a real war would not typically rhapsodize immediately when their loved ones suffer and die in defense of the homeland. The reader sees, finally, that Runeberg tells much truth, bends about as much again, and simply makes up the remainder of *Fänrik Ståls sägner*.

This same medley of fact and fabrication echoes in "Ländshöfdingen" (The Provincial Governor), a late tale recounting a character's refusal to cooperate with the now victorious Russians. After a Russian general demands that Provincial Governor Wibelius relay the Russian demands to the vanquished Swedes and Finns, the governor instead lays his hand upon the Swedish-Finnish law code, suggesting the reverential treatment of a sacred text, and he claims that all the rules that the Finns need bother about are there already. The Russian officer, somewhat improbably impressed with the governor's mettle, bows in respect and walks out of the office. Writing on "Ländshöfdingen," Tore Wretö tells us that the encounter does represent an actual historical occurrence: there really was a Governor Wibelius, and he did, in fact, refuse the Russian demands. There, however, similarities disappear. The encounter, such as it was, took place only in writing, so the wordless departure of the Russian commander took place only in Runeberg's poetic imagination.[159]

No discussion of Runeberg's fictional enterprise would be complete without a consideration of the oddest tale in the collection, "Molnets broder" (The Cloud's Brother). It sets itself apart from the work as a whole, for it is the sole poem without stanzas and rhyme. It is, hence, the least poetic tale, the only one conveyed in real, natural, everyday speech. Most curiously, however, this most real tale of all has no express connection between the incident related and the actual War of 1808–1809, the real background of Runeberg's cycle. Thus, the tale that, according to its form, appears to be least poetic and most realistic turns out, according to its content, least historically accurate and therefore most contrived. In contrast, the other tales, based on actual historical events of the War of 1808–1809, thus the most realistic, appear arranged in artificial verse and turn out to be least convincing realistically!

On another level, if "Molnets broder" seems, in lacking Runeberg's highly elaborate verse schemes, more realistically convincing, then it must also be said, conversely, that the author's attention to an intricate symbolism likewise removes that tale from realistically convincing narrative. No reader can fail to be struck by the tale's unusual, obviously contrived imagery. In a particularly concentrated passage Runeberg unites the poem's central images: an old man rushes at sunset toward the church, where he has heard there was fighting and where he will discover that his adopted son has become a dead hero:

> Gick han ut, som om från glöd han ilat;
> Aftonrodnan var dock bleknad redan,
> Innan kyrkobyn han hinna kunde.
> Så var byn att se i rök och aska,
> Som ett stjernehvalf af skyar härjadt,
> Så låg kyrkan bortom byn på kullen,
> Som en ensam stjerna mellan molnen,
> Så låg tystnad öfver ödenejden,
> Som ett månsken öfver kala hösten.
> Mellan fallna kämpar, vän och ovän,
> Som en skugga öfver skördad åker,
> Gick den gamle. Öfverallt var döden ...

---

[159] Ibid., 137.

>(Forth he went, as though he fled from wildfire;
>But the afterglow had paled to twilight
>Ere he reached the village where the church was.
>It lay half concealed in smoke and ashes,
>Like the starry heaven when clouds obscure it;
>And the church stood on a knoll above it,
>Like a single star amid the vapor;
>While on all the land about lay silence,
>Like the moonlight on bare fields in autumn.
>Mid the fallen fighters, friend and unfriend,
>Like a shadow on a lane of stubble,
>Went the old man. Death was all around him ...)
>
>*Translated by Charles Wharton Stork*

The movement in light imagery from wildfire to the dark shadow of the father is characteristic. The images clearly work with the poem's greater issues: the smoke cloud of war obscures the public life of the town, the religious life of the church shines faintly but distinctly through the vapor, and finally the weak individual father wends his way, a shadow walking the valley of death, up the hill to the church and the dead sacrificial savior.

Darkness, shadow, and obscuring smoke all connect with the intricate central image of the cloud, with which the dead son is continually identified. The richness of the image consists in the opposition it contains: obscurer and life-giver, bearer of ominous storms and refreshing rains, cousin to the smoke of war and night dew. The dead hero is to be one with the stormburst, to be like the raven croaking in the clouds in this poem's opening lines. He spills his blood as the cloud spills life-giving water onto the land, and he evaporates eventually after his earthly appearance.

At the poem's close, the daughter looks over her dead lover in the churchyard and refuses simply to lament her loss, recognizing in it a rightness akin to natural cycles:

>Så skall fosterlandet dig begråta,
>Som en afton gråter dagg om sommarn,
>Full af glädje, ljus och lugn och sånger,
>Och med famnen sträckt mot morgonrodnan.
>
>(For thy native country shall but weep thee
>As the evening sheds its dew in summer,
>Full of joy, of light and peace and bird-song,
>Bosom lifted toward the flush of daybreak.)
>
>*Translated by Charles Wharton Stork*

The intricacy of the symbolism is remarkable. When the dew accumulates on a summer's evening, it just begins an accumulation which will only be reversed at "the flush of daybreak." This dew, the ephemeral earthly manifestation of the vaporous cloud, ties the water/cloud images (and with them, our dead hero) into a cycle of life the poem celebrates. Indeed, many of the *Fänrik Stål* poems, despite their fatal climaxes, have what must be called celebratory endings. An extract from the daughter's song at this final point serves as an epigraph to "Molnets broder," as it could well serve *Fänrik Ståls sägner* as a whole:

> Mer än lefva, fann jag, var att älska,
> Mer än älska är att dö som denne.
>
> (Sweeter far than life I found that love was,
> Sweeter far than love to die as he did.)
> *Translated by Charles Wharton Stork*

The young woman's exultant sorrow, while rather abstractly touching, one must find, realistically, something between improbable and absurd. Here, as throughout *Fänrik Ståls sägner*, our narrator intends to relate the tales of a common ensign, as they came from the ensign's mouth. Told to expect this round unvarnished tale, readers might well smile at their complicity in an obvious fiction, undeniably present.

The pervasive opposition of reality and poeticism keeps always in front of us this realistic narrative's artificial component, even as we read that this is actual history, not artful fiction. Fact and creation — essentially the twin concepts of *mimesis* and *poiesis* that Runeberg as a teacher of Greek knew so well — are pursued in *Fänrik Ståls sägner* so intensely and relentlessly that the entire literary canvas deepens, broadens, and becomes transfigured, before our almost unbelieving eyes, into a lucid document of universal significance. Runeberg has piqued us, by means of his poetic history, with the same dichotomy of truth and imagination that puts us to such considerable exertions in real life. He confronts us with our daily struggles over where in our own lives fact leaves off and fabrication begins. What could be more poetic? What could be more real?

10. *Poetisk Realism* comes to a halt in Finland

Runeberg's legendary status prevents others from following in his footsteps

The "new standards" of Poetic Realism Runeberg established (as Scandinavianists tell us)[160] with *Fänrik Ståls sägner* others in Finland could not match easily, and the banner of the movement he raised so high in his native land did not fly for long there. The poet had quickly become a legendary figure in his own time in Finland, something of a national saint, doubtless inhibiting some bright Finnish talents who might have wished to rival or compete with him. Other younger Finnish writers who may have been adventurous enough to add to the flowering of Poetic Realism were overtaken by political developments which channeled their artistic skills in different directions.

Stepped-up Russian cultural oppression compels younger Finnish authors to write in a different vein

What political happenings prevented younger Finnish writers from embracing Runeberg's Poetic Realism? After the middle of the nineteenth century the Finns, by then already for decades under the autocratic rule of the Russian czars, realized that the dreaded cultural Russification of their land was now occurring with alarming speed. With the establishment of every additional Russian institution on Finnish soil, they saw the blows of the Russian cultural whip growing stronger. Most visibly the Finns noticed this when the lavish gold-domed churches of the Russian Orthodox religion were erected one after the other in their traditionally Lutheran country, and when these new houses of worship received equal status (including equal support from taxation) with those belonging to the established Lutheran faith in Finland. With the growth of the Russian religious influence came the introduction of Russian language study in the schools. Participation in Orthodox religious services presupposed an ability to speak and understand Russian. For people excelling in Russian language study, royal scholarships supported travel in Russia, where promising native sons of Finland would acquire a firsthand knowledge and appreciation of Russian life and manners, and then subsequently return to Finland as the most ideal sort of cultural emissaries. As the cultural Russification of

---

[160] Bredsdorff et al., 124.

Finland gathered momentum, it seemed for the Finns only a matter of time before their nation's absorption into the Russian cultural orbit would be complete. If any doubts lingered, the opening of the telegraph line connecting Helsinki with the Russian capital in 1855, followed by the inauguration of regular rail service from the Finnish capital to St. Petersburg in 1868, made Finnish fears even more of a reality. These two technical events seemed the final knots tied in the subjection of little Finland to the colossal Russian bear. Nothing now seemed to impede a mass transportation of the Russian lifestyle to Finland. Finns could draw no other conclusion when they listened to the boastful speeches of the various representatives of the Russian crown who had come to Helsinki for the elaborate opening ceremonies.

Yet, all of this naturally presented men and women of vision in Finland with the challenge and the urgency to find a means to prevent the seemingly inevitable. The task appeared enormous, indeed almost impossible, but the stakes were high, too — a way to avoid total Russification had to be found. The Finns finally came up with a solution: to Finnicize their nation before the rapidly progressing Russification could reach its final stage. The slogan, "Swedes we are no longer, Russians we cannot become; we must be Finns,"[161] became a rallying cry for the new ideology. This ideology brought about the rise of a national consciousness, a growing sense of Finnish cultural pride unknown during the many centuries when the Swedish Bible, used by the Lutheran clergy in churches all across Finland, had kept the Finns securely within the Swedish cultural orbit.

The literati who followed Runeberg in Finland played a key role in ushering in this new orientation. More effectively than others they took the initiative in countering the stepped-up Russian cultural oppression. They knew, though, that they would only succeed if they could endow Runeberg's Poetic Realism with a pronounced patriotic aim, something which, in the last analysis, was alien to his great art. Runeberg, in his *Fänrik Ståls sägner*, had fictionally exploited some of the saddest events of his early life in Finland — events having to do with the War of 1808–1809 — to transfigure genuine and invented episodes into a timeless message about the pervasive opposition of truth and poeticism in the world; in doing so he became an exemplary Poetic Realist. The younger Finnish writers, his immediate successors, followed in his footsteps inasmuch as they, too, used real facts from Finland's history as the coloring material for their aesthetic intentions. Then, however, they parted company from their older fellow-artist when they recalled events from Finland's storied past specifically to assert the values of the Finnish heritage and so awaken in the

---

[161] Jutikkala with Pirinen, 174.

Finns a sense of national pride, for the purpose of giving them the courage to stand up to the advancing Russian menace. These younger writers felt the hour needed not another *timeless* message mirroring the reality of mankind but a *timely* warning to stop the approaching Russian cultural invasion before it was too late.

Zacharias Topelius and Aleksis Kivi ring down the curtain on *Poetisk Realism* in Finland

Particularly typical for the new direction of Finnish literature in subverting Runeberg's style was the immensely popular historical novel *Fältskärns berättelser* (Tales of a Field Surgeon) in four volumes, published between 1853 and 1867 by the Swedo-Finnish writer Zacharias Topelius (1818–1898). A close friend, as well as a gifted literary disciple of Runeberg, popular consent has placed him foremost among the cultivators of the literary seed Runeberg had planted in Finland's soil.[162] But instead of continuing in his older friend's footsteps as a Poetic Realist, Topelius pressed his pen into the service of the Finnish national movement. His popular novel, although possessing many similarities with Runeberg's *Fänrik Ståls sägner*, primarily tries to arouse in Finnish readers a patriotic interest in their national heritage. They are offered an entertaining history of Finland with the stories of two Finnish families over several generations, commencing with the Thirty Years' War. Far more than in Runeberg's work, historical description overwhelms here. The reader senses an author bent on glorifying Finland's past, even its remote past, but never trying to transfigure historical description and present the distilled essence of reality.

If Topelius, the writer most closely associated with Runeberg, had fundamentally altered the course of Poetic Realism in Finland by joining it to a new stream of literary patriotism, other subsequent Finnish writers deepened the patriotic coloring matter more, guiding Finnish literature into a course even further removed from Runeberg's Poetic Realism.

Aleksis Kivi (1834–1872), the youngest in the triumvirate of the widely-read nineteenth-century writers in Finland (together with Runeberg and Topelius), went so far in his nationalistic, patriotic zeal that he switched from Swedish to Finnish in the late 1860s when he penned his major literary works, though up to then no one had considered Finnish a literary language. The language change served an obvious patriotic intent, as did the many fairy tales and fables from Finnish folklore he used to endow his writing with additional Finnish color. There could be no doubt

---

[162] Yrjö Hirn, "Zachris Topelius vid Runebergs sida," *Ord och Bild* 50 (1941): 481-93.

about Kivi's literary purpose: to offer portraits of Finnish men and women, speaking Finnish, and living in Finnish surroundings. A zealous patriot was busy writing here, but not a Poetic Realist.

Poetisk Realism suspends its functions in Finland and migrates abroad

On the foregoing pages I tried to show that in 1860, when the printer's ink was drying on the second part of *Fänrik Ståls sägner*, Poetic Realism was grinding to a halt in Finland. Meeting the challenge of the Russian cultural invasion in that easternmost flank of Scandinavia prevented Runeberg's literary successors from carrying on where he left off.

Runeberg wrote two additional works of fiction subsequent to the completion of *Fänrik Ståls sägner:* the dramas *Kan ej* (Cannot, 1862) and *Kungarne på Salamis* (The Kings on Salamis, 1863). However skillful and resourceful the author, the literary convention of Poetic Realism did not lend itself to adaptation on the stage. In this respect, the situation in Finland was no different from that in other nations where Poetic Realism flourished. After these unsuccessful attempts at adapting Poetic Realism to drama, Runeberg wrote no further. Within only a few months after completing *Kungarne på Salamis*, he suffered a stroke from which he never recovered.

Yet, if politics and the incapacitation of Runeberg threw Poetic Realism in Finland into a state of *deliquium*, its trans-European activity again only ceased temporarily. The seedlings of Poetic Realism which had sprouted in Finland by Runeberg's hands were transplanted to foreign soil. As mentioned, the flourishing of Poetic Realism in Finland had contributed much to the cultivation of its theory in Sweden. Quickly, too, Runeberg's works of Poetic Realism found a reading public in both Sweden and Denmark. Translations of many of his works appeared in numerous Danish anthologies. The catalog of the Royal Library in Copenhagen lists them in detail. In 1856 the entire first part of Runeberg's magnum opus was published in Copenhagen, with the Swedish and Danish versions printed on facing pages.[163]

The growth and spread of *Poetisk Realisme* in the land of its birth naturally created an ideal climate for the Danish reception of Runeberg's kindred works, and unsurprisingly his oeuvre easily found many appreciative readers in Denmark. Yet, despite Runeberg's undoubted impact in Denmark, judging by the number of Danish translations, his works reached

---

[163] Johan Ludvig Runeberg, *Fændrik Staals Fortællinger* (Copenhagen: Hagerup, 1856).

Danish audiences after the decline of the movement in Denmark had already set in, owing to changed political, social, and economic conditions. These continued to be the overriding factors determining the direction Danish literature was heading, and so, however well Denmark received Runeberg and his brand of Poetic Realism, this reception made no change in the course of Danish literary history.

In Germany the situation was altogether different. There the numerous translations and many critical reviews of Runeberg's works let the energy of Swedish (and Swedo-Finnish) *Poetisk Realism* quicken the tide of Danish *Poetisk Realisme* flowing into Germany at about the same time. I shall now try to show how these two national literary forces together struck the German literary scene, precisely when *Poetischer Realismus* was emerging there. And this, I wish to say, must have helped to galvanize the literary climate in Germany so as to abet markedly the rise of Poetic Realism in the third tongue in which it would flourish.

Fredrika Bremer
Courtesy of *Kungliga Biblioteket*, Stockholm

Johan Erik Rydqvist
Courtesy of *Kungliga Biblioteket*, Stockholm

Per Daniel Amadeus Atterbom
Courtesy of *Kungliga Biblioteket*, Stockholm

Johan Ludvig Runeberg
Courtesy of *Svenska Litteratursällskapet*, Helsinki

SCANDINAVIAN POETIC REALISM TRAVELS TO GERMANY

1. Political conditions abet the flow of Danish literature into Germany

No current of Danish literature ever flowed southward across the Danish language frontier into Germany with as much force as did *Poetisk Realisme*. A unique series of political circumstances made this possible.

What happened politically? On August 6, 1806, the Holy Roman Empire of the German Nation officially dissolved, leaving the duchy of Holstein, hitherto a part of that empire, without any significant legal ties to the rest of the German-speaking world. Within only a few weeks, on September 9, 1806, an Act of Incorporation united this northernmost flank of the former empire to the kingdom of Greater Denmark. This happened altogether naturally, for the king of Denmark was, at the same time, the duke of Holstein. His newly-gained freedom of rule over his duchy, resulting from the dissolution of the Holy Roman Empire, allowed him to realize a long-cherished Danish dream: to supersede the loose personal association of the German duchy with the crown of Denmark by the establishment of a new unitary state.

The next step followed equally logically. If the newly formed united kingdom of Greater Denmark and Holstein (including the duchy of Schleswig) hoped to become a reality in practice as well as in theory, German-speaking Holstein needed to be pulled culturally within the Danish-speaking orbit. Since a single administrative language and a common culture seemed the most effective means of centralizing the new enlarged state, everything had to be done to encourage German-speaking Holstein to become Danish in language and culture — the express desire of the monarch, Frederick VI, as stated in a letter to the Danish poet Jens Baggesen (1764–1826).[164]

To achieve the will of the sovereign several directives promoting the use of Danish in Holstein appeared in quick succession. In 1807 a royal

---

[164] August Baggesen, *Jens Baggesens biographie*, IV (Copenhagen: Reitzel, 1856), 45.

decree required that all ordinances in Holstein be written in both Danish and German. In 1809 Danish as well as German was to be used for all official appointments. Next came the Danish language rescript of 1810, encouraging the introduction and strengthening of the study of Danish language and literature in all the schools of the German-speaking districts. The study of Danish in the German schools quickened. Only four years later, in 1814, a further royal decree for language instruction stipulated that henceforth Danish would supersede French as the most important foreign language taught, with Danish instruction offered on every single grade level, in the upper grades nearly as extensively as instruction in the pupils' native German (seven hours of Danish per week vs. eight hours of German).[165]

This sudden flurry in the study of Danish, as part of the enormous organized effort to encourage the spread of the Danish language and Danish culture beyond the ancient Danish-speaking frontier, provoked a concurrent spectacular revitalization in the study of Danish literature. Particularly for those serving society from positions of higher authority, such as clergymen, competence in Danish meant a level of proficiency only attainable by familiarity with Danish literature. The prefaces to many anthologies of Danish literature read in the German-speaking schools of the realm clarify this with their justifications for anthologies of prose and lyric selections from Danish literature. Specifically, successful German-speaking candidates for ecclesiastical positions in the newly united kingdom had not only to offer simple proof of their knowledge of Danish, but to demonstrate a superior competence in its use. This competence, according to the anthologists, was best acquired through study of the use of the language by the great masters of Danish literature.[166]

Vital for the spread of Danish literature into the German-speaking areas was the institutionalization of such study within a German center of learning. Taking this ultimate step in 1811, a royal decree established a chair for Danish at the University of Kiel. The new professorship served two purposes: to help civil service candidates meet the 1811 promulgation requiring proficiency in Danish for posts in German-speaking areas, and to ensure the training of language teachers for the burgeoning demands for instruction in secondary schools. The aim of the crown, to increase the

---

[165] Jürgen Rohweder, *Sprache und Nationalität* (Glückstadt: Augustin, 1976), 31.

[166] T. Hoyer Jensen, *Dänisches Lesebuch zum Gebrauch in Schleswig-Holsteinischen Volksschulen* (Hadersleben: Seneberg, 1814), i; Detlev Lorenz Lübker, *Neue Dänische Blumenlese; oder Sammlung prosaisch-poetischer Stücke, zum Gebrauch für Höhere Classen und für Freunde der dänischen Literatur* (Altona: Hammerich, 1826), ix; J. P. Sternhagen, *Der kleine Däne* (Itzehoe: Schuberth & Niemeyer, 1835), iii-vi.

appreciation of Danish literature, would be ably served by the prestige of a chair at Kiel, contrasting greatly with instruction in other modern languages, English and French for instance, which lower-ranking lecturers — never professors — taught. Reflecting this desire to cultivate the interest in Danish prose and poetry, the chair entailed wide-ranging travel and many off-campus commitments: besides teaching at Kiel, the professor would address various audiences and give lectures about Danish literature at every convenient opportunity.[167] The German populace of the monarchy was to be exposed to Danish literary gems, and rough interest was to be polished. The inventive plan saw several of Denmark's most capable and illustrious men of letters appointed to this newly created seat of Danish learning within the German-speaking region. Jens Baggesen, the well-known poet, first occupied the position (from 1811 to 1814). After an interval, when the chair remained vacant because of fiscal reasons, Baggesen was followed by Johan Ludvig Heiberg and his Poetic Realist mother Fru Gyllembourg (from 1822 to 1825). Then came in succession the extraordinarily dedicated missionary of Danish culture Christian Flor (from 1826 to 1845), the highly influential novelist and lyricist Carsten Hauch (from 1846 to 1851), and the distinguished literary critic Christian Molbech (from 1851 to 1864).

No better way to plant the seed of Danish literature in a German-speaking territory could have been imagined than the recruitment of this splendid array of outstanding Danish literati for the professorship at the University of Kiel. Danish literature now acquired an unprecedented affluence outside the strictly Danish-speaking world. Success for the travel of Danish literature to the German-speaking world seemed assured, and never more so than when the talented Heiberg, in Kiel, wrote (in German!) his *Formenlehre der dänischen Sprache* (Morphology of the Danish Language) so that his German-speaking students could acquire, as he said in the preface to that work, a heightened sensitivity for the musical beauty of Danish literature.[168]

Small wonder, then, that this concerted effort to spread the treasures of Danish literature should not remain within the territorial confines of those German-speaking districts now incorporated into the newly extended Danish kingdom. Only too naturally, the growing interest in Danish literature (as it was embraced by well-educated Germans in the new southern parts of Greater Denmark) also spilled over further southward,

---

[167] Harald Skalberg, *Aktstykker angaaende det danske Docentur i Kiel* (Copenhagen: Munksgaard, 1932), 145.

[168] Johann Ludwig Heiberg, *Formenlehre der dänischen Sprache* (Altona: Hammerich, 1823), xxiii.

via the medium of the German language, to the various German states outside of and far removed from the Danish state. For instance, what was taught in the schools and read among the educated Germans of Altona, the southernmost outpost of the newly united Danish kingdom, quickly found its way into the big German city of Hamburg, which lay just below Altona's city limits. Significantly, one of the most popular anthologies of Danish literature for Germans at the time, J. P. Sternhagen's *Der kleine Däne* (The Little Dane), appeared, beginning with its second edition in 1844, directly in Hamburg instead of in Itzehoe in Holstein, where the first edition had been published.[169] The compiler doubtless wished to take advantage of the new market for Danish books which had opened in Hamburg.

From Hamburg, Danish literature easily flowed to the rest of Germany. As natural as this thrust of Danish literature from Altona to Hamburg and thence further south of the Elbe River appeared, intention also aided it. The foreword to another widely read contemporary anthology of Danish literature for German readers, *Nordische Harfentöne oder gnomische Blumenlese aus dänischen Dichtern* (Nordic Harp Tones or Gnomic Floral Harvest Gathered from Danish Poets), illustrates the degree of planning for this southward thrust. The compiler of this anthology, Gottlieb Ernst Klausen (1762–1851), was a distinguished pedagogue and orator, knight of the coveted royal Danish *Danebrog* order, the rector of the Gymnasium in Altona, and an uncle of the Minister for Cultural Affairs in Copenhagen. He knew the policies of the Danish government well when he compiled his anthology. He prefaced it with a reverent dedication to Frederick VI of Denmark, the sovereign who was responsible for the Act of Incorporation that added Holstein to the Danish kingdom and who also issued the royal decrees promoting the spread of Danish language and literature to the German-speaking districts.

Klausen's anthology took as its specific purpose, according to its preface, the throwing of a linguistic and cultural net — woven of Danish language and literature — over the newly incorporated areas of the state. The aim of capturing new adherents to Danish literature, however, went beyond the regions immediately below the Eider River, the ancient boundary between German and Danish culture. Indeed, this anthologist says he flings his net deliberately wide, casting in even those regions lying below the Elbe River (by which he means the frontier between the newly extended Danish kingdom and the rest of the German-speaking world) and

---

[169] J. P. Sternhagen, *Der kleine Däne*, 2nd ed. (Hamburg: Niemeyer, 1844).

hoping to woo friends for Danish literature among German-speaking readers living far beyond the new Danish state.[170]

Klausen's wish to kindle an enthusiasm for Danish literature throughout Germany, and not just in the German-speaking parts of the new Danish kingdom, was shared by Christian Flor (1792–1875). He applied for and received the professorship for Danish at Kiel's university, hoping to be so influential, as he wrote his superiors in Copenhagen, that other German universities would take notice and likewise establish chairs for Danish and other Scandinavian literatures.[171] To achieve this goal, Flor traveled, lectured, and published widely, receiving his measure of success. The University of Leipzig followed the example of Kiel, establishing the second seat of learning outside of Denmark proper where Danish literature could be formally studied.[172] Flor's manual for instruction in the Danish language and literature, written in German and published with the University Press at Kiel, sold so well all over Germany that it quickly went through three editions.[173]

2. Novellas of Danish *Poetisk Realisme* are translated into German en masse

Significantly, Denmark's giving literature to Germany coincided with the advent of *Poetisk Realisme* within Denmark. After 1820 the new novellas of *Poetisk Realisme* became the Danish literary instruments par excellence, the vehicles of Danish culture which reached the German reading public with the most force when political forces in Denmark contrived to promulgate Danish literature in Germany. These novellas, after all, most accurately represented what contemporary Denmark offered. Their authors, as we read in Carl Bernhard's anthology of Danish novellas intended for German readers, had blazed a new trail and been enthusiastically received at home, whereas earlier Danish writers, whose works were

---

[170] Gottlieb Ernst Klausen, *Nordische Harfentöne oder gnomische Blumenlese aus dänischen Dichtern* (Altona: Hammerich, 1817), xvii.

[171] Harald Skalberg, "Dänische Lektoren und Professoren an der Universität Kiel," *Deutsch-Nordische Zeitschrift* 1 (1928): 102.

[172] Olaf Klose, "Die nordische Professur in Kiel in der 2. Hälfte des 19. Jahrhunderts," in *De Libris: Bibliofile Breve til Ejnar Munksgaard paa 50-Aarsdagen* (Copenhagen: Munksgaard, 1940), 56.

[173] Christian Flor, *Lehrbuch der Dänischen Sprache, enthaltend eine Grammatik, ein Lesebuch und ein vollständiges Wortregister* (Kiel: In der Universitätsbuchhandlung, 1833, 1835, 1843).

no longer in tune with the bitter reality of impoverished Denmark, had dropped out of sight.[174] Hence, Fru Gyllembourg's nephew states, it is primarily these new writers' "troops which should be boldly led across the Elbe River"; and hopefully there would be an "invasion" of such novellas into Germany.[175]

These new landmarks of Danish fiction soon deluged the German reading public. No later than the end of the 1830s audiences as far south in the German-speaking world as Vienna were discussing Denmark's new literature.[176] Little of this is known today, but Germans everywhere were reading the new Danish novellas in anthologies, in literary journals, and in separate book publications (sometimes even in bilingual editions, with the same text in German and Danish on facing pages).[177]

Danish literature, it was now claimed, had as much to offer as English, French, or German literature.[178] Writers of *Poetisk Realisme* became so well known in Germany that enterprising publishing houses could even undertake the ambitious task of circulating in German translation multi-volume collections of their works. With the appearance of such mammoth collections, *Poetisk Realisme* reached the pinnacle of its influence in Germany.

Fru Gyllembourg saw two different editions of her novellas published in Leipzig between 1834 and 1836.[179] The reception accorded these collections by the German reading public must have been extraordinarily good, for soon thereafter an enterprising publishing house in Stuttgart commissioned a translator to render into effective German prose an imposing seventeen-volume edition of her novellas.[180] Following quickly in the wake of the first German editions of Fru Gyllembourg's novellas came a six-volume set of the novellas of her nephew Carl Bernhard, in 1840 and 1841.[181] This collection, too, must have met with immediate success, for a

---

[174] Carl Bernhard, *Lebensbilder aus Dänemark in Novellen und Erzählungen*, I (Leipzig: Weber, 1840), xxvi.

[175] Ibid., xxiv.

[176] Ibid., xii.

[177] Bernhard, *Das Glückskind* (Copenhagen: Schuboth, 1837).

[178] Sternhagen, vi.

[179] *Erzählungen aus der Copenhagener fliegenden Post*, trans. L. Kruse (Leipzig: Kollmann, 1834-1836); *Novellen vom Verfasser einer "Alltagsgeschichte,"* trans. W. C. Christiani (Leipzig: Kummer, 1835).

[180] *Die Novellen des Verfassers der "Alltagsgeschichte,"* trans. E. Zoller (Stuttgart: Franckh'sche Verlagsbuchhandlung, 1852).

[181] Bernhard, *Lebensbilder aus Dänemark in Novellen und Erzählungen*.

rival publishing firm in Leipzig quickly began to market a more extensive edition of his *Gesammelte Werke* (Collected Works) in fifteen volumes.[182]

Blicher's works were also much in demand. Two volumes of his collected novellas appeared in Altenburg in 1846;[183] in 1849 a competing publisher in Leipzig presented the German public with another, considerably expanded edition of his novellas in six volumes.[184]

As these two collections of Blicher's novellas sold to the eager German public, or were lent out to it via the chains of lending libraries across Germany, Danish Poetic Realism reached the threshold of its new namesake in the German-speaking world. For German Poetic Realism, as we shall see, had its auspicious beginnings in 1848. It is hardly surprising, therefore, that the works of Blicher, the last of the novella writers of Danish Poetic Realism to become widely known all across Germany, anticipated much in the prose of the first of the major novella writers of German Poetic Realism, Theodor Storm.[185]

3. Baron Constant Dirckinck-Holmfeld stirs German interest in the lyric of *Poetisk Realisme*

As men and women far and wide in German-speaking Europe were reading the novellas of Danish Poetic Realism, a remarkable Dano-German, Baron Constant Dirckinck-Holmfeld (1799–1880), stepped forward to encourage a specific German interest in the lyric poetry of that Danish literary movement. Of the many books and essays this versatile man of letters once wrote, forgotten today, at least one work, because of its importance for the international travel of the lyric of Poetic Realism, deserves to be resurrected: his *Nachbildung dänischer Poesien* (Reproductions of Danish Lyrics), published in Copenhagen in 1848,[186] in the

---

[182] Bernhard, *Gesammelte Werke* (Leipzig: Lorck, 1847-1850).

[183] Steen Steensen Blicher, *Novellen* (Altenburg: Pierer, 1846).

[184] Blicher, *Novellen* (Leipzig: Teubner, 1849).

[185] Emanuel Hirsch in Søren Kierkegaard, *Gesammelte Werke*, XXX (Düsseldorf/Cologne: Diederich, 1960), 181; Victor A. Schmitz, *Dänische Dichter in ihrer Begegnung mit deutscher Klassik und Romantik* (Frankfurt am Main: Klostermann, 1974), 142; *Dänische und norwegische Dichtungen* (Heidelberg: Kerle, 1949), 78; Franz Stuckert, *Theodor Storm, Sein Leben und seine Welt* (Bremen: Schünemann, 1955), 447; Roger Paulin, *The Brief Compass, The Nineteenth-Century German Novelle* (Oxford: Clarendon, 1985), 118.

[186] *Nachbildung dänischer Poesien, Zum Gedächtniss der Schweden und Norweger, welche im Kampfe für Dännemark gefallen sind, geweiht von Constant Dirckinck-Holmfeld und*

darkest year of Dano-German relations following the Act of Incorporation.

As noted in the previous chapter, consequent to that Act, Danish policy sought to pull the German-speaking duchy of Holstein (and the German-speaking districts of the duchy of Schleswig) into the orbit of Danish culture. Over the years, this well-conceived, energetically furthered effort on the part of the sovereign, as well as of many Danish political and cultural emissaries, met with much success. The royal capital, Copenhagen, always proved a powerful cultural center from which Danish culture could radiate to the farthest corners of the monarchy. Germany, then without a national capital, had no similar seat of culture to rival it. But the vast strides of the gradual Danisation of German-speaking lands in the duchies of Schleswig and Holstein also produced a side effect: the rise of a corresponding German cultural nationalism. This countermovement, seeking to stop the penetration of Danish culture into ancient German-speaking territory, led to a Dano-German animosity previously unknown in European history. Tensions in the German-speaking areas ruled by the Danish king mounted as rapidly as the Danish cultural domination gained new ground. On March 24, 1848, all hell seemed to break loose when the German population of the duchies rose up in armed revolt to rally around the slogan "We will not tolerate the sacrifice of German territory as a prey of the Danes."[187] It was, in the words of Disraeli, in a moving speech before the British House of Commons, "rebellion in the most unblushing and flagrant manner."[188] After a few months, as a result of intervention on the part of other European powers, a truce was declared; but anti-Danish sentiment continued to run high — in Schleswig, in Holstein, and in all parts of German-speaking Europe. When the new German Federal Diet convened its stormy meetings in Frankfurt, beginning in May 1848, no topic was discussed more frequently and passionately than the controversy surrounding the advance of Danish culture into German-speaking territory. It became the rallying point for the clamor for German unity that eventually culminated in the founding of the German Empire in 1871.[189] "Denmark" had come alive to the German national consciousness, albeit in a negative sense.

---

dargeboten als Scherflein zu dem dänischen Monument für die gefallenen Brüder (Copenhagen: Salomon, 1848).

[187] J. A. S. Grenville, *Europe Reshaped 1848-1878* (Hassocks/Sussex: Harvester, 1976), 89.

[188] *Hansard's Parliamentary Debates*, XCVIII, 514.

[189] Alexander Scharff, *Schleswig-Holsteinische Geschichte* (Würzburg: Ploetz, 1982), 64.

At this juncture, Baron Constant Dirckinck-Holmfeld, a brother of the last Danish ambassador to the German Federal Diet at Frankfurt and a Dano-German equally at home in Danish and German letters (according to source materials available today in the Royal Library at Copenhagen), decided to capitalize on the publicity Denmark was receiving in Germany and turn the German negative opinion of Denmark into a positive one. To achieve his peacemaking mission and woo friends for Denmark, he translated modern Danish poetry into German. He believed poetry the finest instrument available to sharpen man's sense of values. If he could expose the German national consciousness, now so attuned to Danish matters, to modern Danish poetry in German translation, then, he believed, hearts hardened by hatred might mellow. Both within and beyond the lands ruled by the Danish king, Germans hostile to the Danish cultural thrust southward might then reverse their stand, even welcome the inflow of Danish culture into Germany.[190]

Prominent on the opening pages of Baron Dirckinck-Holmfeld's *Nachbildung dänischer Poesien* was his translation of *Poetisk Realisme*'s lyric showpiece, "Glæde over Danmark,"[191] making Møller's famous poem available to the German reading public in translation for the first time. He evidently felt it (and other verse masterpieces of *Poetisk Realisme*) especially well suited to enable German audiences to reflect favorably on Danish culture. He succeeded so well in stirring German interest in this poem that he opened up a considerable "foreign trade" in it. The catalog of the Royal Library at Copenhagen records a long list of other German translations of this poem following in rapid succession. Certainly "Glæde over Danmark," and with it the poetry of Danish *Poetisk Realisme*, now became, consequent to Dirckinck-Holmfeld's initiative, as well known in Germany as the novellas exported from Denmark at the same time.

4. Jens Bergendahl von Schepelern, Adolph von Gähler, and other Dano-Germans add works of Swedish *Poetisk Realism* to the Danish literary current flowing into Germany

Before turning to the German manifestation of Poetic Realism, we may note how the influence of Danish *Poetisk Realisme* in Germany was magnified by the influx of Swedish *Poetisk Realism*, which had gained its first

---

[190] *Nachbildung dänischer Poesien*. Afterword, 15.
[191] Ibid., 7-8.

harbor abroad in Denmark and then spilled over into German-speaking lands. Naturally Denmark, the birthplace of Poetic Realism, first attended to the sister movement from its Scandinavian neighbor. Once in Denmark, however, Swedish *Poetisk Realism* quickly followed the trade route of Danish *Poetisk Realisme* south to Germany.

Many Germans born, raised, or schooled in the kingdom of Greater Denmark after the Act of Incorporation had acquired a taste for Danish *Poetisk Realisme* through the new emphasis on Danish literature in their school curricula. Easily and understandably they developed an interest in the related Swedish literary current and became prime *agents littéraires* conveying to Germany the Swedish works they had come to admire in Denmark.

Two enterprising Danophile literati from German-speaking Holstein — Jens Bergendahl von Schepelern (1801–1864) and Adolph von Gähler (1807–1898) — were the first to add Swedish *Poetisk Realism* to the current of Danish *Poetisk Realisme* flowing south. As with Baron Dirckinck-Holmfeld, nothing is known today about these two adventuresome intermediaries of literature, but a variety of scattered source materials available in the Royal Library at Copenhagen makes it clear how actively these two literati engaged in awakening German interest in contemporary Danish and Swedish literature.[192] They, too, deserve to be resurrected from the oblivion to which literary history has consigned them.

Von Schepelern, the leading spirit of the two, hailing, like von Gähler, from a family German in language and culture, early in life had joined the forces of the new Danish militia that had come to be stationed in German-speaking Holstein after the Act of Incorporation. Once in the Danish militia, he quickly developed strong pro-Danish sentiments. The excellent Danish language skills he managed to acquire, and the strong interest in the novella of Danish Poetic Realism he displayed by imitating that art and writing novellas of his own in Danish, must have brought him quickly to the attention of the cultural emissaries of the Danish crown in Kiel — at that time Fru Gyllembourg and her son Johan Ludvig Heiberg were serving in these posts — for in the early 1820s he was recruited to promote instruction in Danish in Holstein's German school system.

---

[192] For a first introduction to these forgotten Dano-German *agents littéraires* see (from a Danish perspective) *Almindeligt Forfatter-Lexicon for Kongeriget Danmark med tilhørende Bilande fra før 1814 til efter 1858*, ed. Thomas Hansen Erslew, I & II, reprint ed. (Copenhagen: Rosenkilde & Bagger, 1962) and (from a German perspective) *Lexikon der Schleswig-Holstein-Lauenburgischen und Eutinischen Schriftsteller von 1866-1882*, ed. Eduard Alberti, I & II (Kiel: Biernatzki, 1885 & 1886).

He wrote, as one of the byproducts of this teaching appointment, he informs us, a grammar of the Danish language for Germans, published in 1831 in Altona.[193] Since Altona lay just north of Hamburg, his enthusiasm for the Danish cultural thrust southward must have fired him with the missionary zeal to transmit Danish culture to the huge German-speaking population of Hamburg as well. Attempting to woo friends for Danish culture in Hamburg, he would have been following the example of Altona's foremost pedagogue at the time, Gottlieb Ernst Klausen.

Von Schepelern's sense of apostleship in the Danish cultural cause doubtless encouraged him also to embrace Pan-Scandinavianism, which began to flourish particularly strongly in Denmark in the early 1830s, and this must have awakened an interest in Swedish *Poetisk Realism*, then infiltrating Denmark. Whether things happened in this order is difficult to determine today, but von Schepelern did learn of Swedish *Poetisk Realism* around this time, for he decided, no later than 1835, to quicken the movement of Danish literature to Germany by adding to it selected texts from Swedish Poetic Realism.

To do so he founded a new periodical, editing and publishing it with his Dano-German friend von Gähler. In March 1836 their first issue appeared simultaneously at Copenhagen and Leipzig, the respective centers of the Danish and the German book trades. Von Schepelern and von Gähler called their journal the *Skandinavische Bibliothek* (Scandinavian Library), indicating, as stated on the title page, that the journal would offer German-speaking subscribers a "library" comprising translations of some of the best and latest examples of Scandinavian literature. In their first issue they introduced Runeberg to German readers.[194] Apparently receiving from Germany a very positive response, they promptly translated into German another selection from Runeberg's oeuvre and printed it in their second issue.[195]

Following the lead of von Schepelern and von Gähler, others from the German-speaking areas of the Danish king's domains joined in transmitting to Germany those works of Swedish Poetic Realism familiar to the Danes. The Holsteiner Eduard Osenbrüggen (1809–1879) was the first of these subsequent translators. After his exposure to the best of Danish literature at the University of Kiel's center for promoting Danish literature abroad, Osenbrüggen translated into German excerpts from Runeberg's

---

[193] Jens Bergendahl von Schepelern, *Dänische Grammatik für Deutsche* (Altona: Aue, 1831), iii.

[194] *Skandinavische Bibliothek, Eine Zeitschrift, enthaltend: eine fortlaufende Auswahl des Anziehendsten und des Neuesten aus der dänischen, norwegischen und schwedischen Litteratur in sorgfältig bearbeiteten Übertragungen* I, no. 1 (1836): 228-31.

[195] Ibid., I, no. 2 (1836): 238-39.

Fänrik Ståls sägner, that work of Swedish literature the Danes had been quick to nationalize.[196] Osenbrüggen published these successful translations[197] (together with a highly spirited introduction to Runeberg) in 1853 in his *Nordische Bilder* (Northern Pictures) at Leipzig.[198]

Next came Peter Johann Willatzen (1824–1898), another member of the German ethnic minority in Greater Denmark. He had received early in life a thorough schooling in Danish letters. Later he disseminated in Germany both Danish and Swedish Poetic Realism, publishing in 1858 in Rhenish Prussia an anthology of translated Danish texts augmented with Danish-nationalized Swedish masterworks.[199] This anthology served especially well in further awakening German sensibilities to the art of Poetic Realism. Such notable masters as Blicher and Runeberg figured prominently in the volume, and Willatzen took great pains to use particularly felicitous translations, bringing the Scandinavian authors across the Dano-German language frontier in such a way that Germans could almost regard these foreign writers as their own. The German reading public took to these translations of the Poetic Realists from the north so strongly that a second, considerably expanded edition had to be printed to meet the consumer demand after the initial publication sold out.

Of the many Dano-Germans promoting the travel of *Poetisk Realisme* and *Poetisk Realism* into Germany, not all acted out of patriotic Danish or Pan-Scandinavian sentiments (as with von Schepelern and von Gähler) or because of a hearty affection for the new aesthetic embodied in Danish and Swedish literature (Osenbrüggen and Willatzen). Some international agents, such as the Dano-German anthologist Edmund Lobedanz (1820-1882), acted on a more material desire to capitalize on the commercial advantages of exporting northern Poetic Realism. In 1868 Lobedanz compiled the *Album Nordgermanischer Dichtung* (An Album of Northern Germanic Literature), two hefty tomes, in German translation, of texts taken largely from the Danish and Swedish Poetic Realists.[200] Together, these volumes contained the most extensive set of Scandinavian Poetic Realist texts imported into Germany. The German market's appetite for Scandinavian Poetic Realism had gradually increased until competition became intense among compilers of such anthologies, each compiler claim-

---

[196] According to the *Magazin für die Litteratur des Auslandes* (Berlin) 60 (1861): 496.

[197] In the judgment of Erich Kunze, *Deutsch-finnische Literaturbeziehungen, Beiträge zur Literatur- und Geistesgechichte* (Helsinki: Universitätsbibliothek, 1986), 12.

[198] Eduard Osenbrüggen, ed., *Nordische Bilder* (Leipzig: Hinrichs, 1853), 1-10, 76-77.

[199] P. J. Willatzen, ed., *Nordlandsharfe* (Elberfeld: Baedeker, 1858; 2nd expanded ed., 1889).

[200] Edmund Lobedanz, ed., *Album Nordgermanischer Dichtung* (Leipzig: Fritsch, 1868).

ing to offer better translations and larger selections. Such, apparently, were Lobedanz's goals. In the preface to the first volume he justified the publication of this new anthology by deploring the translations in preceding volumes and promising redress, claiming that his collection offered better, more accurate translations. The comparative size of his new anthology also allowed him to excite his readers with the belief that they could now own and read the most comprehensive selection of literary texts from contemporary northern Europe to date. Doubtless, the commercially motivated Lobedanz hoped his anthology would supersede other German anthologies so he could corner the booming market in new literature out of Scandinavia. His intention backfired, however, because of his hastily produced, inaccurate translations and a selection of texts so extensive as to place works by Scandinavian authors of pedestrian talents side by side with masterworks of Poetic Realism. A review appeared almost immediately in the *Magazin für die Litteratur des Auslandes* in Berlin, exposing the inferior quality of this huge anthology, and the sharp criticism must have caused a sensation.[201] Ironically enough, the highly critical attention in such a widely read periodical only served ultimately to make many more German readers aware of the vigorous new literature entering Germany through the efforts of Dano-German intermediaries.

5. Carl August Hagberg and the Brothers Brockhaus introduce the term *Poetischer Realist* to the German literary scene

While the Dano-Germans blazed trails for the importation of Poetic Realism into Germany, Swedish *Poetisk Realism* found other ways of reaching the German literary scene. For instance, the direct ferry route between Sweden and Germany brought across the Baltic the single most important effort in introducing Swedish *Poetisk Realism* to Germany: the entry of the very formula itself into the German critical vocabulary.

In August 1830 two circumspect and influential Leipzig publishers, Friedrich Brockhaus (1800–1865) and Heinrich Brockhaus (1804–1874), traveled to Sweden and established in Uppsala intimate connections to the Swedish muse. They made an especially important contact there (and maintained it after returning to Leipzig) with the university librarian who had issued the great critical "manifesto" for Poetic Realism: Johan Erik

---

[201] Paul Herlth, "Eine Anthologie skandinavischer Dichtung," *Magazin für die Litteratur des Auslandes* (Berlin) 72 (1867): 691-93.

Rydqvist.[202] Directly exposed to the new critical breeze blowing in Uppsala, these two publishers, attempting through their prominent journal *Blätter für literarische Unterhaltung* to mold German taste, naturally wanted to inform their German readership of the exciting events occurring on the Swedish Parnassus. They succeeded in persuading Carl August Hagberg (1810–1864) to write an article for their forum. It was published with the title "Literarische Notizen aus Schweden" (Literary Notes from Sweden) in the September 19, 1838, issue.[203]

Hagberg sought with this essay (unknown to critics today) to instill in the journal's German readership an echo of the excitement Runeberg's Poetic Realism was occasioning among the literary elite of Uppsala. Only seven months earlier, on February 28, 1838, the great sage of Uppsala, Atterbom, had taken up his influential pen to portray Runeberg as "decidedly a Poetic Realist." Now Hagberg, an active participant in the Uppsala circle of literary critics[204] and a glowing admirer of Atterbom,[205] repeated this characterization in German translation on the pages of the Brockhauses' journal. Said Hagberg to his German readers: "Runeberg ist entschieden ein poetischer Realist."[206]

This is the first mention in the German language of the now-famous formula in the context of a direct application to Realistic literature in the nineteenth century. It has gone completely unnoticed by all of the many critics who have addressed themselves to the use of this term in German literary history. Either the philosopher Schelling or the writer Otto Ludwig gets credit for its invention in Germany, and the contest between these two competing claims has always been the whole debate among scholars.[207] Schelling's champions point out that he used this formula in German as early as 1802;

---

[202] Ruben G:son Berg, "Palmblad och Brockhaus," *Samlaren*, n.f. 5 (1924): 50-53.

[203] "Literarische Notizen aus Schweden," *Blätter für literarische Unterhaltung*, Sept. 19, 1838: 1058-60. The article is unsigned, but Ruben G:son Berg assures us that the author could be none other than Hagberg. See Ruben G:son Berg, "Tidiga Svenska Runebergs-Kritiker i Tyskland," *Nya Argus* 21 (1928): 12. His findings are confirmed when we read in Hagberg's travelog *Resa i Europa på 1830-talet*, ed. T. Hagberg (Stockholm: Natur & Kultur, 1927), 133, the following sentence: "I promised Brockhaus an article on Swedish literature for his *Blätter für literarische Unterhaltung*."

[204] Kurt Aspelin, *Poesi och verklighet*, I (Göteborg: Akademiförlaget, 1967), 111-88.

[205] Less than three years earlier Hagberg, writing for a French audience, referred to Atterbom as "une gloire immortelle." In "De la littérature en suède," *Journal de l'institut historique* (Paris) 3 (Jan. 1836): 243.

[206] "Literarische Notizen aus Schweden," 1060.

[207] See René Wellek, *Concepts of Criticism*, 5th printing (New Haven & London: Yale University Press, 1969), 226; and — for the contrary opinion — Richard Brinkmann, *Wirklichkeit und Illusion*, 3rd ed. (Tübingen: Niemeyer, 1977), 3-4.

defenders of Ludwig claim Schelling's notions had nothing to do with the principles governing German *Poetischer Realismus* — credit for naming the German literary movement should go to the first of the German Poetic Realists using the name for the movement, Ludwig.

In truth, neither Schelling nor Ludwig should get credit for introducing the formula *Poetischer Realismus* to the German literary scene. Rather, this term first entered German criticism with Hagberg's essay in the *Blätter für litterarische Unterhaltung*. Once introduced in such a prominent literary forum, it quickly came to the attention of readers all over Germany, at least among those many men and women of literary taste who comprised the main readership of the Brockhauses' journal. Modern German literary historiography stands in need of correction!

6. Swedish *Poetisk Realism* comes to the attention of German readers via other channels

A year had hardly passed when, on January 10,1840, the *Magazin für die Litteratur des Auslandes* in Berlin, the most important forum at the time in Germany for bringing foreign literature to the attention of the German reading public, devoted a lengthy article to praising the work of Runeberg.[208] A Russian critic — the fame of *Poetisk Realism* had apparently spread to all nations touched by the Baltic — describes in great detail to the readers of this journal how a Swedish-speaking Finnish author had uniquely grafted together a stringent realism and poetic melody, innovatively combined poetic fantasy with realistic truth, and so opened up a new chapter in Swedish literary history.

German interest in Runeberg and in the new Swedish Poetic Realism had now been piqued from three different directions: via Denmark, directly across the Baltic from Uppsala, and through the efforts of a critic from Russia. The stage was now fully set in Germany for the reception of Runeberg's masterwork *Fänrik Ståls sägner*. It was twice translated almost immediately after its initial publication in Helsinki in 1848, and it then descended like a thunderbolt upon Germany. Atterbom, the authoritative theoretical apostle of *Poetisk Realism*, initiated placing the masterpiece before German readers. He, with the active collaboration of Runeberg, urged Ida Meves (1809–1890), the daughter of a German lyricist from Swedish Pomerania (Karl Lappe [1773-1843]), to translate it.[209] She published her translation in Leipzig in 1852.[210]

---

[208] *Magazin für die Litteratur des Auslandes* (Berlin) 18 (1840): 17-24.

[209] For splendid background information on this translation see Werner Söderhjelm, "Runeberg inför utlandet," in *Profiler i finsk kulturliv* (Helsinki: Lilius & Hertzberg, 1913), 9-12.

Atterbom had chosen an ideal translator. Her rendering succeeded so well that it gained readers for Runeberg's chef d'oeuvre not only in Germany but also in France, over the frontiers of German-speaking Europe,[211] making it a milestone in the travel of *Poetisk Realism* beyond Scandinavia.

Independently, but practically at the same time, a writer named Hans Wachenhusen (1822–1898) from Wismar — the other traditional trade route, besides Swedish Pomerania, from Sweden into Germany — translated *Fänrik Ståls sägner* into German, publishing it again at Leipzig in 1852, though with a rival publishing house.[212] His translation received much publicity, due to a highly favorable review in the *Magazin für die Litteratur des Auslandes* and probably not least because the reviewer called special attention to Runeberg's unique artistic commingling of *poiesis* and *mimesis*.[213]

Even these simultaneous translations of *Fänrik Ståls sägner* apparently did not satisfy the sudden German demand for this work. More translations followed in quick succession. An exhaustive bibliography compiled by Erich Kunze, the leading interpreter of Finnish literature in post-Second World War Germany, gives all the details.[214] Swedish *Poetisk Realism* had now invaded Germany as forcefully as had Danish *Poetisk Realisme*, and these Danish and Swedish influences contributed to the conditioning of a new literary climate in Germany, siring yet another offshoot of Poetic Realism: German *Poetischer Realismus*.

Additional biographical material on this (now forgotten) contributor to the advance of Poetic Realism in Germany is available in scattered places at the Royal Library in Stockholm.

[210] *Dichtungen von Johann Ludwig Runeberg*, trans. Ida Meves. 1. Bd. *Die Sagen des Fähnrich Stål* (Leipzig: Hartmann, 1852).

[211] A. Geffroy, "Poésies finlandaises de Runeberg," *Revue des Deux Mondes*, XXIV: 7 (1854): 1076-80.

[212] *Johann Ludwig Runeberg's Gesammelte Dichtungen*, trans. Hans Wachenhusen. 1. Bd. *Die Sagen des Fähnrich Stahl* (Leipzig: Lorck, 1852).

[213] *Magazin für die Litteratur des Auslandes* (Berlin) 42 (1852): 463-64.

[214] Erich Kunze, *Finnische Literatur in deutscher Übersetzung 1675-1975, Eine Bibliographie* (Helsinki: Universitätsbibliothek, 1982), 107 ff.

GERMAN *POETISCHER REALISMUS*

1. Julian Schmidt develops a theory of *Poetischer Realismus* at Leipzig

Leipzig's importance for the reception of Scandinavian Poetic Realism

By the middle 1840s Scandinavian Poetic Realism had become known far and wide in the German-speaking world but probably nowhere found a larger audience than in the Saxon city of Leipzig. Two different but not unrelated reasons could be cited. First, Leipzig was important for the publishing industry. Following elaborate celebrations in 1840 of the 400th anniversary of Gutenberg's invention of movable metal type, Leipzig quickly became the undisputed center of the German publishing trade. Books, pamphlets, newspapers, and journals of all sorts came off the presses at Leipzig in ever-increasing numbers as nowhere else in the German-speaking world. Correspondingly, more works of Scandinavian Poetic Realism in translation were printed and circulated in Leipzig than in any other German city.

Poetic Realism from the north also made a particular impact in Leipzig because of the personal efforts of the Brockhaus brothers, the owners of Leipzig's most influential publishing house. Friedrich and Heinrich Brockhaus had acquired a firsthand knowledge of Swedish *Poetisk Realism* when they visited Uppsala in 1830. Returning to Leipzig, they did their share to call attention to the literary revolution engaging the minds of Uppsala's literary elite. On the pages of one of their Leipzig journals they had even introduced, as mentioned earlier, the term *Poetischer Realist* to the German literary public.

Julian Schmidt moves to Leipzig and is attracted to Scandinavian Poetic Realism

Despite the attention that Scandinavian Poetic Realism was receiving at Leipzig, it might never have caught fire as it did, if not for Julian Schmidt (1818–1886). A Prussian pedagogue with a remarkable talent for journalism, he followed the example of so many young men seeking a vocation in writing and publishing, moving to Leipzig. There he soon became, as Friedrich Sengle has rightly pointed out, the "pioneering spirit"[215] of the new literary movement in Germany.

It is one of the scandalous oversights of contemporary literary criticism that so little is known today about this pioneer. Sengle has made much of professional Germanists' "ignorance" of Schmidt's seminal role in the rise of realism in German literature.[216] Henry Remak has bemoaned the lack of attention twentieth-century literary historians have given to Schmidt's journalistic accomplishments.[217] Yet, despite the emphatic reminders of these two prominent critics about this gap in literary historiography, no one has produced a useful biography of Schmidt.[218] Anyone wishing to describe how Schmidt's work galvanized the energies of Poetic Realism in Germany must piece together data from a wide variety of not easily accessible source materials, such as commemorative essays in German newspapers.[219] It is especially difficult to obtain information about the early, formative years that prepared Schmidt for his writing career.

So much, however, seems certain. When Schmidt moved to Leipzig from Berlin in mid-1846 (the frequently cited 1847 is incorrect), he brought with him more than his ambition to embark upon a career as a writer-publisher. He brought a staunch Prussian patriotism and an unshakable belief in a form of Protestantism that insisted on acknowledging the Prussian sovereign as the *summus episcopus* of the Protestant Church.

---

[215] Friedrich Sengle, *Biedermeierzeit*, I (Stuttgart: Metzler, 1971), 265.

[216] Ibid., III (1980), 1054.

[217] Henry H. Remak, "The German Reception of French Realism," *PMLA* 69 (1954): 420.

[218] More than 100 years have passed since the last biography (biographical sketch) of Schmidt was written: by his friend Constantin Rößler in *ADB* 31 (1890): 751-68. It is hardly useful today.

[219] The most informative of these are by 1) Oskar Walzel, "Ein deutscher Kritiker, Zu Julian Schmidts hundertstem Geburtstag," *Beilage des Berliner Börsen-Courier Blattes*, March 5, 1918; 2) C. Ling, "Julian Schmidt, Zu seinem hundertsten Geburtstag am 7. März," *Rheinisch-Westfälische Zeitung*, March 7, 1918; 3) Alex Köster, *Julian Schmidt als literarischer Kritiker* (Bochum: Poppinghaus, 1933).

As soon as he settled down in the more liberal, cosmopolitan center of the German publishing trade, where freedom of the press and religious tolerance enjoyed a more widespread appeal than in Berlin, he became quickly disturbed at reading in Leipzig's free press many an article arguing for ideas counter to beliefs he had grown up with in his philistine Prussian environment. Schmidt was forced, then, into the patriotic position of combatting these attitudes to which Leipzig's citizens were so exposed. Especially distasteful for him were the Austrian proclamations of cultural supremacy over German intellectual life, so much touted in the press of the little Saxon nation squeezed between Austria and Prussia.

The last thing Schmidt wished to see happen was the (at that time in the Saxon press much discussed) prospect of a greater Germany united under the crown of "His Apostolic Majesty," the Catholic emperor of Austria (the so-called *großdeutsche* solution to the problem of German unification). Should that prevail, the Prussian patriot feared, there might follow negative consequences for many venerable institutions he firmly believed in, not least, of course, his beloved Protestant Church.

The pre-condition of Austrian life for centuries had been the preeminence of an imperial court that was the consummation of a divine order sanctioned by the Pope at Rome. The strength and originality of the Austrian imagination appeared in the aura of an affectionate Catholic faith, in its ornate episcopal and archiepiscopal palaces, but no less in a fanciful theater. This institution had been shaped by an extravagant court, by the pomp and circumstance of the papacy, and by the traditions of Jesuit drama. This was the antithesis of everything Prussia stood for and naturally anathema to the ascetic Protestant Schmidt. "Protestant literature," he stated magisterially in 1846, "is concerned with concrete reality," whereas "the cardinal feature of Catholic literature is solely its beautiful appearance."[220] Yet, for many Saxons, including Saxony's Catholic monarch, Vienna with its baroque splendor remained the capital of an empire of considerable consequence; it seemed a more impressive center of political power than Prussia's less-populated, austere Berlin.

The cultural rivalry of Vienna and Berlin in the German power struggle must have made the Prusso-Protestant Schmidt particularly receptive to the breeze of Poetic Realism blowing down into Germany at that time from the land of Gustavus Adolphus, that earlier militant defender of Protestant values against the upward surge of Catholic culture from Austria. Schmidt was, of course, acutely reminded of that Swedish king's anti-Catholic stance when his ideas were revived in the years following the

---

[220] Published two years later in Julian Schmidt, *Geschichte der Romantik in dem Zeitalter der Reformation und der Revolution*, I (Leipzig: Herbig, 1848), 85, 243.

founding in Leipzig of the *Gustav-Adolf-Verein* (Gustavus Adolphus Foundation) in 1832. It was a foundation which had impressed Schmidt,[221] although no critic has noted this. Like Gustavus Adolphus, Schmidt wished, as Ferdinand Lassalle (1825–1864) once taunted, "to callously oust Catholics from the German nation."[222]

The new realistic literature from the Scandinavian north offered Schmidt the perfect antidote to the fanciful Catholic cultural wave flowing into Saxony from the south. For Poetic Realism had its roots in the geographic orbit that had remained more exclusively Protestant than any other part of Europe and — what must have been particularly appealing to Schmidt's Protestant prejudices — the movement's founder (Møller), as well as two of its brightest stars (Blicher, Runeberg), were even Protestant clergymen.

How could Schmidt have failed to take an interest in Poetic Realism? Of course, he had to be aware of it first, but how could he miss it, given the publicity it received in the journalistic circles where he, with his career ambitions, was seeking entry? His determination to be a success in the vocation that brought him to Leipzig must have made him eager for personal contact with the influential Brockhaus brothers. After all, besides their many publishing enterprises, they controlled the most important daily newspaper in Germany, the *Deutsche Allgemeine Zeitung*. Schmidt was anything but a shy and timid soul, if we are to believe the description of his personality given by Gustav Freytag (1816–1895).[223] He must have elbowed his way into their offices at the earliest opportunity after arriving in Leipzig. And who could have given him a better introduction to Swedish *Poetisk Realism* than these returnees from Uppsala?

He also must have learned about the Scandinavian literary movement in his extensive conversations with Meïr Goldschmidt. Not a single one of the various miscellaneous German publications about Schmidt ever mentions these conversations, but Goldschmidt's diaries and letters do. They inform us that soon after his arrival in Leipzig from Copenhagen on October 12, 1846, he met regularly with Schmidt and other literati at a local tavern, to apply their collective intelligence to the criticism of literature.[224] Goldschmidt records that he was more impressed with Schmidt than with

---

[221] See the statement about the foundation in Julian Schmidt, *Geschichte der deutschen Nationalliteratur im neunzehnten Jahrhundert*, II (Leipzig: Herbig, 1853), 313.

[222] Ferdinand Lassalle, *Herr Julian Schmidt, der Literaturhistoriker* (Leipzig: Röthing, 1862), 100.

[223] Gustav Freytag, *Gesammelte Werke*, I (Leipzig: Hirzel, 1887), 153.

[224] Hans Kyrre, *M. Goldschmidt*, I (Copenhagen: Hagerup, 1919), 102-3.

any other member of that intimate circle of Leipzig's fastidious minds. Apparently, the feeling was mutual, for the two decided to continue their dialogue on literature daily over dinner, without the rest of the company.[225] Every day for three weeks Schmidt's curiosity about Danish *Poetisk Realisme* could receive, in a congenial atmosphere, the best schooling possible, and from an ideal native informant.

Schmidt's mission as a journalist

Before the year 1846 drew to a close, Schmidt understood what his mission was to be. The Swedish and Danish literary models had provided him with the imaginative concepts he needed to put his journalistic talents to work tipping the cultural scales in favor of the Protestant north and securing at the same time Germany's unification under the crown of Prussia. On May 1, 1847, he joined the editorial staff of the *Grenzboten*, a weekly journal for "politics and literature" at Leipzig. He lost no time in putting his powerful pen to work on a programmatic theory for a new realistic literature in Germany. It was the duty of the critic, he believed, to teach the present and future writers of the nation.[226] If his prescripts could change the literary climate of Germany, he hoped to reduce the infatuation with the fanciful Catholic art that abetted Austria's cultural dominance.

Schmidt was messianically visionary, tirelessly energetic, clairvoyantly articulate, defiantly biting, and he knew how to enlist all these resources in effective journalism. In less than a year, on March 14, 1848, he advanced to editor-in-chief of the *Grenzboten*. From that day forward his effort to persuade writers and would-be writers to become Poetic Realists stepped up to a crusade of a fury perhaps unmatched in previous journalism.

Significantly, on the day before Schmidt's crusade reached full blast, Prince Clemens von Metternich (1773–1859), the most conspicuous symbol of the Austro-Catholic will to dominate German-speaking Europe, had been toppled. All Germany was in revolutionary uproar. Schmidt knew an ideal historic hour had arrived to put his message across with the greatest possible force, and he took full advantage of it. This is not to argue that the revolutions of March 1848 were the sole source of Schmidt's programmatic theory, but they certainly provided the indispensable backdrop he needed for his escalated critical campaign to teach new writers.

---

[225] *Breve fra og til Meïr Goldschmidt*, ed. M. Borup, II (Copenhagen: Rosenkilde & Bagger, 1963), 223, 227.
[226] Walzel, "Ein deutscher Kritiker."

Schmidt's theory unfolds

In Schmidt's first public statement as editor-in-chief he wrote that it was a time when "the most unheard-of dreams had become reality."[227] The statement revealed at once his conviction that in the wake of the political ferment of the day reality was all that counted. In literature it was to count no less than in politics, as he explained in the July 1848 issue of the *Grenzboten*. Prior to the revolutions, he said, "public life [Schmidt meant the politics of Catholic Austria which, through Metternich, ever-increasingly dominated Germany] had been so wretched" that Germans everywhere had taken refuge in an "abstract literature." Romantic literature's fanciful divertissements had provided an escape from an oppressive political order. But current events had suddenly and drastically altered the course of belles lettres. Politics, he said, had at last become the domain of every literate citizen, and so the literature of fantasy or escape should not be tolerated any longer. On the contrary, literature was to become "engulfed in life itself."[228]

These statements echo Schmidt's announcement two years earlier of the superiority of Protestant literature over Catholic literature: the Protestant emphasis on reality opposed to the Catholic focus on decorativeness in art.[229] Yet, against the revolutionary backdrop his pronouncements carried more conviction and certainly came before readers in a more persuasive form.

In subsequent pages of the *Grenzboten* Schmidt expounded his programmatic theory with unflagging zeal, never losing sight of the goal he had recognized since March 1848, and with newfound clarity. In the same July 1848 issue he delivered, for instance, a withering attack on French literature, particularly as represented by François René de Chateaubriand (1768–1848) and his cohorts.[230] Schmidt takes them to task for missing the point in their portrayal of reality. They depict reality, he says, only to contrast it with the object of their belief or, for some, the object of their disbelief: "the Catholic conception of heaven juxtaposed in purity against the base life on earth." Since a strong religious faith — or the ostentatious rejection of one — thus becomes the central issue at stake in portraying reality, the latter is subordinated to the former; and consequently, Schmidt concludes, the French have not taken the real world seriously.

---

[227] *Die Grenzboten*, 1848, II, 253.

[228] Ibid., 1848, III, 1-4.

[229] Schmidt, *Geschichte der Romantik*, I, 85, 243.

[230] *Die Grenzboten*, 1848, III, 154-66.

A more aggressive early attempt to change literary taste came in the autumn of 1848, when he sought to expose the ills of contemporary Danish literature, i.e., the literature that had superseded *Poetisk Realisme*. After the fading of *Poetisk Realisme*, Hans Christian Andersen increasingly dominated the muse of Germany's neighbor to the north. He had inaugurated a new literature of post-Poetic Realism in Denmark; it emphasized amusement and sentimentality, de-emphasizing reality. Schmidt avoids attacking Andersen directly, perhaps because he knew him personally,[231] perhaps because he secretly admired Andersen's extraordinary ingenuity as a writer,[232] or perhaps — what seems most likely — because Andersen was so esteemed in Europe that it would have been almost suicidal for a young critic to attack such a luminary. Instead, he singles out Henrik Hertz (1798–1870) as his critical target. In 1846 three different German translations of Hertz's play *Kong Renés Datter* (King René's Daughter) appeared in Berlin, Leipzig, and Oldenburg, only one year after the original edition in Denmark. The German public had enthusiastically embraced this play set in troubadour-era Provence, far removed from the reality of the day. Now, in early 1848, another quixotic play by Hertz, *Svend Dyrings Hus* (Svend Dyring's House), had been translated into German. Schmidt feared that this Romantic pastiche might also have wide appeal in Germany. He therefore issued a warning to the German public about the unrealistic nature of most recent Danish literature and of this work in particular. *Svend Dyrings Hus*, he tells us, "lacks the bold strokes" essential to literature. The play is "musical" and not "plastic" as it should be. It would have been better, Schmidt says, if Hertz had transferred his poetic view from the "nocturnal side of nature" to the "animated world of daylight." As it stands, however, the play so lacks realism that it resembles life in no way. Only those works, he adds, which are distinguished felicitously by realism can convey a genuine poetic sensation to the reader. Picturesquely, he sums up his criticism by saying: "There beats more poetry in the pitter-patter of a simple fisher-maiden's heart than in the stiff grandezza of all the phantoms in history, from the prophet Samuel right on down to the seeress of Prevorst in the nineteenth century, not forgetting the witches of the Middle Ages."[233]

Less striking than Schmidt's censure of contemporary French and Danish literature, but no less illustrative of the literary reform he sought, is

---

[231] *H. C. Andersens Dagbøger 1825-1875*, eds. K. Olsen & H. Topsøe-Jensen, IV (Copenhagen: Gad, 1971-1976), 217.

[232] *Die Grenzboten*, 1848, I, 207-15.

[233] Ibid., 1848, IV, 416-19.

the mixed blessing he bestows on Wilhelm Meinhold (1797–1851), one of the popular German authors of the day. In the first *Grenzboten* issue of 1849 Schmidt reviews Meinhold's latest novel, *Sidonie von Bork, die Klosterhexe* (Sidonia the Sorceress), adding his own measured voice to the large contemporary chorus of Meinhold eulogies. Schmidt points to the highly successful depiction of historical reality, down to minute detail. But this praise, as he impresses upon the reader, must also be tempered with the sobering realization that Meinhold's conception of reality is not always genuine. At times it degenerates into a feigned reality that clearly feeds on the sermonizing of a clergyman turned poet. Schmidt warns that Meinhold's poetic reality could delude us; but insight would show, Schmidt says, that the clergyman-author was more interested in a supernatural world than in the observable one.[234]

The summer of 1849 brought another significant step for Schmidt's theory of Poetic Realism. It came in a critique of Berthold Auerbach (1812–1882) and his fashionable school of literature. This essay sets itself against the "poets of detail," as it calls the school's adherents. Since the previous summer, following the revolutions, Schmidt had publicly criticized Auerbach's collection of *Schwarzwälder Dorfgeschichten* (Village Tales from the Black Forest), the second volume of which had appeared in 1848, after the first in early 1843. Because these pre-revolutionary tales were attracting European attention, Schmidt sought to make the public aware that they did not convey a universally accepted picture of reality: only offbeat provincial images, the minutiae of rural Black Forest life, however lovingly portrayed by Auerbach, representing but a small corner of the world. Auerbach may have captured a few picturesque moments, Schmidt says, but this reality holds up only as local color. Against the broad actual life of the general public, it breaks down.[235]

Schmidt reiterates this position when he objects, in the same essay, to Leopold Kompert's pre-revolutionary collection of tales, *Aus dem Ghetto* (Tales from the Ghetto), also published in 1848. Schmidt considers Kompert (1822-1886) one of Auerbach's most gifted imitators, focusing like Auerbach on the authenticity and ethnic character of a local region or on the mundane realities of life in a far corner of Germany. Schmidt admits that Kompert paints the life and manners of his native Jewish settlement in German-speaking Bohemia with warmth and accuracy. Yet, these charming descriptions and delightful anecdotes are rigidly limited to the "stagnating, narrow pond of the ghetto," far removed from the fresh,

---

[234] Ibid., 1849, I, 237-38.

[235] Ibid., 1849, III, 181-86.

broad "mainstream of life." They present unique and thus idealized situations rather than reality itself.

Schmidt's position in designing his theory of Poetic Realism with regard to the realism of Auerbach and Kompert may be summed up as follows: although Auerbach in the *Schwarzwälder Dorfgeschichten* and Kompert in *Aus dem Ghetto* have depicted daily life in a seemingly authentic manner, they have done so imperfectly. Their truth, restricted to the idyllic world of the peasants in the Black Forest or to the inhabitants of isolated Jewish communities in Bohemia, gives only a partial picture of reality, one separated from the "mainstream of life"; hence, it is mixed with falsehood.

Schmidt's stubborn insistence that literature must be realistic climaxed a few months later when he turned to English literature and condemned William Harrison Ainsworth's Gothic novel *The Lancashire Witches*. The reception accorded this novel by German readers had been spectacular: almost simultaneously with publication in England in 1849, an English-language edition came out in Leipzig; and virtually at once three different publishing houses commissioned translations into German. The enthusiastic German reception of this novel, which reveled in incredible supernaturalism, must have horrified Schmidt, for he set out to curtail Ainsworth's sudden popularity with a review dismissing the novel contemptuously. Ainsworth (1805–1882) is "unsurpassed," he says, when it comes to "conjuring up the horrors of hell." Drawing on *The Lancashire Witches* and five other works by Ainsworth, Schmidt shows how unsparingly the English novelist presses upon his reader a dazzling phantasmagoria of witches, devils, ghosts, exotic spirits, spurious romances, fantastic prophecies, spells, and curses; in short, the very antithesis of what is real. Yet, of all Ainsworth's literary capers, in Schmidt's estimation, the ultimate *embarras de richesses* occurs in *The Lancashire Witches*. To Schmidt, this novel is sheer madness: far too long has such "insanity in fictional form" been tolerated by the German reading public. "The nightmare of madness," he concludes, "belongs in the lunatic asylum." It should not find a haven "in the sunlight of fiction."[236]

By 1850, with this frenzied denunciation of Ainsworth's novel, Schmidt had become obsessively dedicated to making German fiction consonant with universally recognized reality. In the two years since the great watershed of March 1848 he had become a messianic advocate for realistic literature.

The year 1850, however, also saw the vigorous emergence of another dimension to his campaign to promote Poetic Realism. He now argued

---

[236] Ibid., 1850, I, 114-16.

that not only must literature be realistic in order to be poetic, it must also be poetic in order to be realistic. On the very first pages of the 1850 issue of the *Grenzboten* he makes this clear.[237] He addresses himself to the writers of March 1848, those *Märzpoeten* already infected by the revolutions, who thus no longer could content themselves with the Romantic tones of pre-revolutionary literature. Rejecting the conventions of pure fancy, the March writers directed their attention rather to the issues of the day, such as civil freedom and even revolution itself. These writers, Schmidt allows, rightly substituted reality for idealism, but they also joined hands with the politicians, and so lost sight of literature's true calling. Schmidt argues that literature must not prejudice itself in favor of a single political viewpoint and thus be reduced to a cog in the partisan machine. If the pre-March writers had sought to escape reality by conjuring up imaginative dream worlds, he says, the March writers, in revolting from the past, contented themselves too easily with disclaiming the unreal attitude of pre-revolutionary fiction. But it is not enough for post-revolutionary fiction to reject illusion; the new spirit also demands a new, enduring form, more universal than either patriotic sketches of provincial reality or tendentious weapons of political controversy.

Two of Schmidt's rejections illustrate in particular his impatience with the March writers: Alexander von Ungern-Sternberg (1806–1868) and Ferdinand Freiligrath (1810–1876). He felt they had fixed their gazes, and thus their literary themes, too closely upon the political-journalistic world. These two literati had opposed each other during the strife of 1848: Ungern-Sternberg supported the royalist camp and Freiligrath the republican, but both committed in Schmidt's opinion the same cardinal sin: turning literature into a forum to support a specific political conviction. In reviewing Ungern-Sternberg's novel *Die Royalisten* (The Royalists), Schmidt even denies that it is a novel.[238] Schmidt notes that it negatively describes the insurrection in Berlin on March 18 and 19, 1848, from a royalist point of view. This, he adds, is objectionable party politics in literary disguise.

Schmidt levels a similar criticism at Freiligrath's *Neuere sociale und politishe Gedichte* (Modern Social and Political Poems), the first of which appeared in 1849. Reviewing these poems, Schmidt claims that Freiligrath has wasted his poetic talent,[239] simply sprinkling "spices on the food of the democratically incited masses," essentially the same thing Ungern-

---

[237] Ibid., 1850, I, 5-13.

[238] Ibid., 1848, IV, 80.

[239] Ibid., 1851, III, 54-57.

Sternberg did for the monarchists. Of course, Schmidt lets us know, one pugnacious turn deserves another. If royalist authors like Ungern-Sternberg try to outdo one another in heaping insults on the republicans, we should not be surprised that republican writers, like Freiligrath, eagerly deride their adversaries: quid pro quo. But this shows, Schmidt continues, that Freiligrath does not rise above the political issues of the day either, for he portrays a crudely confined, sociopolitical reality; his poetry has lapsed into propagandist doggerel, thus "devoid of genuine artistic vitality."

With the rejection of the writers of March 1848, Schmidt's theory of Poetic Realism had attained full maturity. Now his stubborn edict that the themes and images of real life must prevail had been complemented by the equally harsh demand that the portrayal of real life must be transfigured, as the Swedish school of Poetic Realism had insisted, to give the reader a distilled, coherent, and personal vision of the essence of reality. Excesses of fancy and escapism were condemned, but realistic literature was to be shunned if its poetic substance had withered into artificial incrustation.

By the beginning of the 1850s, the widening circle of *Grenzboten* readers knew what the contentious Prussian critic expected from post-revolutionary literature in Germany. Yet, the fight for Poetic Realism had not ended: his doctrinaire proselytizing continued undiminished. As the Viennese critic Emil Kuh (1828–1876) put it, Schmidt spurred "the horses of realism" ever onward.[240]

But Schmidt had nothing new to add to his theory. All his subsequent criticism is belligerent maintenance of the position he had already fully developed. Even the best of his later reviews, his merciless condemnation of *Die Ritter vom Geiste* (The Knights of the Spirit), a novel by Karl Gutzkow (1811–1878), in 1852, and his brusque dismissal of Annette von Droste-Hülshoff's novella *Die Judenbuche* (The Jews' Beech-Tree), in 1859, offer, in spite of some compelling insights, nothing fundamentally new. Schmidt merely reminds us that reality does not preside over the details of these works. Schmidt cites the portrayal of Prince Egon von Hohenberg as typical of Gutzkow's runaway imagination. Schmidt finds it incredible that a character supposed to be a key representative of the nobility should be depicted sitting at a table in his castle with journeymen carpenters, jesting with them in carefree intimacy while his servants stand stiffly in gala dress holding champagne bottles. Scenes so unbelievable, Schmidt says, occur again and again.[241]

---

[240] Gottfried Keller, *Gesammelte Briefe*, ed. C. Helbling, III/1 (Berne: Benteli, 1952), 188.

[241] *Die Grenzboten*, 1852, II, 41-63.

In Droste-Hülshoff's novella, Schmidt informs us, "the reader is left in the dark with regard to no less than four different murders; it remains unclear who committed them and why they were committed." Hence, obscurity veils the whole composition, typical of Droste-Hülshoff's penchant for letting everything "terminate in death and for covering all the details with the dust of the grave." "That may have something to do with Romanticism," he adds, "but for the reader wishing to be convinced realistically, such nebulosity is too much to accept." Schmidt concludes by saying that Droste-Hülshoff has "misused" her talent for writing realistically.[242]

This commentary on *Die Judenbuche* is shattering for literary historians accustomed to viewing the work as a document of Poetic Realism[243] rather than an opus by a pre-revolutionary "strict Catholic writer," as Schmidt on another occasion called her,[244] for whom a divinely inspired, mystical order uniting everything on earth — and all above and below — transcended the more limited world of visible reality. The theory behind this critique, however, does not go beyond what Schmidt developed a decade before. Between March 1848 and the early 1850s the leaven for the new movement in German literature had been fully prepared.

Schmidt's programmatic theory had set German *Poetischer Realismus* on the course that determined its basic principles. As Wilhelm Dilthey (1833–1911) has said, Schmidt was "victorious" in his struggle to change the course of German literature.[245] Yet, it would be underestimating the influence of Scandinavian Poetic Realism in Germany if credit for ushering in the new German literary movement went solely to Schmidt. For one thing, Schmidt's theory might never have developed had he not become acquainted with Scandinavian Poetic Realism in Leipzig. Moreover, when the many translations of Scandinavian Poetic Realist works reached a wide audience in Germany, they certainly helped to condition the literary climate that made it possible for *Poetischer Realismus* to take root. Furthermore, the importance of 1848 should not be underestimated. This singularly disastrous and amazing year in German history formed the

---

[242] Ibid., 1859, IV, 449-54.

[243] E. K. Bennett, in *A History of the German Novelle*, 2nd ed., revised and continued by H. M. Waidson (Cambridge, England: University Press, 1974), 129, claimed: "Droste-Hülshoff's Novelle can be said to represent Poetic Realism in a form which is hardly surpassed by anyone except perhaps by Gottfried Keller." Many others have echoed Bennett's claim.

[244] Schmidt, *Geschichte der deutschen Litteratur von Leibniz bis auf unsere Zeit*, V (Berlin: Hertz, 1896), 402.

[245] Wilhelm Dilthey, "Julian Schmidt's Literaturgeschichte," *Deutsche Rundschau* 52 (1887): 153.

backdrop for the unusual German receptivity to Danish and Swedish Poetic Realism. In no other part of Europe had *Poetisk Realisme* and *Poetisk Realism* been translated so profusely as in Germany just before and after 1848. Significantly, it was a Danish critic, Georg Brandes, who became one of the first, if not *the* first, to recognize that 1848 was the Rubicon dividing German literature of the nineteenth century.[246]

2. Schmidt's brother-in-arms Otto Ludwig

Ludwig not Freytag

The theoretical seed of *Poetischer Realismus* Schmidt had germinated matured into a powerful literature. As the movement developed over half a century, it grew more equable, richer, and stronger, with a wealth of novellas, novels, and lyrics. As in many dynamic literary movements, some writers of German *Poetischer Realismus* stayed close to the theoretical spring while others strayed afar.

The closest brother-in-arms of Schmidt was Otto Ludwig (1813–1865), a fact not generally recognized by literary historians. Instead of coupling Schmidt and Ludwig they have preferred to link Schmidt to Gustav Freytag (1816–1895). Instead of viewing Ludwig's novel *Zwischen Himmel und Erde* (Between Heaven and Earth, 1855–1856) as the prototypical illustration of Schmidt's programmatic theory, they bestow the honor commonly on Freytag's dubious novel *Soll und Haben* (Debit and Credit, 1855). This has come about due to a legend spread by Hermann Marggraff (1809–1864), the editor of the *Grenzboten*'s competing *Blätter für literarische Unterhaltung* in Leipzig. Marggraff, always quick to sneer at his successful editorial rival Schmidt, laid the faults of Freytag's novel at Schmidt's door by trouncing it as Schmidt's theory put into practice.[247] Later critics, ignorant of the misattribution and the malice behind Marggraff's commentary, have repeated it ad nauseam.

A French *homme de lettres*, René-Gaspard-Ernest Saint-René Taillandier (1817–1879), writing in the *Revue des Deux Mondes* soon after the

---

[246] Georg Brandes, *Hovedstrømninger i det nittende Aarhundredes Literatur*, 5th revised ed., VI (Copenhagen: Gyldendal, 1924), 323. Brandes made the observation in a lecture at the University of Copenhagen in 1871, but it could well be that the idea occurred to him (and was written down) at an earlier date.

[247] *Blätter für literarische Unterhaltung*, June 21, 1855: 445-52, esp. 445. The crucial paragraph is now conveniently reprinted in Hartmut Steinecke, *Romantheorie und Romankritik in Deutschland*, I (Stuttgart: Metzler, 1975), 305, n. 36.

novels of both Freytag and Ludwig appeared, comprehended immediately and objectively that Ludwig's, rather than Freytag's, was the landmark of the literature that emerged under Schmidt's critical auspices. But Taillandier's remarks were never taken seriously, perhaps never even noted outside France. Freytag's realism may have something to do with the new climate ushered in by Schmidt, Taillandier grants, but it was Ludwig's novel which successfully embodied Schmidt's principles. Freytag's *Soll und Haben* was singularly inferior by comparison. "If the novel of M. Freytag only possessed the poetic power and precision characteristic of M. Otto Ludwig's work," Taillandier says on one occasion, "what a great novelist he could have turned out to be!"[248]

Unfortunately, Marggraff's, and not Taillandier's, observations have been cited so often by literary historians. Taillandier's essay should be resurrected from the oblivion to which it has been consigned. German Poetic Realism deserves to be judged by its best product closest to its spring, not its worst. This is more urgent today than ever, for doubts have appeared, as Jeffrey Sammons has pointed out, about whether Freytag's opus can any longer be called "literature."[249] How could the practice of early *Poetischer Realismus* be illustrated by a work that cannot even be called literature?

It is easy to see how Marggraff's cynical commentary has gained such wide acceptance. Schmidt and Freytag had met in Leipzig in early 1848. Quickly they must have sensed a common belief in the Protestant ethic and a burning desire to exclude Catholic Austria from German affairs to pave the way for German unification under the Protestant king of Prussia. Each harbored the ambition to work for this cause by means of the pen. Shortly after their first meeting, Schmidt became editor-in-chief of the *Grenzboten*. As he lacked the money to assume ownership of the journal alone, he offered Freytag the chance to purchase a half interest. They became co-owners and co-editors for thirteen years. These facts have given literary historians the circumstantial evidence to couple the names of Schmidt and Freytag and perpetuate the false legend about their literary affinity.

Critics have not observed sufficiently, however, that the editorial collaboration between Schmidt and Freytag was by no means happy. They kept their editorial duties rigidly separate; they really did not collaborate at all. Schmidt assumed responsibility for articles on literature and art; Freytag wrote on politics and the theater (which never became a forte of Po-

---

[248] Saint-René Taillandier, "Le Roman de la Vie domestique en Allemagne," *Revue des Deux Mondes*, XXVII: 8 (1857): 33-65, esp. 50.

[249] Jeffrey L. Sammons, "The Evaluation of Freytag's *Soll und Haben*," *German Life & Letters* 22 (1968-1969): 322.

etic Realism). At first, the two men lived under one roof, but soon they must have discovered their incompatibility, for they moved to separate quarters. They worked and lived apart. Within a year, they rarely saw one another. Schmidt managed the journal's affairs during the summer months, and Freytag did the same in the winter. When Schmidt was in charge, Freytag would move out of town.[250] After five years of co-ownership of the *Grenzboten*, and despite the fact that they were two young men of about the same age, they still addressed one another with the formal *Sie*.[251] Was this a close, collaborative friendship, as we read so often in modern criticism? Critics would do well to note what each thought of the other. Schmidt once wrote to Freytag: "In our personalities and in our temperaments we are the opposite of one another."[252] Freytag recollected later: "Schmidt became impossible to work with."[253]

With regard to Freytag's oeuvre and, in particular, his novel, *Soll und Haben*, we never get the impression Schmidt considered them models of his theory of literature. Of course, in his regular appraisals of so many of the latest works of literature, both German and foreign, he could hardly avoid "advertising" his partner's contributions. The two men had, despite their personal differences, a good financial arrangement; each needed the other in order to continue earning a living from the journal. Nevertheless, this did not deter Schmidt from finding fault with Freytag's fiction.[254] But with *Soll und Haben* he had to be more careful, for Freytag had flattered him and practically solicited a favorable review when he prefaced that novel with a maxim from Schmidt. Feeling this time that he had to avoid using adverse words, Schmidt damns the novel with faint praise.

In his three-page review[255] Schmidt offers hardly more than a detailed synopsis of the plot, which substitutes for genuine critique and makes the novel appear, at best, wearisome or, at worst, insufferably dull. Schmidt does not convince us that the novel rises above the strictly descriptive even when he mentions some of its virtues: the emphasis on the portrayal of "the typical," the apt language, and the graceful organization of details.

---

[250] A gold mine of information about Schmidt and Freytag at the *Grenzboten* is the unpublished, handwritten Ph.D. dissertation of Adolf Thiele, "Gustav Freytag, der Grenzbotenjournalist," Münster, 1924.

[251] Schmidt, *Geschichte der deutschen Nationalliteratur im neunzehnten Jahrhundert*, v.

[252] Ibid., vi.

[253] *Gustav Freytag an Salomon Hirzel und die Seinen*, ed. A. Dove (Leipzig: Hirzel, 1902), 135.

[254] Kenneth Bruce Beaton, "G. Freytag, J. Schmidt und die Romantheorie nach der Revolution von 1848," *Jahrbuch der Raabe-Gesellschaft* (1976): 19.

[255] Schmidt, *Geschichte der deutschen Litteratur von Leibniz bis auf unsere Zeit*, V, 582-85.

Nowhere does he indicate that this novel had for him the power to transfigure reality and make it genuinely exciting. That Schmidt deemed this novel "dreary" (the adjective the legendary Friedrich Gundolf associated with Freytag's fiction)[256] is clear when he later reveals his feelings in his discussion of another contemporary novelist, Friedrich Spielhagen (1829–1911). Spielhagen "surpassed Freytag," Schmidt says, "with the brilliancy of a narrative artistry and the colorfulness of character portrayal."[257] To be sure, Schmidt tempers this statement with comments about weaknesses in Spielhagen, which gives the impression that, in his estimation, Spielhagen was not a very successful writer either. We are not sure whether Schmidt thought less of Freytag or less of Spielhagen, but we are certain he thought neither a prototypical Poetic Realist. In contrast to these unenthusiastic responses, Schmidt is elated with Ludwig's success at giving realistic description a fictionally transfigured meaning: "He [Ludwig] knows how to transform impressions of everyday life into a poetic reality."[258]

Before we look more closely at Ludwig's contributions to Poetic Realism, it should be pointed out that another prominent Poetic Realist, Theodor Storm, also had a series of disparagements for *Soll und Haben*. He stated categorically and repeatedly — for emphasis, as he wrote to his friend Fontane — that that novel was "poetically sterile," "insipid," "unimaginative," "imprecise," and even "puerile."[259] Nowhere in Freytag scholarship has there been any mention of Storm's rejection of *Soll und Haben*, but the novel could hardly be a paradigmatic text of Poetic Realism when such a prominent Poetic Realist as Storm held it in such contempt.

Zwischen Himmel und Erde

In comparison with Freytag's poetically arid *Soll und Haben*, the novel by Ludwig, *Zwischen Himmel und Erde*, is, as Gail Finney properly insists, "a model example of Poetic Realism."[260] Had it not had this significance,

---

[256] Georg Lukács, *The Historical Novel*, trans. H. & S. Mitchell (London: Merlin, 1962), 246.

[257] Schmidt, *Geschichte der deutschen Litteratur von Leibniz bis auf unsere Zeit*, V, 585.

[258] *Die Grenzboten*, 1857, IV, 410.

[259] *Theodor Storm—Theodor Fontane Briefwechsel*, Kritische Ausgabe, ed. J. Steiner (Berlin: Erich Schmidt, 1991), 102, 107.

[260] Gail Finney, *The Counterfeit Idyll* (Tübingen: Niemeyer, 1984), 92. Finney augments her comment with an absorbing discussion of this novel in the context of Poetic Realism (92-100). The most comprehensive analysis of the novel was written by William J. Lillyman: *Otto Ludwig's "Zwischen Himmel und Erde," A Study of its Artistic Structure* (The

Julian Schmidt certainly would not have acclaimed it as "a work of the first magnitude, one of those few from our century which can be predicted with some assurance to outlive our own generation."[261]

As with Schmidt's theory of literature and so many early works of *Poetischer Realismus*, this novel might never have been written had not the author received his literary baptism in the fires of 1848. Living in Saxony, he had experienced these in all their horror. Early in March 1848 the flurry of revolutionary agitation had spread to that part of Germany, and unrest and uproar rapidly encompassed the kingdom. Leipzig was placed under military occupation. Ludwig, closely observing the events, wrote at the time to a friend that eight thousand soldiers were encamped around the city, so that food became scarce and prohibitively expensive. In the capital city of Dresden, he went on to say, one riot followed another. For the economy of the entire nation, as well as for the welfare of its population, Ludwig also noted, the revolution was catastrophic. Industry and commerce had become paralyzed. Everywhere men were out of work; starvation ran rampant.[262] This horrible state of affairs continued for more than a year. On May 3, 1849, the citizens of Dresden, in a last desperate effort to bring about a change, tried to take the government arsenal by storm. Royalist troops fired into their midst and into the barricades set up all over the city. The king, fearful of mob violence, fled. Anarchy erupted, and blood flowed freely in the streets. Peace came only later in the month when Prussian troops marched into the unhappy kingdom and ruthlessly quelled every vestige of rebellion.

For Ludwig, the revolutionary outburst he had witnessed caused deep concern over the function of literature. He wrote in May of that year that the escapist belles lettres in vogue before 1848 were now completely out of fashion and would not be easily revived. The other type of literature, however, which had rejected the conventions of pure fancy and supported political issues, hardly seemed an alternative. "For every flake of gold

---

Hague & Paris: Mouton, 1967). It is indispensable for all scholarship on this novel. Other noteworthy modern analyses are by 1) Keith A. Dickson, "'Die Moral von der Geschicht': Art and Artifice in 'Zwischen Himmel und Erde,'" *Modern Language Review* 68 (1973): 115-28; 2) Lionell Thomas, "Otto Ludwig's *Zwischen Himmel und Erde*," *Proceedings of the Leeds Philosophical and Literary Society* 16 (1975): part 2, 27-38; 3) Jörg Schönert, "Otto Ludwig: *Zwischen Himmel und Erde (1856)*, Die Wahrheit des Wirklichen als Problem poetischer Konstruktion," in *Romane und Erzählungen des Bürgerlichen Realismus, Neue Interpretationen*, ed. H. Denkler (Stuttgart: Reclam, 1980), 153-72.

[261] Schmidt, *Charakterbilder aus der zeitgenössischen Literatur* (Leipzig: Duncker & Humblot, 1875), 186.

[262] "Otto Ludwigs Stellung zur Revolution von 1848 nach seinen Briefen an Ludwig Ambrunn," *Otto Ludwig-Jahrbuch* 11 (1939): 83-84.

which political literature contained," he whimsically said, "there were ten barrow-loads of gravel and mud covering it."[263] He realized, just as Schmidt did, that an altogether new style seemed called for.[264]

The finest fruit of Ludwig's experiences in the Saxon revolutions of 1848–1849 is *Zwischen Himmel und Erde*. In an important critical statement about the story, Ludwig tells us what he sought to portray in the main body of the narrative: the central figure, Apollonius, turns his fearful, tender conscience into a passion clouding his intelligence. Ludwig says he intends to show the typical fate of a man with too much conscience. In contrast, his brother Fritz is to illustrate too little conscience. And each aggravates the other's weakness, the too-conscientious making his vicious brother worse, who, in turn, makes the former more timorous. This is the predictable fate of the overly conscientious person: he gets a headache, so to speak, from what others drink.[265] Ludwig thus presents an inescapable reality — the necessity to choose between right and wrong, virtue and vice — and the consequences of a clash between people choosing opposites, especially within a family.

But the novel does not unfold this very genuine concern for ultimate values in everyday life simply and straightforwardly, as Ludwig's summary does. Remarkably, real life — the natural development of the two real passions, the obvious contrast between the characters — comes fictionally garbed as reminiscence. The narrator begins capriciously, boldly telling the end of the story. Memory weaves the novel's realistic fabric, transfiguring and spiritualizing it from a different point in time — some thirty years later — lifting it out of the realm of real time (no note appears in the story of dates and geographic locations). Living in peaceful retirement in his advanced years, Apollonius recollects scenes from the drama a generation earlier between him and his brother. In his mind's eye he eagerly retraces certain events from his youth, while deliberately forgetting others. The reality of the past has been fictionalized in retrospect and assumes a new, fanciful appearance. Colored, partial, and biased, the remembered experience distorts and falsifies the original facts, as the Victorian critic George Henry Lewes (1817–1878) once keenly detected.[266] Autobiographically, Apollonius presents himself more like a saint than a human being.

Thus, an overriding conflict gives this novel its Poetic Realist structure and meaning. The conflict, however, is neither that of the two brothers

---

[263] Ibid., 91.

[264] Ibid., 83.

[265] *Otto Ludwigs Gesammelte Schriften*, ed. A. Stern, VI (Leipzig: Grunow, 1891), 223.

[266] *Westminster Review* 14 (1858): 499.

nor that of virtue and vice, as often claimed. Rather, it is the fictionally superimposed conflict between an experienced reality and its subsequent autobiographical transformation in an imaginative memory not bound by reality. Fact and fiction, reality and imagination then become the dominant points of interest in the novel. The reader, once realizing this, faces the crucial question: which is reality and which imagination? On one level of the narrative, the past seems to be factual, whereas the spell of recollection, which projects that historical past in a reordered, distorted, and falsified fashion, seems imaginary. But that territory of memory, giving a new life to certain past events, is the sole world directly presented in the narrative, while the prior events it recalls can only be imagined.

The novel speaks about the fundamental roles of fact and imagination in human life. The narrator seems to struggle as much with these two opposing spheres as did Ludwig himself, in an extensive set of philosophical exercises (written concomitantly) on Shakespeare, where he pondered the dualistic structure of *Poetischer Realismus*.

Ludwig's philosophical exercises on *Poetischer Realismus*

Ludwig's multifarious jottings on Poetic Realism delighted Schmidt as much as had *Zwischen Himmel und Erde*, and they are just as important for understanding Poetic Realism in Germany. Alas, they were not left in publishable form. Paul Merker's historical-critical edition of Ludwig's oeuvre (1912–1922) did not include them, since only six of the projected eighteen volumes were ever published. Several attempts to put the reflections into a surveyable order seem variously unsuccessful, if we compare different editions and read what each editor writes about the inaccurate readings of his predecessors. Léon Mis (1873–1964), a (now forgotten) French philologist, had perhaps succeeded best in making Ludwig's arguments intelligible, in two books, in 1922 and 1929.[267] These might have sparked attention for Ludwig's ponderings, if not published in France. They never became known in Germany, for the importation of French books into Germany virtually halted in the 1920s because of the lack of valuta in the postwar, debt-ridden nation. All of this has greatly hampered the scholarly study of Ludwig's reflections. Yet, they should not be left by the wayside, for they distinctively illuminate *Poetischer Realismus*. As Eric Bentley has said, Ludwig "ought to be famous everywhere" for these stud-

---

[267] Léon Mis, *Les "Études sur Shakespeare" d'Otto Ludwig* (Lille: Imprimerie Centrale du Nord, 1922; 2nd rev. ed., Paris: Gamber, 1929).

ies, "because they probe into the nature of literature with skill and even genius."[268]

For the specific bearing of these theoretical exercises on *Poetischer Realismus*, it is important to note that they are in the form of an imaginary dialogue with Julian Schmidt. With the woeful lack of attention these reflections have received, not surprisingly their connection with Schmidt has gone unrecognized. Alfred Schwarz, for instance, observes correctly that Ludwig "speaks extempore, as if in leisurely conversation across the room."[269] But Schwarz seems unaware that the figurative conversational partner is Schmidt. Yet, Ludwig wrote once to the guiding spirit of *Poetischer Realismus* in Leipzig that he was filling a notebook with analyses of literature, and that these pages upon pages took the form of imaginary letters to his mentor.[270] Under the titanic shadow of Schmidt, Ludwig filled many such a notebook with probing inquiries into the nature of literature.

Ludwig drew heavily from twin springs: the phantom conversations with Schmidt and the actual ones in oral and written form. (They had met in Dresden and corresponded.) A devoted disciple of Schmidt, he moved more and more within the orbit of Poetic Realism. The bulk of these real and imagined conversations focused on Schmidt's antipodal principle: literature must stay true to actuality and yet operate in a poetic realm. Reality and fantasy were the twin bases, according to Ludwig, of a work of literature. The marriage of the two creates, as he put it, "a world that stands midway between the objective truth of things and the law which our [i. e., the poet's] mind is impelled to read into them."[271] Speaking of Shakespeare he said: "By and large there is no writer who, for instance, remains so faithful to the truth of life, and yet his details put him thoroughly into the realm of fantasy."[272] On another occasion the preoccupation with Shakespeare led him to the realization that the drama as a literary genre was, in essence, the marriage of two arts: the poetry of the fictional play and the acting on the real stage.[273]

---

[268] Eric Bentley, *The Playwright as Thinker* (New York: Harcourt, Brace & World, 1967), 265.

[269] Alfred Schwarz, "Otto Ludwig's Shakespearean Criticism," in *Perspectives of Criticism*, ed. H. Levin (Cambridge, Mass.: Harvard University Press, 1950), 100.

[270] *Ludwigs Gesammelte Schriften*, VI, 420.

[271] Ibid., V, 459.

[272] Ibid., V, 271.

[273] Bentley, 58.

The indissoluble marriage between the two opposing poles, fiction and reality, which increasingly compelled Ludwig, also made him acutely aware of the term *Poetischer Realismus*. Conversing with Schmidt, he knew that this formula lent a marvelous precision to the antipodal principle, the basis of his comrade's apostolate.[274] Ludwig's use of the formula has given rise to the incorrect notion that he invented it. "Otto Ludwig devised the term 'Poetischer Realismus,'" René Wellek has said.[275] "The term was coined by Otto Ludwig," we read in the standard reference work on German Poetic Realism by Walter Silz.[276] Carrying the notion further, it has been claimed that Ludwig was father to the new German literary movement's theory.[277] But Atterbom, as noted before, had coined the term, specifically to refer to post-Romantic literature, and Hagberg and the Brockhaus brothers had introduced it into the German critical vocabulary long before Ludwig.

Ludwig could have heard the term from the Brockhaus brothers, whom he knew well, possibly also from Schmidt or from the many other men of letters he knew in Saxony — most likely, however, from the lips of his friend Adolf Stern (1835–1907). Stern, a professor of literature in Dresden who saw Ludwig often, had strong ties to the Swedish muse. He corresponded extensively, for instance, with Carl Rupert Nyblom (1832–1907), a noted Runeberg scholar and a pupil of Atterbom and subsequent occupant of the very chair for aesthetics at Uppsala previously held by his teacher. Stern dedicated his *Studien zur Literatur der Gegenwart* (Studies in Contemporary Literature) to the king of Sweden. He must have been unusually well informed about Swedish *Poetisk Realism*. He was the first person to write that Schmidt's *Grenzboten* had propagated "die Theorie des poetischen Realismus."[278] How could Ludwig fail to learn of the term from this intimate friend who must have been well acquainted with it?

If we would be giving Ludwig too much credit, however, to assign the coinage to him, or to consider him and not Schmidt as the theoretical father of the new literary movement in Germany, we must not underrate the importance of his philosophical writings. Thinking and writing so inten-

---

[274] *Ludwigs Gesammelte Schriften*, V, 264, 458.

[275] René Wellek, *Concepts of Criticism*, 5th printing (New Haven & London: Yale University Press, 1969), 230.

[276] Walter Silz, *Realism and Reality: Studies in the German Novelle of Poetic Realism*, 4th printing (Chapel Hill: University of North Carolina Press, 1965), 12.

[277] Heinrich Reinhardt, *Die Dichtungstheorie der sogenannten Poetischen Realisten*, (Würzburg: Triltsch, 1939), 37-89.

[278] Adolf Stern, *Geschichte der neuern Litteratur*, VII (Leipzig: Bibliographisches Institut, 1885), 96.

sively under the patronizing influence of Schmidt, and concisely defining his mentor's literary creed with the revived formula *Poetischer Realismus*, Ludwig became Schmidt's true comrade and disciple, a prime figure in the budding movement.

In this zealous disciple the movement's chief arbiter saw his theoretical program mirrored, confirmed, and splendidly reworded. "I was absolutely amazed," Schmidt once said, "at how perfectly we agreed in our judgments. But how exquisitely he can express his judgment!"[279] Schmidt knew how much he owed the early implementation of his program to Ludwig's writings and conversations. "You have fought and won the battle [for literature in our time]," he wrote in an open letter to Ludwig at the beginning of his book on Schiller.[280] His brother-in-arms agreed: "It was not until I read the dedication in J. Schmidt's book on Schiller that I had the courage to see ... what had been right in front of my eyes for so long."[281]

In 1860, still in the midst of his ponderings on the concept of *Poetischer Realismus*, Ludwig became seriously ill. He was not yet fifty, but he never recovered. To the end, in early 1865, he continued his phantom conversations with Schmidt on Poetic Realism, jotting his thoughts down as they came. He knew time was running out to organize all his reflections in a publishable treatise. Rather than leave them to posterity in a disorganized form, he ordered them destroyed only a few months before his death. One box of manuscripts was lost this way. The rest were saved through the intervention of a friend. These deserve to receive more attention than they have heretofore. Despite their incomplete and unfinished state, they offer an impressive series of compelling insights into the enigma of reality and imagination that Ludwig, like his fellow theorists in Uppsala, insisted on calling *Poetischer Realismus*.

---

[279] Schmidt, *Charakterbilder aus der zeitgenössischen Literatur*, 186.
[280] Schmidt, *Schiller und seine Zeitgenossen* (Leipzig: Herbig, 1859), iv.
[281] *Ludwigs Gesammelte Schriften*, VI, 18.

3. Continuing *Poetisk Realisme* on German-speaking soil: Theodor Storm

Storm versus Schmidt

If Ludwig was a brother-in-arms to Schmidt, Theodor Storm (1817–1888),[282] another early German Poetic Realist, seems as removed from the programmatic initiator as possible. They never met or corresponded and probably would not have wanted to. Schmidt was a chauvinistic Prussian patriot attracted to Scandinavian Poetic Realism as an alternative to the decorative Austro-Catholic art which he viewed as an obstacle to the unification of Germany under the Prusso-Protestant sovereign. Storm, in contrast, hated Prussia. "Go to hell," he indignantly replied to his friend Fontane's request that he write a poem commemorating a Prussian military victory.[283]

Although it would be difficult to imagine any two contemporary German men of letters further apart in political attitudes than Schmidt and Storm, their names will, nevertheless, always remain linked in the annals of *Poetischer Realismus* as two of its towering sponsors.

Storm between Denmark and Germany

Storm was a native of the little town of Husum, near the Dano-German language frontier. The sovereign then, both above and below the frontier, was the king of Denmark. This geographic stroke of fate had caused Storm to drink heavily at the fountain of Danish literature. This has not been sufficiently recognized in Storm scholarship; only one Danish Germanist, Leif Ludwig Albertsen, has forthrightly stated that Storm was "thoroughly at home in the Danish language and literature."[284]

With so little known about this subject, even among Storm critics, it may be beneficial to review some of the facts here. In the nine years Storm attended the Latin grammar school in Husum (1826–1835), he regularly

---

[282] The literature on Storm is vast. Two excellent general studies in English are by 1) A. Tilo Alt, *Theodor Storm* (New York: Twayne, 1973); and 2) David A. Jackson, *Theodor Storm, The Life and Works of a Democratic Humanitarian* (New York & Oxford: Berg, 1992). The best modern general study in German is by Winfried Freund, *Theodor Storm* (Stuttgart: Kohlhammer, 1987).

[283] *Storm—Fontane Briefwechsel*, 121.

[284] Leif Ludwig Albertsen, "Theodor Storm zwischen Dänemark und Deutschland," *Slesvigland* 5 (1984): 134.

received at least as much formal instruction in Danish as in German. The *Regulativ für die Gelehrtenschule der Stadt Husum* (Regulations for the Grammar School of the Town of Husum) of 1827[285] lists every week in the *Quarta* three hours of instruction in Danish and three in German. In the *Tertia* it prescribes two hours each in Danish and German, in the *Secunda* and the *Prima* one hour each in each language. The teaching of Danish was taken so seriously that the principal himself, Peter Friedrichsen (1790–1873), not only took personal charge of the instruction in Danish, as the *Schulprogramm* (School Report) of 1831 states, but also actively encouraged experts in Danish, such as Detlev Lorenz Lübker (1773–1852), to edit texts of Danish literature to make them more easily accessible to the pupils.[286] His emphasis on teaching Danish literature is all the more striking next to the small attention he gave to the teaching of German literature. In Friedrichsen's annual report for 1829, for instance, he lists in detail the Danish texts the pupils read but makes no mention whatsoever of any German literature. That was a "luxury," an account of Storm's school days informs us, which the pupils were left to read (or not) on their own.[287]

With such schooling in Danish letters, Storm had no trouble passing the obligatory state examination in Danish at the University of Kiel. His examiner, the Dano-German jurist Nicolaus Falck (1784–1850), certified that "Candidate Storm can read Danish well, with a good pronunciation, and can also translate Danish prose and poetry accurately and with ease."[288]

Yet, if Storm had acquired a familiarity with Danish culture, he belonged, nevertheless, to the German-speaking minority population in the lands governed by the Danish monarch. Between 1848 and 1850, when the German minority rose up in rebellion against its sovereign, Storm's life was affected markedly, more so than the lives of any of the other Poetic Realists touched by the revolutions elsewhere in the German-speaking world. This was the bloodiest and most anguishing of all the German insurrections; both Julian Schmidt and Friedrich Engels (1820–1895) said

---

[285] A copy of this rare booklet and the Annual Reports of the school are preserved in the archives of the Hermann Tast Gymnasium in Husum.

[286] Detlev Lorenz Lübker, *Neues dänisches Lesebuch*, 2nd ed. (Schleswig: Kgl. Taubstummen Institut, 1843), i.

[287] Joachim Rohweder, "Aus der Jugendzeit Theodor Storms," *Schleswig-holsteinische Zeitschrift für Kunst und Literatur* 1 (1906): 535.

[288] A photo of the certification is reproduced in Karl Ernst Laage, *Theodor Storms Welt in Bildern* (Heide: Boyens, 1988), 62.

that the revolutionary movement first really came to life when these northern rebellions erupted.[289]

How the revolutions affected Storm's life has been more acutely observed by a Danish historian, Knud Fabricius (1875–1967), than by literary critics, perhaps because Fabricius commanded a deeper insight into Danish political and military events.[290] The rebellion of the Germans in the duchy of Schleswig, in which Storm's native Husum was located, began on March 24, 1848. Within a month Danish troops occupied Husum, seeking to crush the insurgents. Soon on the brink of anarchy, the town tottered for over two years between the exigencies of mutinous warfare and the tyranny of martial law.

The tumult caused by this revolutionary war moved Storm profoundly.[291] He wrote vivid accounts of his anguishing experiences for a rebel newspaper. As the rebellion progressed, he became increasingly impassioned. On May 1, 1849, he demanded outright sedition against the crown of Denmark; on October 5 he publicly refused to obey the laws handed down by the new military government. Most important, the revolution, the harsh military occupation, and the oppressive political conditions which had suddenly engulfed him all forcibly alienated him from the fairy-tale literary activity of his pre-revolutionary days.

In his early manhood as a subject of the Danish king, Storm had been infected by the unrestrained fantasy so integral a part of the post-Poetic Realistic literature in Denmark after the middle of the 1830s. He had not been altogether different from Hans Christian Andersen. But that sort of Danish literature, as Julian Schmidt had said, was out of tune with the rugged realities of revolutionary times.

Storm now felt obliged to revolt against that form of Danish literature as much as he revolted against the Danish crown. Because of his harrowing experiences in the rebellion, he could no longer pay allegiance to the crown; nor could he view literature as a flight from reality into a fairy-tale land of fantasy. He had to look for a more realistic, down-to-earth literary vehicle. He turned from Copenhagen and the North to Germany, southward. There a new realistic literature had sprung up in 1848: the *Märzliteratur*, represented by Freiligrath and Ungern-Sternberg. Rather than pure fantasy, topical issues of the day prevailed in this fiction. Storm em-

---

[289] Schmidt, *Geschichte der deutschen Litteratur von Leibniz bis auf unsere Zeit*, V, 462; Karl Marx and Frederick Engels, *Collected Works*, VII (New York: International Publishers, 1977), 421.

[290] Knud Fabricius, *Sønderjyllands Historie*, IV (Copenhagen: Reitzel, 1937), 458.

[291] The details have been given best by Anna Simonsen, "Theodor Storm og Danmark," *Sønderjydske Aarbøger* 1 (1950): 140-52.

editions of Storm's collected works or the many translations, followed the speculative publication of 1850 until, finally, the copyright expired in 1918 and it entered the public domain.

Storm's novella portrays a compelling reality inescapably facing all mankind: the evanescence of human life and happiness. It offers a poignant poetic lesson on the nature of reality; but it also steers the reader unrelentingly into reality, for it unflinchingly marks the limits of man's ability to cope with the obtrusively destructive force of transience.

With a few bold strokes, Storm paints a childhood happiness gradually but steadily destroyed by the passing of time. While still young and in school together, the characters Elisabeth and Reinhard are happy. The flux of time, however, forces them apart. Reinhard matures and leaves primary school, where he has been together with Elisabeth, for a boys' secondary school. Now he can share only his after-school leisure with his childhood companion. Seven years later he loses even leisure hours with her, for his secondary education is completed and he moves away to study at a distant university. The reader witnesses Elisabeth's and Reinhard's last happy day together. When the subsequent six months between June and December have drifted by, the previous warmth of affection has faded into the forced chill of prolonged separation. The further passage of time only intensifies their estrangement; two more years sever their ties so thoroughly that Elisabeth agrees to marry someone else. The years bring Elisabeth and Reinhard to the final realization that the enchantment of youth has gone forever.

Thus, the reader of *Immensee* learns how human happiness erodes with time, but the novella has another message also. Fused with this portrayal of the fragility of human happiness is a countervailing thought. In spite of his sensitivity to the destructive effects of time, the narrator seems confident that the power of memory can overcome his apprehensions. Immediately before and after the story of the passing of human happiness, the narrator relates how Reinhard, as an old man, relives in his memory the same joyful scenes that he had once known. Through recollection the aged Reinhard can detach himself from his immediate surroundings and recapture his lost happiness as if it had not been obliterated by time.

A third thought follows: closely interwoven with the narrator's sensitivity to the ravaging of time and his apparent ability to ease this haunting concern through the counterweight of memory is his awareness that this power of memory will prove deceptive. In the closing chapter, just as earlier happiness had eroded, the power of memory, too, will be engulfed by time: the aged Reinhard's memory dwells in a body increasingly prey to senility and final dissolution.

Here the novella ends. The poetic insight into reality the reader gains from *Immensee* is disquieting indeed, but certainly real life is acutely presented. It is not surprising that man's helplessness should emerge so distinctly in this realistic portrayal: Storm composed *Immensee* in deep despair caused by the disruptive political and military events around him.

Hardly had Storm finished *Immensee* when the mutinous turmoil hit him again even harder. On August 1, 1850, before *Immensee* could even be published, another brigade of Danish royalist troops entered Husum and immediately began to stamp out all vestiges of the local insurrections. This provoked further rebellion and more bloodshed throughout the adjacent countryside. Storm witnessed horrors: as he wrote in an anguished letter to a friend on October 14, 1850, the wounded poured into the town, hundreds and hundreds of them, not only soldiers but women, children, and old people, bodies mangled, mutilated, and seared by bullets.[295] The author grew increasingly depressed, as his letters show. He found intolerable the new state of siege declared by the military government and eventually felt he had to go into exile, a fate he endured for eleven despondent years. Exile, however, only sharpened his defeatism and made him work all the more, with unabated vigor, toward contouring the same hard reality which had poetically shaped *Immensee*.

Aquis submersus

Of all his subsequent novellas, Storm praised none more lavishly than *Aquis submersus* (Beneath the Flood), completed during the winter of 1875–1876. "I am convinced," he said in a still unpublished letter to his publishers, Elwin and Hermann Paetel, "that I am offering you herewith the best work in prose that has ever come from my pen."[296] Such lavish words were never repeated for any other novella. Critics today often seem unaware that the author apparently thought this his best work, as we shall see when later we address ourselves to *Der Schimmelreiter*. But many have regarded this novella as second to none in Storm's literary legacy. Albert Köster (1862–1924), Storm's faithful editor, classified it as a "crowning achievement in the art of novella-writing; without any haggling or bargaining one can make the claim that it has remained Storm's masterpiece."[297]

---

[295] *Theodor Storm—Hartmuth und Laura Brinkmann Briefwechsel*, Kritische Ausgabe, ed. A. Stahl (Berlin: Erich Schmidt, 1986), 25.

[296] *Theodor Storm—Paul Heyse Briefwechsel*, Kritische Ausgabe, ed. C. A. Bernd, II (Berlin: Erich Schmidt, 1970), 119.

[297] Storm, *Sämtliche Werke*, ed. A. Köster, I (Leipzig: Insel, 1919), 50.

Other critics, too, have referred to it variously as Storm's *Meisterstück*, *Meisterwerk*, or *Meisterschuß*.[298] In the United States George Madison Priest of Princeton (1873–1947) called it the author's "best work";[299] Calvin Thomas of Columbia (1854–1919) asserted that "the art of Storm" had "culminated in *Aquis submersus*."[300] In a college edition of 1942 we read: "*Aquis submersus* ... is frequently acknowledged to be Storm's greatest work."[301] The list of such opinions could be supplemented almost endlessly, confirming again and again the prominent place this novella deserves in any study of Poetic Realism.

In the novella, as in its precursor (*Immensee*), time sweeps away the obliterated delights of childhood.[302] The joy the main character, Johannes, had thought permanent ends when the time comes for him to study abroad. In the next five years conditions change so much that the pleasures of former days prove to be gone forever. The drift of time encircles the carefree happiness of youthful love with fear. Johannes and the girl he loves, Katharina, hope that time will remain at a standstill, precisely what it cannot do. The hours Johannes spends with Katharina painting her portrait slip away with each stroke of his brush. The following events rapidly make it imperative, if he is to regain his lost bliss, for him to establish a home for Katharina soon. But the more he races against time, the more he loses. Though badly wounded and in need of rest, he leaves his sickbed too early in order to earn enough money to return to Katharina before Christmas. His wound heals so poorly that by Christmas his condition is worse. Day after day passes, as he notes with anguish, his separation from Katharina prolonged even further. By spring, when he is able to return, the last friend who could have helped him has died, and, in a situation similar to *Immensee*, Katharina has married someone else. He has returned too late. In the next five years things worsen further: his illegitimate child

---

[298] The opinions are cited in *Storm—Heyse Briefwechsel*, II, 225.

[299] George Madison Priest, *A Brief History of German Literature* (New York: Scribner's, 1909), 305.

[300] Calvin Thomas, *A History of German Literature* (New York: Appleton, 1909), 377.

[301] *Deutsche Novellen*, eds. A. van Eerden & B. Ulmer (Boston: Houghton Mifflin, 1942), 213.

[302] This account of *Aquis submersus* is based on the analysis in C. A. Bernd, *Theodor Storm's Craft of Fiction,* 2nd ed. (Chapel Hill: University of North Carolina Press, 1966), 11-53. Critical discussions of this novella are numerous. A particularly engaging (but frequently overlooked) commentary (over fifty pages!) can be found in P. M. Boswell, ed., *Theodor Storm, Aquis submersus* (Oxford: Blackwell, 1974). The most recent modern interpretations include 1) Roy C. Cowen, *Der Poetische Realismus* (Munich: Winkler, 1985), 235-47; 2) Winfried Freund, *Theodor Storm*, 90-103; 3) Robert C. Holub, *Reflections of Realism* (Detroit: Wayne State University Press, 1991), 132-51.

is born, and with the days and years the yearning for what he has lost increases, only to be thwarted by time. In the end Johannes has to realize that his child, the symbol of his entire life's joy, is dead, engulfed in the dark waters of oblivion. "Aquis submersus, aquis submersus" are the final chilling words of the chorus.

Complete as this flood seems, coupled with it in the poetic composition of the novella is the countervailing force of reminiscence. The whole story about Johannes is preserved in a hand-written memoir that salvages for posterity Johannes's former happiness, long after it has been submerged in time. But the memoir's pages yellow and fade. Symbolically, a motto pointing to the transience of all things appears over the door of the house where the memoir is kept. The implication becomes trenchant as we learn that the motto uses an antiquated dialect no longer a vehicle of communication.

But just when the reader starts to realize that the memoir, too, will fall prey to time, the narrator strives to allay this fear by resorting again to memory. He turns to the most vivid means known to him of recalling the past: pictorial commemoration. The narrator counteracts his fear of the memoir's fading by resorting to the power of painting to perpetuate Johannes's childhood joy. But even this fails. Worms eat away at the paintings' frames. The paintings themselves fall apart and are thrown away. "Aquis submersus, aquis submersus" at the end applies not only to the obliteration of Johannes's youthful joy and his entire life's happiness but to the perpetuating medium of pictorial commemoration as well.

On this disquieting note the novella ends. As with *Immensee*, the reader closes *Aquis submersus* chilled by the realistic depiction of man's ineffectual struggle against mortality and decay. In comparison with *Immensee*, however, the additional set of unreliable mnemonic devices has galvanized the tension between annihilation and life. Reading *Aquis submersus* yields, thus, a more poignant poetic lesson and a more engaging vision of reality, of human extinction and man's ability and inability to deal with it. Storm had learned now to paint "in oils" rather than as formerly "in watercolors."[303]

Der Schimmelreiter

Storm produced seventeen novellas after *Aquis submersus*. One triumph of Poetic Realism followed another. His final novella was *Der Schimmelreiter* (The Rider on the White Horse), completed in 1888.

---

[303] For the distinction, see Bennett, *A History of the German Novelle*, 171.

Storm could not find for it the high words of praise that he used for *Aquis submersus*. Writing to the Countess Emilie Reventlow (1834–1905), he even disparaged *Der Schimmelreiter* as "no masterpiece."[304] But the history of its reception has placed it certainly no lower than, and often even higher than, *Aquis submersus*. Almost immediately after its appearance it was acclaimed in the *Grenzboten* as the pinnacle of Storm's art.[305] No one has done more to give credence to this judgment than Thomas Mann, who, in 1930, referred to *Der Schimmelreiter* as "the masterpiece which crowned his [Storm's] life-work."[306] Who, after 1930, would have cared to argue with Mann?

During the writing of the novella Storm was alternately more despondent and more joyful than ever in his life. Despondent, because his physician had told him his life was drawing to a close with terminal cancer. Joyful, because, after he collapsed at hearing this news, his brother, a physician, held a hocus-pocus *concilium* with two other doctors and reported that the verdict of cancer was nonsense — he was not dying after all! Storm's spirits rebounded in undisguised jubilation.

Doubtless because of the initial diagnosis, Storm chiselled the gloom of life's end, the ebbing-away of happiness, into this work much more scrupulously than in any other of his novellas. The (funeral) cortège of passing hours, days, weeks, seasons, and years assumes a visibility not known earlier. Curiously, in this narrative as soon as we meet the main character, Hauke Haien, we are told about Euclid. Euclid, we ask, why the mention of this mathematician at the start of Hauke's story? We hardly reflect on the importance of Euclid and mathematics when we are invited to take part in a mathematical exercise: to count the almost unbelievable number of clock and calendar references as the story unwinds. Thus, the narrator insists on time's inexorable passing. This does not seem to have been noticed by the novella's many interpreters,[307] but the examples are

---

[304] Ferdinand Trömel, "Theodor Storms Briefe an die Gräfin Emilie Reventlow," *Schriften der Theodor-Storm-Gesellschaft* 25 (1976): 44.

[305] *Die Grenzboten*, 1889, I, 82.

[306] Thomas Mann, *Essays of Three Decades*, trans. H. T. Lowe-Porter (New York: Knopf, 1947), 286. The German essay, many times reprinted, was first published in *Theodor Storm, Sämtliche Werke*, ed. F. Düsel, I (Berlin: Knaur, 1930), 7-26.

[307] The secondary literature on *Der Schimmelreiter* is vast and growing fast. Indeed, it is probably safe to say that no single work of Poetic Realism has commanded more critical attention in recent years than this novella. The fullest treatments include 1) Reimer Kay Holander, *Theodor Storm: Der Schimmelreiter* (Frankfurt am Main: Ullstein, 1976); 2) Paul Barz, *Der wahre Schimmelreiter* (Hamburg: Kabel, 1982); 3) Winfried Freund, *Theodor Storm: Der Schimmelreiter, Glanz und Elend des Bürgers* (Paderborn: Schöningh, 1984). Other major recent interpretations are by 1) John M. Ellis in *Narration in the*

overwhelming, once one starts to count: "... by the time winter was past and the gooseberries were blossoming again," we read at the beginning of Hauke's story. A long season on the calendar is over, and it is early spring again. But early spring does not tarry long, for soon "the beanfield blossomed" and it is late spring. From "Easter to Martinmas" (November 11) Hauke worked on the dike. Then we learn what happens "at the end of October"; a few lines later "All Saints' Day" (November 1) arrives. Soon it is Christmas. Next we hear that "winter has returned again" and before long it is February. And so it goes throughout the story.[308] Counting these references we become ever increasingly aware of transience from page to page. Particularly at the beginning of paragraphs the narrator reminds us that more time has passed, e.g., "the year following," "After yet another year," "Several years had passed," "Summer and autumn passed," "three years had gone by," etc.

Correspondingly, life's happiness and life itself pass. With every passing hour and year things worsen. The ominous clouds of disaster, destruction, and death descend continually, just as the "Ge*zeit*en" (the "tides" = time, e.g., "even-*tide*") of the sea ceaselessly pound, weaken, and eventually destroy the man-made dikes, bringing the end to all life on their inner rim. Death looms heavily in this novella: life's happy moments, such as Hauke's wedding, are barely mentioned, whereas sorrowful events, such as his father-in-law's funeral, are treated at length. Eventually, in the dark of night the hostile tides breaking through the dike, destroying all in their path, consume Hauke, his family, everybody and everything he loved, all that he lived and worked for.

The novella, however, does not end on this chilling note. Storm once again designs a system of narrative frames that keeps the life of Hauke from the tempest of oblivion. First, a Frisian saga, a folk recollection, keeps his memory alive. Soon enough, however, this commemorative medium weakens: different versions of the saga arise. To forestall further distortion of the saga, the recollection of Hauke is put in writing: an ac-

---

German Novelle (Cambridge, England: University Press, 1974), 155-68; 2) Wolfgang Frühwald, "Hauke Haien, der Rechner: Mythos und Technikglaube in Theodor Storms Novelle 'Der Schimmelreiter,'" in *Literaturwissenschaft und Geistesgeschichte, Festschrift für Richard Brinkmann,* ed. J. Brummeck et al. (Tübingen: Niemeyer, 1981), 438-57; 3) Thomas Heine, "Der Schimmelreiter: An Analysis of the Narrative Structure," *German Quarterly* 55 (1982): 554-64; 4) Roy C. Cowen in *Der Poetische Realismus,* 304-16; 5) Margaret T. Peischl, "The Persistent Pagan in Theodor Storm's *Der Schimmelreiter,*" *Seminar* 22 (1986): 112-25; 6) Mark G. Ward, *Der Schimmelreiter* (Glasgow: University French & German Publications, 1988); 7) Alfred D. White, *Storm: Der Schimmelreiter* (London: Grant & Cutler, 1988).

[308] A detailed accounting is given in C. A. Bernd, "Theodor Storm," in *Deutsche Dichter des 19. Jahrhunderts,* ed. B. von Wiese, 2nd ed. (Berlin: Erich Schmidt, 1979), 571-72.

count in a magazine. But this commemorative medium also falls to nothing before time. The young boy who read the story can no longer find the magazine article fifty years later nor even remember in which magazine he had once read about Hauke. The details of the story, nevertheless, remain preserved in his memory. But aging and death will also erase this inscription of Hauke's story.

Will memory, man's most powerful ally against the destructive power of time, prove, in the last analysis, powerless? In all of Storm's novellas we are led to believe this will happen. But it does not, after all; for the life and happiness of Hauke in *Der Schimmelreiter*, of Johannes in *Aquis submersus*, of Reinhard in *Immensee*, indeed of all the characters in Storm's novellas have been rescued from extinction by yet another superimposed commemorative frame: art, the fictional novella, in which the stirring lives of Storm's characters continue to move us as if they were sitting beside us. Of course, some day Storm's novellas could lose their appeal for readers and be forgotten. Then the nullification of remembrance would, indeed, be complete, and time would have ultimately carried the field. Does Storm think this will happen? We never know for sure. His drama of ephemerality and reminiscence remains unresolved.

Storm, the lyricist

Storm became famous as a Poetic Realist not only for his dramatic novellas but also for his lyrics.[309] As the earliest of the major novella-writers and lyricists of *Poetischer Realismus*, he was not unlike the earliest of his predecessors in *Poetisk Realisme:* Poul Martin Møller. Each raised both genres to high distinction in his linguistic orbit. The parallel careers of Storm and Møller as practitioners of both the novella and the lyric show, of course, how closely aligned *Poetischer Realismus* and *Poetisk Realisme* were with one another and how different Poetic Realism was from literary realism elsewhere in Europe. Neither in English, French, nor Russian realism of the nineteenth century do we find the major writers in prose composing gems of verse. England produced memorable verse while realism flourished, but not by Dickens or Thackeray. Swinburne, Tennyson, Browning, and the Pre-Raphaelites were thoroughly at odds with prosaic Victorian realism. Similarly, in France the likes of Balzac, Stendhal, and

---

[309] Splendid introductions to Storm's poetry are on the opening pages of P. M. Boswell, ed., *Theodor Storm* (Leicester German Poets) (Leicester: University Press, 1989), 5-33; and 2) L. Zagari, ed., *Theodor Storm, Liriche* (Rome: Edizioni dell'Ateneo, 1969), vii-cxii. These two lengthy discussions are usually omitted (wrongly) in the "select" bibliographies of Storm.

Flaubert provoked poets such as Baudelaire, Verlaine, and Mallarmé to compose strikingly anti-realistic verse. In Russia the age known for the prose realism of Turgenev, Tolstoy, and Dostoyevsky conspicuously lacked lyric impulses. "Don't ask the reason," Turgenev wrote to Polonsky in 1869, "why there are no poets. There aren't any because there aren't any."[310]

Storm as a lyric poet had quickly gained a high visibility when the versatile Theodor Fontane compiled an anthology of German poetry entitled *Deutsches Dichteralbum* (An Album of German Poets) in 1852 and placed a poem by Storm on the opening page. As if to make doubly sure that the readers understood Storm to be the outstanding poet of the day, Fontane saw to it that the lyric voice of the poet from Husum resounded louder than that of any other post-1848 poet. Fontane's anthology sold rapidly. Before the decade closed, the fourth edition was on display in the windows of German bookshops. As fast as Germans bought the anthology, the fame of the lyricist Storm spread.

Fontane's effort to identify Storm as an outstanding lyrical talent did not end with assigning prominence to Storm in his anthology. The more Fontane became acquainted with the poetry of the second half of the nineteenth century, the more he became convinced that Storm's poetry possessed qualities superior to everything the age was producing as lyric poetry. "Ten lines of Storm's verse," Fontane commented in 1883, "outweigh the entire annual production of all those who presently reign supreme as champions of the lyric."[311] In 1888, the year of Storm's death, Fontane concluded that Storm was "the finest lyricist Germany had produced since Goethe."[312] A year later he went a step further: Storm's lyrics were, he said, "equal in quality to the very best ever written" in German.[313] More recently, Thomas Mann has corroborated Fontane's judgment. Mann said:

> In this ten times sorted and sifted lyrical treasure, gem stands almost next to gem. There is a constant, thrilling, concentrated power of expression about life and the emotions, a skill at shaping in the simplest form, which in certain poems — however old you are, however often you read them — unfailingly bring the catch in the throat as you are seized by that sweet and ruthless and woeful sense of life.... At least half a dozen pieces are

---

[310] I. S. Turgenev, *Works and Letters* [title in Russian], Section *Letters*, VIII (Leningrad & Moscow: Nauka, 1964), 20.

[311] Fontane, *Sämtliche Werke*, XXI/2, 246.

[312] Ibid., XXI/2, 86.

[313] Ibid., XXI/1, 498.

worthy to stand beside the best and highest in feeling and language and possess the unmistakable traits of immortality.[314]

"Meeresstrand"

Of these half-dozen poems Mann felt immortal, none has appeared with more persistence, in one anthology after another from the mid-nineteenth century on, than "Meeresstrand" (Seashore). First published in 1856 in the second edition of Storm's *Gedichte* (Poems), it was the only one in the group Storm deemed worthy of inclusion in his *Hausbuch aus deutschen Dichtern seit Claudius: Eine kritische Anthologie* (Book for the Home of German Poets since Claudius: A Critical Anthology, 1870). When the Swedish poet and critic Anders Österling (1884–1981) once sought to bring Storm's verse to the attention of a larger audience in Sweden, this was the first poem he chose to discuss.[315] Manfred Hausmann, a contemporary German poet, has ranked it among the ten most beautiful poems ever composed in the German language:[316]

> An's Haf nun fliegt die Möwe,
> Und Dämm'rung bricht herein;
> Über die feuchten Watten
> Spiegelt der Abendschein.
>
> Graues Geflügel huschet
> Neben dem Wasser her;
> Wie Träume liegen die Inseln
> Im Nebel auf dem Meer.
>
> Ich höre des gärenden Schlammes
> Geheimnisvollen Ton,
> Einsames Vogelrufen —
> So war es immer schon.
>
> Noch einmal schauert leise
> Und schweiget dann der Wind;

---

[314] Mann, *Essays of Three Decades*, 272-73.

[315] Anders Österling, *Dagens gärning* (Stockholm: Bonnier, 1921), 169.

[316] Manfred Hausmann, "Unendliches Gedicht, Bemerkungen anläßlich der Lyrik Theodor Storms," *Abhandlungen der Akademie der Wissenschaften und der Literatur in Mainz* (1962): 42.

Vernehmlich werden die Stimmen,
Die über der Tiefe sind.[317]

(Laguneward flies the seagull
As day gives way to night.
The wet-glazed flats at ebbtide
Reflect the evening light.

Gray fowl in flocks are darting
Close to the water's brim.
Like dreams appear the islands
In mist, remote and dim.

I hear the eerie ferment
In mud banks off the shore,
The lonely cry of the seabird —
Thus was it evermore.

Again the wind wails softly,
Then slowly sinks to sleep,
And now are heard the voices
That hover over the deep.)

Translated by Gerd Gillhoff, revised by C.A. Bernd[318]

At its more obvious biographical level, "Meeresstrand"[319] reflects Storm's despondency in the 1850s over the horrors of the recent rebellion against the Danish crown. The poem nostalgically seeks out the seaside

---

[317] This poem exists in many versions. Storm printed it in various revisions. Different editors have also printed differing texts. The version here is reproduced from P. M. Boswell's exemplary volume *Theodor Storm* (Leicester German Poets), 36.

[318] The unrevised parts of this translation are reprinted, by permission of Johanna Gillhoff, from G. Gillhoff, A Collection of German Poetry (unpublished, 1973).

[319] The most elaborate analysis of this poem to date has been provided by Paul Merker, "Theodor Storm: Meeresstrand," in *Gedicht und Gedanke*, ed. H. O. Burger (Halle: Niemeyer, 1942), 274-87. To read this piece of criticism is like seeing the poet conduct a magnificent orchestra. Noteworthy, too, is the interpretation by Wilhelm Schneider, *Liebe zum deutschen Gedicht*, 5th ed. (Freiburg i.B.: Herder, 1963), 105-13. An interesting Russian assessment of this poem is by Tamara Silman, "Theodor Storms Gedicht 'Meeresstrand,'" *Schriften der Theodor-Storm-Gesellschaft* 25 (1976): 48-52. The most recent study is by Elfriede Stutz, "Verskundliche Notizen zu Storms Gedicht 'Meeresstrand,'" in *In Search of the Poetic Real, Essays in Honor of Clifford Albrecht Bernd on the Occasion of his Sixtieth Birthday*, eds. John F. Fetzer, Roland Hoermann, Winder McConnell (Stuttgart: Heinz, 1989), 243-53.

town Storm fled after a Danish military garrison occupied it. Storm, now exiled far from the sea, evokes images and sounds of his lost seaside homeland. The vividness of his native shorescape shows the poet's acute sensitivity to reality. Though physically remote, he still sees the wet mud flats and the fog-shrouded islands beyond, still perceives the never-varying flow of the tides; and, though inaudible, the sharp cry of the seagull still reaches his ears distinctly.

Above all, Storm attends to the annihilation to which all life is subject, and from which, he senses, no escape is possible. Was Storm predicting that his native shore, now held by the Danish occupation forces, would somehow perish? Or was he foreseeing an even more complete annihilation from furious floods loosed by an incomprehensible force from the unknown beyond? In his utter despair, both thoughts doubtless merged. Annihilation raged in his blood like an obsessive passion, passed into his verse as a transfiguring element, and he practiced a depressing, elegiac dirge on life's evanescence.

The poem consists of two equal parts. The first two stanzas rely on visual stimuli: the poet sees the last gull seek evening refuge in the harbor as day departs, and he sees the eventide flow over the desolate expanse of mud flats bared by the ebbtide. Then the darkness deepens: the eye's objects grow dim. The seagull, so clear in the gathering twilight of the first stanza, gives way to blurred and fading images: gray wings (presumably of seagulls) scurrying indistinctly along the shore, wavering contours of islands dying on the foggy horizon.

The last two stanzas appeal to the ear. The descending darkness has fully shrouded earth and sea, and all things visible have passed away. The poet can only hear the bubbling, from decomposing life in the ooze, and the last call of a lonely bird, still awake (still alive?). Strangely, a dash now follows in the poem, indicating, like a musical fermata, a hold or pause. The mysterious sound of decay and the chilling shriek of the gull linger in the darkness beyond their time and, in a bar of full rest, the sting of death penetrates with a harrowing sensation into the ear. It is the abiding message of passing time. A shudder of wind makes itself heard before it, too, dies with the hours and the day. Then comes the grand finale: the ghostly foes ensconced in night, the sinister voices of nocturnal fear and fantasy. All join in one last chorus.

Amid this song of confrontation between life and death, pinned at its center, is an element of extreme personal involvement: the *Ich*. The first word of the third stanza (of four), this lone first person is caught at the intersection of the visual and the acoustic halves. Deeply anchored in the poem's heaviest line (nine syllables), it hangs irretrievably trapped within the gruesome sights and sounds of transience, forever bound to their collage of decay, like the crumbling shore to the perpetual motion of the tides.

In the center of the poem man — with heavy heart — witnesses with his senses night descending around him. He sees the light of his day slowly, irresistibly fall into shade. As light vanishes, his ears tell him all semblance of permanence is ebbing away: the final outcry in the gloom, then the deathly silence when the last breath of wind brings the last day of his life to its end. Nothing stirs save those mysterious voices beyond the grave, audible only when the life of the everyday world no longer interposes.

Man not only sees and hears life and death interlocked about him but finds himself teased and haunted by the echoing dualities. The aria of transience is plentifully garnished with acoustic effects that constantly echo man's life-death struggle. In particular, the height and depth of the vowels reiterate this. In the first line the vowels start out muffled or low-pitched (*An's Haf nun*) and then become high-pitched (*fliegt die Möwe*). Back down the scale at the beginning of the second line, they grow muffled once more (*Und Dämm'rung*); at the end of that line they ascend again to the high pitch (*bricht herein*). In counterpoint, the second two lines make the reverse pattern audible: descending, the high vowels at the beginning of both lines (*Über die*; *Spiegelt der*) contrast sharply with the ends of the lines, where the vowels first fall precipitously, then rise (*feuchten Watten*; *Abendschein*). This effect, carried through the stanzas in various interplays, not only gives a rich, orchestral coloration to the poem but also reflects the interweaving of life and death. The purest concentration of equally pitched vowels resounds in the last two lines, as a final fusion seems to occur between the previously alternating highs of life and lows of the grave. The heart monitor — to use a modern analogy — seems to level off to an ominous hum.

The poem, in short, offers a disquieting meditation on the reality of human destiny. Man confronts a somber script of his life's cycle, with the four "seasons" of his short "year" on earth — as the number of stanzas (four) suggests — a life that knows only the steady passing of its daylight, the inevitably approaching dissolution in a darkness without dawn. Via the eye, death is made to appear as certain as the arithmetically calculated construction of the verses and the contrived pairing of features: in the only two eight-syllable verses, the life of the islands, still visible on the horizon, is tied to the nocturnal voices, only audible when life has departed. Via the ear, "Meeresstrand" becomes a shattering experience, as the melody of vowels and rhymes, of iambs, trochees, dactyls, and anapests, transports the chilling message into the emotions, like the unabating rhythm of the roaring breakers along the shore.

4. The little giant: Gottfried Keller

Keller and Storm

Gottfried Keller (1819–1890), a dwarf in physical stature but a towering giant in Poetic Realism, was a Swiss writer two years Storm's junior. He had prepared himself for a career in *Poetischer Realismus* more intensively and extensively than any other writer-contributor of lasting radiance.[320] Lacking a family's demands on his attention, he spent long hours in the lending libraries of his native Zurich devouring the literature of his contemporaries and the critical reviews of their works. No other Poetic Realist knew more about the accomplishments of his competitors than he. Of all the rivals he came to admire, he esteemed none more highly than the "Star of the North" (his epithet for Theodor Storm).[321] He followed Storm's literary career from its earliest stages until the very end. He had learned about the "Star of the North" from his familiar libraries, from mutual friends, and from corresponding with Storm himself. Seven editions of their correspondence have appeared in this century, making it into something of a classic on the practical criticism of literature. Both Keller and Storm learned via this correspondence to temper and sharpen aesthetic judgments and broaden their visions of Poetic Realism. Together, they took pleasure in the successes of their competitors and shook their heads in dismay over their rivals' blunders. From one another each got the literary schooling every writer secretly covets but few obtain.

Keller's calling to *Poetischer Realismus*

Keller's avid interest in the life and work of Storm was important for his own vocation in letters — more important than most critics have been prepared to admit. But other factors also contributed to his career in Poetic Realism. As noted, Keller probably very early familiarized himself with Fru Gyllembourg's works in translation in lending libraries. We know that he read in periodicals the literary commentaries of Julian Schmidt, and he followed Otto Ludwig's growth as a Poetic Realist.

---

[320] The literature on Keller is considerable. Good modern general studies in English are by 1) J. M. Lindsay, *Gottfried Keller, Life and Works* (London: Wolff, 1968); and 2) Richard R. Ruppel, *Gottfried Keller: Poet, Pedagogue and Humanist* (New York: Lang, 1988). In German the best study is by Gerhard Kaiser, *Gottfried Keller, Das gedichtete Leben* (Frankfurt am Main: Insel, 1981).

[321] *Theodor Storm—Gottfried Keller Briefwechsel*, Kritische Ausgabe, ed. K. E. Laage (Berlin: Erich Schmidt, 1992), 116.

Like Ludwig's and Storm's, Keller's calling to Poetic Realism came after his baptism by fire as a writer during the revolutions of 1848–1849. He had, in fact, felt revolutionary turmoil as early as November 1847, when civil war between cantons favoring states' rights and those for federal supremacy embroiled Switzerland. With the ashes of that civil war hardly cool, in February 1848 another insurgence broke out: the inhabitants of the canton of Neuchâtel rebelled against the crown of Prussia and tried to overthrow its governors over them. All Switzerland sided with the insurrectionists, of course, in their fight against the foreign yoke.

But however these events agitated and inflamed the passions and temper of the Swiss, the revolutions which swept Paris, Vienna, and Berlin in early 1848 dwarfed them. Electrified by these colossal events, as he called them, Keller hurried to the public library in Zurich each day, absorbing with growing trepidation the various journalistic disquisitions on the spreading fires of revolt. By early October 1848 he feared that the stormy times would gnaw at his life and even uproot him.[322]

Such were his feelings when he left Switzerland to study at the University of Heidelberg in the grand duchy of Baden. It was a momentous decision: only a few months earlier a terrible civil war had convulsed Baden, and the embers of rebellion were still everywhere smoldering. An eyewitness of September 1848 recorded:

> Nothing can be more uneasy and disquieting than the appearance of the Duchy of Baden. In Heidelberg, ultra-revolutionary students have come to a total schism with their moderately and vaguely revolutionary professors; and it is at present difficult to see how any understanding is to be effected between teacher and scholar, so as to render the university a seat of learning of any other kind than that of subversive principles. In this part of Germany the revolutionary fermentation appears far more active, and is far more visible ... than even in those hotbeds of revolutionary movement, Austria and Prussia.[323]

The worst came after Keller entered the unhappy duchy. The ferment and agitation of 1848 continued to mount in the following year and exploded anew, more violently than before. In May 1849 the grand duke of Baden was forced to flee. Anarchy followed, and soon the vapor of cannon and the reek of blood engulfed the duchy. Heidelberg, Keller's residence, became the eerie citadel of a harsh Polish military dictator; swarms of soldiers and horses crowded into the little university town, requisitioning all available space and even sleeping in the streets.

---

[322] Keller, *Gesammelte Briefe*, II (1951), 454; IV (1954), 17.

[323] *Blackwood's Edinburgh Magazine* 64 (1848): 378-79.

Keller lived through a reign of terror. One of his teachers at the university, Ludwig Häusser (1818–1867), vividly recorded the details.[324] The horror began in late May 1849, when guerilla warfare erupted just north of the town. Häusser chronicles the bloodbath ensuing throughout the adjacent countryside. On June 5, in neighboring Weinheim, university students who had joined the rebel cause were shot down or committed suicide in order to avoid capture. On June 13 another ghastly slaughter occurred at nearby Waldmichelbach. On June 15 hundreds more died in fighting along the Neckar River near Heidelberg. On June 21, as a result of the Battle of Waghäusel, innumerable others lay dead or dying on the roadsides just south of the town. Streams of panic-stricken civilians and soldiers, hungry, ravaged, and blackened by gunpowder, then poured into Heidelberg; the university hospital overflowed with the wounded.

Two days later Heidelberg itself was besieged. Keller writes of the horror gripping the populace, of the cannons set up right in front of his window to ward off attack. And he tells of the rebels putting the gun to their own wounded rather than let them fall into enemy hands.[325]

From 1847 on Keller had these appalling sights about him, forcibly in their most gruesome form while he was at Heidelberg, and they affected him profoundly. His rough initiation into the cruel realities of the day inevitably affected his literary calling radically. On July 23, 1849 — the very day the bloody revolution in Baden was finally and mercilessly crushed south of Heidelberg at Rastatt — Keller commented in a letter that he had made up his mind to abandon his Romantic lyric poetry, for he no longer had any use for vehicles of subjective expression. Instead, he longed for a literary form more oriented toward the actuality of life such as he had recently witnessed; he hoped to find it in the drama.[326]

He set out to write a historical drama, *Der Sonderbund* (The Separate Alliance), about the first revolution he had experienced. But try as he might, he failed to produce the specific characteristics he sought for literature. If the Romantic lyric seemed to him too poetic to be in tune with the realities of the day, his attempts at drama seemed too full of current events, too devoid of the timelessness of the Romantic lyric.[327] Dissatisfied with both the subjective lyric and the objective drama, Keller turned to the premier vehicle of Poetic Realism, the dramatic novella.

---

[324] Ludwig Häusser, *Denkwürdigkeiten zur Geschichte der Badischen Revolution* (Heidelberg: Winter, 1851), 479-598.

[325] Keller, *Gesammelte Briefe*, I (1950), 97, 281-83.

[326] Ibid., IV (1954), 345-46.

[327] Ibid., I (1950), 299.

Romeo und Julia auf dem Dorfe

Of all the dramatic novellas bringing Keller fame, none has attracted more attention than *Romeo und Julia auf dem Dorfe* (A Village Romeo and Juliet).[328] In the year of its initial publication, 1856, the writer Berthold Auerbach acclaimed it as "a work of art which had few equals in German literature."[329] Both Julian Schmidt and Theodor Storm called it "a gem of literature."[330] George Henry Lewes, never generous on post-Goethean German fiction, called it a "chef-d'œuvre."[331] Edith Wharton (1862–1937) declared it an "immortal tale told in terms that will bear comparison with its prototype" and "on a level with Balzac's 'La Grande Bretèche' and Tolstoy's 'The Death of Ivan Ilyich.'"[332]

Rich in realistic candor and poetry, the novella is an extraordinary document of Poetic Realism. Storm's dramatic novellas addressed reality by exhibiting an astonishing willingness to grapple with the perpetual reality of death in man's life; Keller's art derives from a more tantalizing concern with the elusive nature of reality. As in Storm's tales, everything in this novella begins with a most faithful observation of actual life, but reality appears now as a contradictory mystery. The difficulty of distinguishing between the actual and the imaginative (always colliding with one another) is ever before the reader. The narrator constantly reminds us that the most crucial problem of all lies in recognizing what is real and what is not real.

---

[328] Critical discussions of this novella are numerous. Interesting recent studies include 1) M. Swales, "Keller's Realism, Some Observations on *Romeo und Julia auf dem Dorfe*," in *Formen realistischer Erzählkunst, Festschrift for Charlotte Jolles*, ed. J. Thunecke (Nottingham: Sherwood, 1979), 159-67; 2) G. A. Wells, "Kellers Erzählkunst in 'Romeo und Julia auf dem Dorfe,'" *Wirkendes Wort* 94 (1984): 169-81; 3) Gerhard Kaiser in *Gottfried Keller, Das gedichtete Leben*, 296-315; 4) Yoshio Abe, *Gottfried Kellers "Romeo und Julia auf dem Dorfe"* (Berne: Lang, 1989); 5) Robert C. Holub in *Reflections of Realism*, 101-31.

[329] *Allgemeine Zeitung* (Augsburg), April 17, 1856: 1722.

[330] Schmidt, *Geschichte der deutschen Litteratur von Leibniz bis auf unsere Zeit*, V, 577; *Storm—Heyse Briefwechsel*, II, 21.

[331] *Westminster Review* 14 (1858): 515.

[332] Gottfried Keller, *A Village Romeo and Juliet*, trans. A. C. Bahlmann, Introduction by Edith Wharton (New York: Scribner's, 1914), xix-xx. It is generally not known that Wharton was more enamored with Keller's tale than these comments indicate. Her missionary zeal to persuade more Americans to appreciate Keller's tale had, for instance, led her to spend many long hours working at improving the Bahlmann translation. E. M. and S. B. Puknat discovered this while examining Wharton's unpublished correspondences in the files of Charles Scribner's Sons in New York. See E. M. and S. B. Puknat, "Edith Wharton and Gottfried Keller," *Comparative Literature* 21 (1969): 246.

Keller had mulled over this story as he awoke to life's bitter truths at Heidelberg. In January 1848, only a few months after his arrival, he was molding it into an epic poem.[333] But following the collapse of the Badensian revolution in July 1849, and in line with his decision to abandon the lyric in favor of the drama, he aborted the poem and started to think of the story as a drama.

The impetus for this dramatic idea came from a book by a local professor, one then generating tremendous academic excitement in Heidelberg: G. G. Gervinus's *Shakespeare* (1849–1850). Gervinus (1805–1871) had argued that the dramatic substance of Shakespeare's *Romeo and Juliet* was to be found in the collision of the leading characters' idyllic love with reality. Gervinus postulates this counterplay between the subjective realm of fancy and palpably real circumstances at the beginning of his analysis; for him it produces the dramatic linkage of the disparate scenes and disparate characters.[334] Gervinus's theory, however disputed among Shakespeare scholars, offered Keller the potent dramatic kernel he needed. He seized it: this collision of chimeric reverie with the unsettling real world expressed precisely what he, as a would-be epic poet, felt when his world of fantasy shattered on the revolution outside his Heidelberg window.

Gervinus's essentially dramatic kernel did not, however, germinate under Keller's nurture into a drama. Keller transplanted it to the novella. The more succinct form of the new "sister of the drama," as Storm had called the novella,[335] accommodated the same central conflict that Gervinus had seen driving Shakespeare's *Romeo and Juliet*. But the novella also could focus more closely on the conflict itself than could drama. In Gervinus's conception drama called for a greater wealth of vivid characters, the portrayal of more variegated scenes, and the inclusion of an array of subordinate plots. Had Keller been as interested as Gervinus in the organic development of the conflict between the idyllic world and external reality, he might have written another drama. But Keller wished to present the conflict itself, not its development, and for this purpose the novella was more suitable. In the novella the essential conflict Gervinus had extracted from Shakespeare's *Romeo and Juliet* could stand out sharply, in bold relief and devoid of everything nonessential.

Keller critics have been surprisingly reticent about noting the importance of Gervinus's theory for the inception of *Romeo und Julia auf dem Dorfe*. In spite of Keller's comment that he had found in Gervinus's book

---

[333] Keller, *Gesammelte Briefe*, I (1950), 276-77.

[334] G. G. Gervinus, *Shakespeare*, 2nd ed., II (Leipzig: Engelmann, 1850), 3.

[335] Lukács, *Soul and Form*, 72.

a rich lode of ideas for further embellishment — precisely when this novella was shaping up in his mind[336] — the critics have pointed to an account in a Zurich newspaper as the narrative's sole source. This traditional thesis needs emendation. The colorless newspaper account did bear on the epic poem Keller wanted to write prior to the harrowing civil war. But the seed out of which the stirring novella grew — indeed which even supplied its title — sprang rather from Gervinus's exciting commentary. Gervinus's theory corresponded to Keller's experience during the Badensian revolution; the newspaper article did not. In Keller's own revolution in prose the pithy, dramatic novella supplanted the long verse narrative. It demanded a crisp dramatic conflict, such as the one postulated by Gervinus, to replace the pallid newspaper report as compositional center.

The novella splits irreconcilably: in the first part two farmers' selfish *real*-estate interests dominate, and in the second — discordantly — two young adolescents' fairy-tale-like love does so. The initial realistic description of peasant greed and cutthroat competition for land gives way to their children's quixotic pursuit of dreamy love. These opposites collide symbolically on a bridge as narrow and shaky as the narrative linking the two parts of the story.[337]

Both farmers, Marti and Manz, angrily leap onto the bridge from opposite banks of the stream; in the middle they meet, pummel each other in the face with their fists, and grapple, each trying to send his rival into the waters beneath. But just as Marti appears about to succumb in the curious battle of vengeance, the two children — Manz's son Sali and Marti's daughter Vrenchen — jump into the fray, to aid their respective fathers. But the interests of Sali and Vrenchen soon conflict with those of their embittered elders, for rather than tip the balance the nineteen-year-old boy and the seventeen-year-old girl enrapture each other. Suddenly they lose interest in the economic triumph of one family over the other. Stepping between the combatants, they break up the death-match and seal their affection. Sali looks into Vrenchen's face; she smiles. Before parting they clasp hands. The beating of their unseen hearts had outdone the beating of their fathers' bloodied fists.

The palpable greed of the two peasants had become more and more consuming since the beginning of the tale. Now it withers away fruitlessly. The affections of Sali and Vrenchen, hardly developed in the first part of the story, now suddenly mature into a blissful romance. The clash of the

---

[336] Keller, *Gesammelte Briefe*, I (1950), 352-53.

[337] See Fontane's incisive comment on the two discordant parts: Fontane, *Sämtliche Werke*, XXI/1, 257-58.

down-to-earth interests of Marti and Manz with the lofty romantic hopes of their children — vividly figured on a bridge between two opposite banks — changes the direction of the narrative dramatically, as the lightning above starkly lights up the stormy events on the darkened bridge below. The bridge scene becomes, then, the fulcrum of the seesaw balancing the two antiphonal parts of the novella.

The recurring alternation of the two forces in seesaw fashion is actually anticipated in miniature in the narrative's opening pages as we see Marti and Manz plowing the soil of their two fields in opposite directions. As the one proceeds up the hill, the other moves downward on the other side. When the peak of the cap of the descending farmer tips forward over his brow, the ascending farmer's falls back on his neck. The sartorial distinction constantly alternates between them, depending upon which direction they plow. They act strictly selfishly, craving to make Mother Earth more productive to increase their own material wealth. This basic greed is divorced from anything human, ethically or aesthetically. For them, the only thing that matters is the augmentation of tangible possession. The happiness and well-being of others never enter into their calculations. Even unlawful acquisition of *real*-estate does not disturb their consciences.

Colliding directly with this opening narrative about the sangfroid of the two landed proprietors is what seems another separate narrative interspersed throughout it: the romantic story of carefree happiness shared by the young children Vrenchen and Sali. Like oil and water, the two tales compete to attract the reader's attention. When the focus sharpens on the pastoral bliss of the children, the objective realism of the tillers of the soil drops from view; when the fathers' stark reality returns to the foreground, the childhood idyll recedes.

The two distinctive strands of narrative — the realistic and the idyllic — stand out in even bolder relief in the narrator's treatment of the ground on which they take place. The separate fields delineating each of the two realms embody the clash of opposites and the inevitable domination of the real over the fanciful. The realm with the most solid foundation is, of course, the farmland of the two humorless, hardworking men, land dedicated not to idle pleasures but only to the production of dividends from the earth and capital gains at the marketplace. Everything said about the two men's real assets sharpens our appreciation of the hard facts of everyday life, of the real necessity of earning a livelihood in competitive society. At loggerheads with this very realistic world of workaday behavior is an idyllic world of make-believe. It stands in between the two farmers' plowed fields and, thus, in the way of their efforts to expand their assets. This middle realm seems especially devoid of reality in contrast with the two other properties. It is covered with weeds and stones and is therefore unproductive. And it is nobody's legal possession, since the apparent owner, unable to prove his birth by a certificate or a reliable witness, has no birthright to the land he would otherwise inherit. Since he does not really exist — in the eyes of the law — he has no valid claim to any real estate. Lacking a real owner, the land is then left to be occupied by children at play. With their unfettered imaginations, they turn it into a paradisal world of make-believe. It is a realm of irrational, childlike babblings, innocent bliss, and romantic dreaming, as distant from workaday reality as are the robust farmers' lives from fairy-tale pleasure.

The two realms collide when the aggressive farmers plow their way, furrow by furrow, into the primeval paradise between their fields. They bid competitively for title to the ever-narrowing strip of land (left to the whims of weeds, rocks, and wild imagination) to make it a source of produce. This will leave room neither for the children's bucolic play nor for the heir-without-proof to lay any further claim to the property.

The fathers' driving industriousness smashes this realm of the fictitious owner and of the children's fantasy. The heir apparent is disenfranchised, the children are expelled from the dreamlike playland, and the fanciful idyll succumbs to the domination of palpable reality. At the end of the novella's first part all that seems important is the sordid wrangling of the fathers for material assets. The children's play and the fictitious owner's claim cease to matter. The seesaw has tipped markedly in favor of undisguised reality.

Now follows the crucial bridge scene, the fulcrum of the novella. The balance reverses. Reality recedes, and imagination takes over. The fathers' money and real estate lose prominence, then vanish. Make-believe, no longer limited to childish games, blossoms into an enchanted love affair.

After the clash on the bridge, the narrative arches from reality's shore to the land of fantasy. Sali loses sight of the real world about him, transforming his old home (in his altered state of mind) into a heavenly Jerusalem. Sali's father, forced to abandon his property, invests in a squalid tavern, haven to the outcasts of society. Sali's mother becomes ludicrous, more of the world of folly than of everyday Swiss life. A mood of pathetic comic relief dominates the descriptions. It seems Sali's parents have become cloudy exiles from reality and found a grotesque refuge.

Vrenchen's father, too, has relinquished his real estate; in exchange, he takes up residence in a lunatic asylum where, now completely deprived of reason, he becomes oblivious to the world around him. His imbecile antics offer the same comic relief as the Manzes' tavern. Vrenchen's mother has also departed from visible reality, at the hand of death.

The real world is increasingly drawn into the world of fantasy at this stage: a peasant woman believes both Vrenchen's and Sali's invented story about their impending marriage and their equally fictive tale of newly acquired wealth, departing as far from reality as had their parents. A gullible innkeeper fooled by appearances improbably believes the lovers a rich couple.

The core of the novella's idyllic second half is the fairy-tale life of Vrenchen, appropriately referred to now as a princess, and that of her Prince Charming, Sali. With the sale of his silver watch, the keeper of real time, Sali signals their final abdication of the physical world in favor of a dream province. Rid of this last remnant of reality and with the proceeds of its sale he can now commit fully to the imaginary. A mock wedding in "The Garden of Paradise," a beautiful country locale, highlights this commitment. Significantly, homeless vagrants, out of touch with reality by means of inebriation, frequent this garden. The official performing the marriage lacks genuine claim to the privilege: he has no baptismal certificate, no secular proof of his birth — no Christian birthright and no citizenship. To the church and state, twin custodians of the wedding rite, he does not exist. The marriage, hence, is null and void in the real world.

After this ceremony, too irregular for legal recognition, there follows a bizarre wedding procession, transporting the couple even further from normalcy. It resembles the nocturnal procession of a witches' sabbath. The carnivalistic betrothal is sealed by counterfeit wedding rings.

A nocturnal scene of mystic-romantic ecstasy aboard a haybarge adrift in the middle of a river climaxes this fantastic simulation of bourgeois joys. Sali carries his bride onto the boat and unmoors it, casting aside ties to reality. Pilotless and in waltz-like fashion the boat winds its way downstream. The consummation of the mock marriage between young dreamers then fulfills a romantic yearning for music, love, and death as the lovers slip beneath the cold waters together. In this romantic death the impossible marriage becomes possible.

Keller added an anticlimactic epilogue in 1874. It tells us the opinion shared by local pundits and arbiters of the press, once harsh daylight breaks, revealing the suicide: shock and disgust. The godforsaken nuptials of Vrenchen and Sali, their wanton disrobing, and their departure from this life naked (the Victorian critic George Henry Lewes once said ladies could not read the story)[338] clashed too much with the prevailing mores of the mid-nineteenth century. Yet, which is true: the actual love affair of Sali and Vrenchen or the pretended beliefs of mid-nineteenth-century readers?

Keller further reinforced his poetic argument about the collision of the actual and the imaginative when he published this tale in a collection of

---

[338] *Westminster Review* 14 (1858): 518. In Denmark, too, the tale was condemned at the time for its "indecency." See Keller, *Gesammelte Briefe*, IV (1954), 161-62.

novellas entitled *Die Leute von Seldwyla* (The People of Seldwyla). Seldwyla is a town, according to the preface, so real that it could be anywhere in Switzerland. But it is also so fictitious that it can be found nowhere in Switzerland. It is inconceivable that in the life of a Swiss town neither a church, a school, nor a marketplace plays a significant part, yet so it is in *Romeo und Julia auf dem Dorfe*. The twin Seldwylan characteristics obviously conflict: if the town is real, it cannot be fictitious; if fictitious, it cannot be real. Linking this novella with a collection bound by the common feigned reality of Seldwyla, therefore, Keller reaffirms once more the tantalizing dichotomy which had given this novella its purport.

"Abendlied"

Not only a supreme master of the novella of Poetic Realism, Keller also, like Storm, was one of the literary movement's most accomplished lyricists. No poem has done more to insure his abiding place among lyricists of *Poetischer Realismus* than "Abendlied" (Evensong), composed in 1879.[339]

Only a few days after reading the poem, Storm dispatched a letter to Zurich to congratulate his Swiss friend. Storm called the poem "the purest lyric gold" and went on to say: "I've read it many times, again and again, to myself and to others, and everyone who heard it was touched by it. I extend to you, dearest friend, my sincere congratulations. Such gems are rare. Even the best poets produce only a very few poems of such quality."[340]

It is not hard to understand why Storm rated this poem so highly. In "Abendlied" the song of time and death so central to "Meeresstrand" echoes again:

> Augen, meine lieben Fensterlein,
> Gebt mir schon so lange holden Schein,
> Lasset freundlich Bild um Bild herein:
> Einmal werdet ihr verdunkelt sein!

---

[339] The most brilliant analysis of this poem has been overlooked in Keller scholarship: S. S. Prawer, *German Lyric Poetry, A Critical Analysis of Selected Poems from Klopstock to Rilke* (London: Routledge & Kegan Paul, 1952), 174-77. Other engaging interpretations are by 1) Wilhelm Schneider in *Liebe zum deutschen Gedicht*, 78-85; and 2) Gerhard Kaiser in *Gottfried Keller, Eine Einführung* (Munich & Zurich: Artemis, 1985), 10-20.

[340] *Storm—Keller Briefwechsel*, 47.

Fallen einst die müden Lider zu,
Löscht ihr aus, dann hat die Seele Ruh';
Tastend streift sie ab die Wanderschuh',
Legt sich auch in ihre finst're Truh'.

Noch zwei Fünklein sieht sie glimmend steh'n,
Wie zwei Sternlein, innerlich zu seh'n,
Bis sie schwanken und dann auch vergeh'n,
Wie von eines Falters Flügelweh'n.

Doch noch wandl' ich auf dem Abendfeld,
Nur dem sinkenden Gestirn gesellt;
Trinkt, o Augen, was die Wimper hält,
Von dem goldnen Ueberfluß der Welt![341]

(Eyes, ye treasured windows of my sight,
Have so long allowed me precious light;
Letting hosts of images delight,
Ere the fall of nature's darkening night.

When some day your weary lids must close,
Light fades out, the soul can find repose;
Gropingly her shoes aside she throws,
Lays her in her coffin so morose.

Yet two sparks she sees aglow on high,
Like two stars that charm the inner eye,
Till they flicker, and they too must die,
Wafted off on wings of butterfly.

Still I linger on the evening weald,
With the sinking sun to share the field,
Drink, O eyes, all that the lashes shield
Of the golden wealth the world doth yield.)

Translated by D. G. Wright[342]

 The first stanza opens under the shadows of a descending eventide, as the poem's title indicates. Yet, something of the glad light of day can still

---

[341] Text taken from Keller, *Gesammelte Gedichte* (Berlin: Hertz, 1883), 33.

[342] From *Anthology of German Poetry through the 19th Century*, 2nd revised edition (New York: Ungar, 1972), 229. Reprinted by permission.

be perceived. The poet's eyes, in the twilight of his life, still admit the wondrous sights of this world. Hence the poet has cause for delight and is serenely happy. S. S. Prawer has masterfully shown how this blissful satisfaction echoes through the beginning verses up to the disruptive colon of the third line: the caressing words *lieb*, *hold*, and *freundlich* constitute major points of emphasis in the stanza, reinforced by the endearing diminutive *Fensterlein*, by the many liquid consonants and the constant rhyme on *ei*, associated with *Schein*, light. Daylight joy has not yet departed, but life's brief day is inexorably waning: after the extended pause at the end of the third line, the heavy-sounding *u* of *verdunkelt* signals the gathering darkness.

The second stanza intensifies the feeling of life's ebb. The gloomy *u* of *verdunkelt* becomes the rhyming vowel and dominant sound of the stanza, lingering on at each line-end. The foreboding doom of *verdunkelt* has now supplanted the first stanza's cheerful light, *Schein*. A weary human being with the failing faculties of old age — suggested by the uncertain groping associated with *tastend* — approaches his appointed end. He lays aside his walking shoes. Having completed his journey though life's daytime, he is ready for the inevitable repose that follows within the dark confines of either the coffin or the grave (*finst're Truh'*). This, the final image, could mean either but probably means both of these.

The third stanza begins with an image of the final moments of the poet's departing life-light. The eyes, so long the windows of his soul, appear now in his final hours as two faintly flickering candle flames near extinction. Prawer's classic analysis of this poem shows how the final departure from this life comes musically to the ears of the listeners: in the third stanza's concluding two lines, the stresses, hitherto so heavy, become less marked (as though a heart were ceasing to beat), and the last signs of life fade away with the whispering sounds of the consonants *f*, *w*, *s*, and *l*.

> Wie von eines Falters Flügelweh'n.
> (Wafted off on wings of butterfly.)

In the barely audible sound of the last dying breath of *weh'n* (wafting away), musically linked by rhyme to *vergeh'n* (passing away), life has expired.

Much in Keller's "Abendlied" to this point discloses a remarkable affinity to Storm's "Meeresstrand": the interplay of musical sound and realistic portrayal in the form of a *Lied;* a melody evoking a meditation on the ephemerality of human life. With vigorous pictorial imagery Keller reminds us — as had Storm — of the ebbing of life. Eventide falls at the end of man's day on earth. The darkness ever deepens. Earth's joys dim. The eyes gradually close. Life is finally snuffed out. The orchestral accompaniment of vowels, consonants, rhymes, and stresses — just as in Storm's poem — carries this song of transience effortlessly into the ear, profoundly affecting the listener. The unwavering, slow trochaic measure suggests the certainty of life's passing, like the interminable, plangent waves of Storm's poem.

The fourth stanza, though, is radically different from Storm's poem. As the first line strikingly demonstrates, a change in the music jolts the listener: out of the lulling trochaic monotony burst three consecutive stressed syllables:

> Doch noch wandl' ich auf dem Abendfeld
> (— — — ᴜ — ᴜ — ᴜ—)
> (Still I linger on the evening weald)

The word *noch* receives unexpected stress in the poem's stringent trochaic pentameter. This emphasis — and this line — thus stand out from the rest of the poem. Hence, the poet, despite the fast-falling eventide of his life, emphasizes that he is *still* walking life's path, *still* very much alive. Images also turn the clock back from final dissolution. The poet paints an exuberant picture of the magnificence he enjoys, the last golden rays he walks in. The last word, *Abendfeld*, Keller coined to unite time and place, suggesting at once the eventide of life and the rich fields of autumn, with the grain at its fullest, ripest, and most plentiful. The setting sun floods the horizon, radiating golden superabundance. At the end, we have a heavy, lingering stress on *Welt*. Everything in this stanza contrives, therefore, to produce a genial affirmation of life, in counterpoint to the first three stanzas: a triumphant celebration of life against death's surety.

Implicitly, Keller's song understands the reality of time and decay, but also that joy is essential to life, even as death impends. It knows nothing of the crueler dualism that sees human life as gloom to be consummated miserably in death. It neither overlooks nor embraces transience and death: they stand forth just as sharply as in Storm's song, but tellurian delights soothe the inevitable sting. Still, this poem is not escapist. It is a poem not of flight, but of courage, insisting on the unabashed affirmation of a life both precarious and fleeting. A wordsmith's craft has rendered a vision as realistic as it is serene.

Der grüne Heinrich

Keller surpassed Storm when he composed, in addition to his dramatic novellas and realistic lyrics, the mightiest German novel of his time: *Der grüne Heinrich* (Green Henry).³⁴³ Neither Storm nor any other Poetic Realist in any national current excelled in three different genres. Revised and rewritten throughout most of his life, this novel rightly seems the flagship of the movement, in the opinion of many, "the paradigmatic text of the German realist vision."³⁴⁴ When the final version appeared in 1879 and 1880 (in four volumes, with a total of 1,364 pages), it dwarfed everything else Poetic Realism produced. When Keller died ten years later, this novel was in its eighth edition. By 1919, the year before the copyright expired, it was in its one hundredth.

It was not, however, just a public success: the best critics have consistently praised it highly, more than any other German novel of the epoch. Julian Schmidt was one of the first. He labeled an early version, printed in 1854 and 1855, one of the most ingenious books in years, the work of an extraordinarily talented novelist.³⁴⁵ Storm grew so intrigued by this novel that he reread it annually for the rest of his life.³⁴⁶ Fontane considered it the crown of Keller's career.³⁴⁷ More recently, Thomas Mann referred to it as "a book altogether out of the ordinary," one which "I read with the greatest pleasure and sympathy, with ever growing admiration for the cleanly displayed wealth of vitality ... [and for] the delicious precision of its language."³⁴⁸

The novel had quickly found extraordinary favor in the motherland of Poetic Realism. Indeed, the reception in Denmark was more spontaneous than anywhere else. The novel had hardly appeared in print when Georg Brandes, the master critic in Copenhagen, rushed to proclaim Keller "the greatest living German writer."³⁴⁹ Only three years after its first appearance

---

³⁴³ Noteworthy analyses of this novel are by 1) Roy Pascal in *The German Novel* (Manchester: University Press, 1956), 30-51; 2) Bertil Romberg in *Studies in the Narrative Technique of the First-Person Novel* (Stockholm: Almqvist & Wiksell, 1962), 237-75; 3) Wolfgang Preisendanz in *Wege des Realismus* (Munich: Fink, 1977), 127-80; 4) Martin Swales in *The German Bildungsroman from Wieland to Hesse* (Princeton: University Press, 1978), 86-104; 5) Gert Sautermeister in *Romane und Erzählungen des Bürgerlichen Realismus*, 80-123; 6) Gerhard Kaiser in *Gottfried Keller, Das gedichtete Leben*, 12-249; 7) Richard R. Ruppel in *Gottfried Keller*, 1-33.

³⁴⁴ Russell A. Berman, *The Rise of the Modern German Novel* (Cambridge, Mass.: Harvard University Press, 1986), 79.

³⁴⁵ *Die Grenzboten*, 1854, I, 405; 1855, III, 166.

³⁴⁶ Keller, *Gesammelte Briefe*, III/1 (1952), 407.

³⁴⁷ *Fontanes Briefe in zwei Bänden*, ed. G. Erler, II (Munich: Nymphenburg, 1981), 354.

³⁴⁸ Mann, *The Genesis of a Novel*, trans. R. & C. Winston (London: Secker & Warburg, 1961), 147.

³⁴⁹ *Correspondance de Georg Brandes*, ed. P. Krüger, III (Copenhagen: Rosenkilde & Bagger, 1966), 362.

a Danish translation surfaced. (It took eighty years for an English translation to do so.) Keller was much impressed. He wrote to his translator in Copenhagen (the versatile poet Holger Drachmann, 1846–1908), saying (for the benefit of his Danish readers) that he had written an autobiographical novel but reworked the facts of his life quite freely, with inventions and alterations for the purpose of making good fiction. The stories of childhood and schooldays were essentially true, but those about his love affairs were all fictitious.[350] This confession reveals his desire that the novel be thought a real record of his early life and yet a poetic reflection of it. The medley of fact and fiction familiar from *Romeo und Julia auf dem Dorfe* reappears in a new garb.

This orchestration works best in the passages — if we believe Keller — most thoroughly contrived: the ones about love affairs. Untrue to autobiography, nevertheless they show the genuine ache of mature love in the life of Heinrich, the hero; and as such they make up the most important phase of his entanglement with reality. Love makes the boy shed the green bark he must relinquish to embrace full manhood. Heinrich's sampling of love jars as much as the discord between fact and fiction in the novel as a whole. Lithe as a dancer he flits between two women: the ethereal Anna, attractive for idealistic rather than sensual reasons, and Judith, awakening the adventurous carnal itch but frustrating his spiritual longing. Each embodies one side of his entanglement with love, one the ennobling requisites of spiritual welfare, the other the natural desire for physical passion. Heinrich is torn between precise counterparts of his split desire for feminine affection. The key sentence, poised fittingly at the center of the novel, in the last paragraph at the end of the first half, tells us: "I felt that I was torn in two, and I wanted to hide myself from Anna with Judith and from Judith with Anna."

This touches the heart of Heinrich's exposure to love. The relationships are so contrived and yet are meant to seem so real. Which of the two women offers real love and which only dream love? Ostensibly, love with Anna is more genuine: she matters most to Heinrich; his love for her proves more enduring, as he withdraws finally from Judith. The short-lived connection to Judith seems more masculine fantasy than love. For all its sensual attraction, this love is never consummated. Heinrich even refuses to call his affection for Judith "love." He cannot bring himself to introduce her to his family as the one he loves. This love, hence, lacks commitment, unlike real love.

Yet, Heinrich's love for Anna is also unreal. He does not love Anna as a man would a woman. His feeling of attachment lacks the richness to

---

[350] Keller, *Gesammelte Briefe*, IV (1954), 255.

make it abiding, while his love for Judith, on the other hand, is wholly natural, arising from an immediate, mutual attraction. It has spontaneous vitality. Heinrich and Judith are genuinely infatuated with each other. One thus might say this love is more real than Heinrich's love for Anna.

Keller called the love scenes the most complete products of his poetic imagination. Next to them, in other episodes, he eased into autobiography. These more genuine bits retrace Heinrich's early life, up to the threshold of maturity but short of erotic experience. As such, these episodes are — Keller to the contrary — less real than those describing the love affairs, which, after all, were crucial for the actual transformation of Heinrich from boy to man. Whether less or more real, however, these portions addressed to Heinrich's early life also reveal the same fictional theme of Heinrich capering on a tightrope between reality and fantasy.

In the putatively non-autobiographical love sections Heinrich had vacillated between two women. Now, in the autobiographical ones, he moves between two locales: the verdant countryside of his native Switzerland and the strange, foreign Bavarian capital city, Munich.

In Switzerland, Heinrich mingles with the rugged landfolk who subsist as herdsmen and tillers of the soil. They keep close with nature, the seasons, sunshine and rain, times of sowing and harvest. They seldom lose sight of hard realities, forming a sober, practical commonwealth devoid of romanticism and rarely rising beyond preservation and increase of their own material goods. Not flights of idealism or imaginative subtleties but practicalities, especially haggling over money, occupy men's leisure hours. Heinrich, a native of this world, is not entirely at home in it. His real calling, he feels, is as an artist. So he abandons the Swiss agrarian setting for "the city of the arts": Munich. There his imaginative nature, his lack of stability, the fullness of his fantasy, and the intensity of his emotion would find a congenial abode. But if the sturdy farmers of Switzerland were more elemental than imaginative, the citizenry of the glittering royal capital of Bavaria was so thoroughly smothered by the artificialities of civilization that it no longer had roots in reality. Elaborate festivals, exclusive masquerade balls, the splendor of the royal court, patriotic fervor devoid of practical reasoning, and, above all, the Bohemian world of the artist take precedence. As Heinrich tries to assimilate, to identify himself with this wholly abstract world, centered around a fictional preoccupation with the improbable and the fancies of the grotesque, his paintings become more and more abstract, eventually losing all contact with reality.

But which place is the real world of Heinrich: his native Switzerland, whose extreme practicality never satisfies his imaginative longings and where he never feels at home, or this foreign, fairy-tale-like Bavaria, where his abstract paintings so thoroughly ignore real life that they do not sell and he cannot earn a living? Ostensibly, the granite of the Swiss Alps holds the stronger attraction, for there he returns. In Munich he lives on thin air, wastes his time, and gets into debt; leaving, he sees himself as a mental and moral failure. Yet, when he returns to Switzerland, he finds hardly any reality to which he can assent. Roots are not really established. He goes about earning his livelihood with no absorbing interest. He remains unanchored in a family life, and his passions lack vitality. The Swiss society, which he has rejoined on the surface, becomes as fictitious as it is devoid of actual political and social conflicts, mercantile enterprises, banks, factories, or productive pastures. Heinrich sustains himself in a Switzerland perhaps more artificial than real. In Munich, in contrast, he was involved in a genuinely throbbing life, one that corresponded more to his real interests.

Reality and artificiality, hence, intertwine as intensely in the autobiographical parts as in the more fictional strands of this novel. The same double keynotes sound again and again, until the reader is unsure which is dominant.

Most strikingly, *Der grüne Heinrich* begins and ends with death: death encircles this whole chronicle of truth and distortion. It is palpable in the first paragraph:

> The little cemetery surrounding the church — the latter's whitewash still glowing despite its age — has never been extended; its soil consists literally of the dissolved bones of previous generations. It is impossible that even to a depth of ten feet there could be a grain of that soil that has not undertaken its journey through the human organism and that has not helped, at some time in the past, to plow over the rest of the soil. But I am exaggerating and forgetting the four pinewood boards which go into the ground at each new burial, and which spring from an equally ancient race of giant trees growing on the verdant hills round about. I am forgetting, furthermore, the coarse, honest linen of the shrouds which grew in these fields, which was spun and bleached here, which belongs to the family just as much as the pinewood boards, and which does not prevent the soil of our churchyard from being just as pleasantly cool and black as any other. The greenest of grass grows here; and roses, together with jasmine, proliferate in such heavenly disorder and exuberance that there is no need to plant individual shrubs on any new grave, for every grave has to be dug out of a forest of flowers, and only the grave-digger knows precisely where, in this chaos, the tract begins that has to be dug anew.

In the novel's closing sequences, death looms even larger. The penultimate chapter dwells on the burial preparations for the narrator's mother, just deceased, and on the darkness in his life which followed as soon as "the grave of my poor dear mother was closed." The final chapter tells of his living death thereafter, in a quiet and obscure, unpretentious but regular employment. This sorrowful existence goes on "without the hope of a brighter life." Everything is "tinged with gloom." Finally realizing that this is "no life," he wishes to escape, but he cannot. He meets again the robust, sensuous Judith — for whom he once felt such passion — and stays with her. They renounce, however, "what the world calls happiness," forego "making themselves man and wife," and continue to see each other only as cousins, "sometimes daily, sometimes weekly, sometimes only once in a year." This love turns sterile, this life loses its vitality. Notably, the autobiography does not continue past the narrator's discovery that he is interring himself in this living death (he is still comparatively young when he stops chronicling his life). There can be no prospects for a viable future.

The somberness and despondency of the novel's beginning and end sharpen the ominous symphonic discord between truth and fiction; the futility of resolving the discord emerges and remains the prevailing mood of this ingenious, enigmatic symphony.

Wilhelm Petersen: fiction in reality and reality in fiction

Interpreters of *Der grüne Heinrich* have missed that it found an extension in real life when a Dano-Prussian privy councillor named Wilhelm Petersen (1835–1900) discovered himself mirrored in the fictional Heinrich. "I am a sort of *Grüner Heinrich*," he wrote in a letter to Keller.[351]

Who was this deputy of the protagonist in the world of reality? Biographical sources[352] say that he came from a long line of Petersens in the capital city of the land that had given birth to Poetic Realism. Early in his life he refused the required oath of allegiance to his sovereign, King Christian IX of Denmark, and then entered the Prussian civil service. Discharging his duties faithfully until sixty-five, he retired from public life and died soon after. His obituaries suggest that his public service was exemplary and that he was blessed with singular good fortune all his life. A regular and steady advancement in government, the honor and respect of the community he served, a loving family — those were the fruits of untiring labors in a society whose principles he fully condoned.

---

[351] *Mein lieber Herr und bester Freund, Gottfried Keller im Briefwechsel mit Wilhelm Petersen*, ed. I. Smidt (Stäfa: Gut, 1984), 41.

[352] Biographical information about Wilhelm Petersen was obtained from 1) Petersen's granddaughter in Hamburg, Anne-Marie Petersen (orally); 2) Lorenz Petersen, *Wilhelm Petersen zu seinem hundertjährigen Geburtstage am 20. Januar 1935 — seinen Enkeln von seinem Sohn gewidmet* (Glückstadt: Augustin, 1935). See also C. A. Bernd, "Wilhelm Petersen," *Schleswig-Holsteinisches Biographisches Lexikon* III (1974): 208-10.

But Wilhelm Petersen's life had another — a more poetic — dimension, well-documented in his extensive correspondences with several of the important poets of his time.[353] He had a creative spirit unwilling to be regulated by the timetables of social responsibility; he longed for the bright color of a Bohemian world and the more exhilarating atmosphere of a life unshackled from convention.[354] He felt his career in civil service enslaved him, suffocated him in a straitjacket of facts, deeds, and practicalities; that his espousal of the ethics of bureaucratic hard work divorced him from the refreshment of art. "Life without art," he said in his first letter to Keller, "is but a shadow, empty and desolate."[355] To Storm he wrote that "only artistically creative life is worth living."[356] But the stifling mechanism of bureaucracy left little room for the avidly desired flights of imagination. Hence, he felt keenly the irritating dullness of his humdrum existence and remained unable to accommodate himself inwardly to his pragmatic life as a public official. Even as a very young man he had wished not to be tied down in an unpoetic world of communal security, nor had he wanted to assume the responsibilities of family life. The freedom of the poet and painter attracted him more. Parental pressure kept him from following his imaginative disposition, but in spite of his destiny his gaze always remained fixed on the poetic life he could not lead. He published poetry anonymously in journals of the day. When official duties did not clamor for his attention, he would paint and model with clay. He allowed himself the luxury of frequent and expensive rail travel to visit Keller, Storm, and other writers. He bestowed lavish gifts on them, forcing his own family to contend with a more meager income than otherwise for a household with a Prussian privy councillor as paterfamilias. Often he escaped the slavery of his official and family obligations by fleeing to Italy, where he wandered, sometimes in solitary contemplation, sometimes in company with an art historian, from one art gallery or baroque church to another.[357]

But recognition for his activity in the arts eluded him. His verse, his paintings, his sculptures, and his expertise in Italian Renaissance art got

---

[353] 1) *Mein lieber Herr und bester Freund, Gottfried Keller im Briefwechsel mit Wilhelm Petersen*; 2) *Theodor Storm—Wilhelm Petersen Briefwechsel*, Kritische Ausgabe, ed. B. Coghlan (Berlin: Erich Schmidt, 1984); 3) extensive unpublished correspondences with other writers in the Bavarian State Library (Munich) and the Schleswig-Holstein State Library (Kiel).

[354] *Storm—Petersen Briefwechsel*, 25-26.

[355] *Mein lieber Herr und bester Freund*, 41.

[356] *Storm—Petersen Briefwechsel*, 109.

[357] *Mein lieber Herr und bester Freund*, 50.

only scant praise and were quickly forgotten. In contrast, his professional accomplishments were duly recorded (in glowing terms) in the annals of the Prussian civil service. Which was the real world for Petersen, which the artificial and empty one?

The frustration of reaping unwanted success in public life while missing any reward in the poetic world led Petersen to start a fictional chronicle of his life — glibly imitating *Der grüne Heinrich* — but this attempt to project the discord in his life into an autobiographical novel proved as futile as his other attempts at art. If the conflict between his public and poetic self could not be resolved in the real world, it could not be harmonized in fiction either.

One option remained for this genuine "poetic realist" not destined for the ranks of Poetic Realists in literature: the original version of Keller's novel, imaginatively translated into his personal reality, could be tempered by facts from his own life and presented to readers in a new, more persuasive form, closer to actual experience. Keller then, on the dogged insistence of the civil servant/artist, deftly brought a further aspect of reality into the novel which had meant so much to Petersen. When a revision of the novel appeared in 1879–1880, in the closing chapters it became the fictionally disguised portrait of the twin faces of Wilhelm Petersen, who had muscled his way into the poetic fabric. The living death of Heinrich, with which the rewritten novel breaks off, reflects the mature wisdom of the practical official knowing that the abysmal disjunction of his public and private lives would remain unreconciled for as long as he lived, who knew and said that his deeply-felt love for the fictional Judith could never be consummated in real life.[358]

Keller never tired of recounting the debt he owed to his Prussian Heinrich for the rewritten *Grüner Heinrich*.[359] Approaching death, he expressed the wish to see the wise bureaucrat Petersen — the frustrated artist — once more. Petersen immediately left his official duties in the town of Schleswig near the Dano-Prussian frontier and made the long trip to Zurich to be near, one last time, to the dying author of the novel which he thought "second to none in the world,"[360] his "most treasured earthly possession."[361]

---

[358] Ibid., 151.
[359] Ibid., 148.
[360] Ibid., 65, 276.
[361] Ibid., 135.

5. The latecomer: Conrad Ferdinand Meyer

Continuing the novella of *Poetischer Realismus*

Conrad Ferdinand Meyer (1825–1898), another author from Zurich, was not one of the founding fathers of *Poetischer Realismus*.[362] He came to the movement about thirty years after 1848 had ignited it. Yet, he came to occupy an exalted position in it. With Storm and Keller he belongs to the triumvirate of canonical novella-writers in German Poetic Realism.

Julius Rodenberg (1831-1914), the erudite editor of the literary monthly *Deutsche Rundschau* (German Review), was the first to recognize the three as a group towering over all others in the movement. Rodenberg, who promoted many works of Poetic Realism through his widely circulated journal, granted Meyer the same extraordinary treatment previously given only to Storm and Keller: the *Deutsche Rundschau* would publish every novella the author wrote immediately, without need for further editorial approval.[363]

Other influential contemporary men of letters have also unequivocally acknowledged this trio's position at the apogee as Poetic Realist novella-writers. The versatile Prussian author and diplomat Rudolf Lindau (1829–1910), for instance, named them first among the best German-language novella-writers at the time.[364]

The trend has continued. In 1952 Victor Lange called them the "three mid-century authors who come closest to representing human beings and attitudes with the reconciliating ease and the wise acceptance of the world about us that is ... attached to the word 'realism.'"[365] In 1954 Walter Silz called them "the three supreme masters" of the novella of Poetic Realism.[366] Recently, in 1985, Gail Finney has again reaffirmed their canonical

---

[362] The best modern introduction to Meyer's life and works is by Marianne Burkhard, *Conrad Ferdinand Meyer* (Boston: Twayne, 1978). This book, by a relative of the poet, offers personal insights not otherwise available.

[363] *Conrad Ferdinand Meyer und Julius Rodenberg, Ein Briefwechsel*, ed. A. Langmesser (Berlin: Paetel, 1918), 73.

[364] Fontane, *Sämtliche Werke*, XXI/1, 327.

[365] *Great German Short Novels and Stories*, ed. V. Lange (New York: Random House, 1952), xv.

[366] Silz, *Realism and Reality*, 151.

position: "In addition to Storm, the most representative poetic realists are Gottfried Keller and Conrad Ferdinand Meyer."[367]

Though Keller, Storm, and Meyer stand linked auspiciously together, Meyer varies markedly from the earlier two. Baptized by the fires of revolution, they had chosen their themes from everyday reality; Meyer, thirty years later, deserted daily life as overgrazed in favor of a new historic reality. This difference has prompted some modern critics, most notably the Cambridge literary historian Edwin K. Bennett (1887-1958), to dissociate Meyer from Poetic Realism altogether.[368] But such a separation misses the dynamism of the movement, its power to twist, turn, and strike out in new directions without losing its identity. If Storm and Keller show an invigorating clarity of purpose, close to the wellsprings, Meyer contributes to a deeper, broader, and fuller current. Storm and Keller are neither more typical nor more perfect examples of this Helicon.

The most acute, perceptive, and incisive observer of Meyer's role was German Poetic Realism's theoretical apostle, Julian Schmidt. In a scandalous oversight, modern criticism has ignored Schmidt's two essays relating Meyer to the movement. Gathering dust in the now-forgotten periodical *Preußische Jahrbücher* (Prussian Annals),[369] they show conclusively the difference between the contemporary themes of everyday reality chosen by the early German Poetic Realists and the historically remote themes of Meyer to be, contra Bennett, a reason to link Meyer to his predecessors and to give him equal esteem. Schmidt shows with special acumen that Meyer's stress on the past was consistent with the realistic conception of literature that came out of the revolutions, even the logical and natural extension of that conception at a time when thirty years had cooled the revolutionary fires. Far from corrupting Poetic Realism, Meyer had revitalized it in its old age.

The details of Schmidt's argument deserve note and all the more so because Meyer himself was much impressed with the way the critic viewed him.[370] Schmidt begins with the skepticism of men of letters in the early days of German Poetic Realism toward historical fiction, responding to the Romantic penchant for the remote corners of the past, their particular delight in "once upon a time." The early German Poetic Realists had fought this Romantic turning-back-the-clock. The turmoils of 1848–1849 had

---

[367] Gail Finney, "Poetic Realism: Theodor Storm, Gottfried Keller, Conrad Ferdinand Meyer," in *European Writers: The Romantic Century*, eds. J. Barzun & G. Stade, VI (New York: Scribner's, 1985), 915.

[368] Bennett, *A History of the German Novelle*, 215-30.

[369] *Preußische Jahrbücher* 44 (1879): 608-13; 53 (1884): 264-83.

[370] *Briefe Conrad Ferdinand Meyers*, ed. A. Frey, I (Leipzig: Haessel, 1908), 171.

brought home that today's affairs, and not yesterday's, really counted. Hence, they rejected sending the mind wandering through the picture galleries of history. They substituted a literature about contemporary life.

But after some years the movement had run this course. Contemporary reality was wearing thin. Subjects started reappearing in one work after another. The monotony would have been fatal, so farsighted Poetic Realists searched for unworn themes, which they found in history. They found real life in actual records of the past and recast it into fiction. This broadened the movement in ways inconceivable earlier, when history was taboo. Still, the thrust of Poetic Realism was intact — the life of the past was as real as the life of the present.

As Schmidt points out, not all who so turned to history succeeded in translating the reality of the past into fiction. He refers to the popular fiction of the talented contemporary Prussian Egyptologist Georg Ebers (1837–1898). Steeped in the Egyptian past, Ebers's knowledge supplied him with dazzling material. But all he did was to place conventional tales of the present in picturesque Egyptian disguise. He did little justice to history, says Schmidt, only by costuming modern characters in colorful ancient Egyptian garb, by giving their language a touch of the obsolete, and by raising a stage-setting reminiscent of the world near the old Nile. Ebers did not portray the real life of ancient Egypt; he merely feigned that reality.

Meyer's contribution to Poetic Realism stands out against this background. Where Ebers failed, Meyer succeeded spectacularly. As Schmidt shows, Meyer's tales leave the reader with the distinct impression that the related events of the past actually occurred, and that the characters really lived. Meyer's episodes illustrate those issues and lives which really mattered, which actually shaped history.

Der Heilige

Meyer debuted impressively as a Poetic Realist with *Der Heilige* (The Saint), published in three installments in the opening pages of the November, December, and January 1879 and 1880 issues of the *Deutsche Rundschau*.[371] Not his first (nor the last) novella, it alone, however, pro-

---

[371] There is a considerable body of literature on *Der Heilige*. The most important modern interpretations are by 1) W. A. Coupe in *Conrad Ferdinand Meyer, Der Heilige*, ed. W. A. Coupe (Oxford: Blackwell, 2nd impression, 1971), xi-xxxvi; 2) Gunter H. Hertling, *Conrad Ferdinand Meyers Epik: Traumbeseelung, Traumbesinnung und Traumbesitz* (Berne: Francke, 1973), 92-109; 3) Luciano Zagari in *Conrad Ferdinand Meyer, "Il Santo,"* ed. L. Zagari (Rome: Salerno Editrice, 1982), 7-31; 4) Roy C. Cowen in *Der Poetische Rea-*

pelled him into the forefront of Poetic Realism, prompting Schmidt to the *laudatio*. Schmidt acclaimed Meyer for this novella even before the third installment appeared in print.[372] *Der Heilige* also quickly won Meyer the affection of Storm.[373] Keller, never sympathetic to Meyer,[374] hurried to admit that his cross-town competitor had written a splendid work.[375]

The praise of this novella spread most widely, however, when another ardent admirer of Meyer's historical fiction, Johannes Haußleiter (1851–1928), lauded it in the most influential daily newspaper in the German-speaking world at the time, the *Allgemeine Zeitung*.[376] If Schmidt had attended to the realism of Meyer's work, Haußleiter now emphasized its drama. He reminded readers, thus, of a cardinal feature of the novella of Poetic Realism: that it should be a prosaic "sister of the drama."

Schmidt had also pointed to the dramatic life of Meyer's novellas,[377] even though he was primarily concerned with their historic content's agreement with the main requirement of Poetic Realism. But it remained essentially for Haußleiter to develop this point by focusing on what he, too, agreed was Meyer's strongest work: *Der Heilige*. Meyer, reading Haußleiter's analysis, called it "excellent."[378] Seldom, in the history of criticism, have we been afforded such an opportunity of knowing how an author liked his work to be read, yet, as with Schmidt's commentaries, Haußleiter's essay remains neglected today. It deserves better.

Haußleiter identifies as central to *Der Heilige* the drama between temporal and eternal values, between the body and the soul, civil power and sacerdotal jurisdiction, secular state competence and the mission of a divinely inspired church. History, according to Haußleiter's reading of *Der Heilige*, has recorded this clash in the conflict of loyalties faced by Thomas à Becket, the twelfth-century English statesman canonized by the Catholic Church. The contradictory historical reality and the contradictory personality present an inherent drama. Becket goes from Chancellor of Eng-

---

lismus, 247-62; 5) Robert C. Holub in *Reflections of Realism*, 152-73. The studies by Coupe and Zagari are invariably omitted (wrongly) in the "select" bibliographies pertaining to this novella.

[372] *Meyer—Rodenberg Briefwechsel*, 64.

[373] *Storm—Heyse Briefwechsel*, II (1970), 89.

[374] Werner Kohlschmidt, *Dichter, Tradition und Zeitgeist* (Berne: Francke, 1965), 355.

[375] Keller, *Gesammelte Briefe*, III/2 (1953), 369; IV (1954), 204.

[376] *Allgemeine Zeitung* (Munich), April 8, 1887: 1441-42; April 9, 1887: 1450-51.

[377] *Preußische Jahrbücher* 53 (1884): 273.

[378] *Briefe Conrad Ferdinand Meyers*, II, 130.

land to Archbishop of Canterbury, from chief aide to the despotic King Henry II of England to primate of the King "not of this world."

Early on, Becket, with little apparent regard for right or wrong, zealously strives to strengthen royal power, often at the expense of ecclesiastical prerogatives. He is an ardent abettor of a Caesarism bent on reducing the church to submission to the crown, and for a good reason.

The church was the most formidable obstacle to supremacy for Henry. Insistent on preemptory clerical rights, it would not tolerate the substitution of civil courts of appeal for legal matters involving a member of the clergy — and there were many clergy. It also insisted on sole power over Christian marriage and the tables of consanguinity, thus over inheritance. This considerable power greatly irritated the absolutist king. Salt in the wound, the church was a foreign power: Rome. Henry counted on his able chancellor to curb papal interference in English affairs, but he knew to expect a hard contest. A few decades earlier the Pope had humbled the German emperor at Canossa: the world had seen a mighty emperor in the dust before the "Vicar of Christ." This papal triumph had dazzled Europe and had set the Petrine tiara scintillating with a brilliance never seen before.

As the story of Becket continues, Henry chose well his time to act: a new Pope had a passion for augmenting the Vatican's coffers. He would not easily offend any sovereign supplying money. This left only the Catholic "Primate of All England," the Archbishop of Canterbury, as the source of ecclesiastical opposition to the crown. Cunningly, Henry causes his friend and pliant advocate, Becket, to be appointed to the archbishopric: a perfect scheme for submission of church to state, with Becket the chief instrument in the plan.

Here the other side of Becket's contradictory personality comes into focus. Once installed in the archiepiscopal See of Canterbury, the former servant of secular power exhibits equal tenacity in service to his divine master. He switches sides. Astonishingly, the luxury- and splendor-loving Becket casts aside all interest in worldly riches and chooses to go about in the raiment of penance. Followed by a motley crowd of beggars, sick, lame, and blind, he invites the lot to dine at his table, once the place of lords. He becomes a militant advocate of spiritual power, indeed to such an extent that, as Haußleiter puts it, he is "more popish than the Pope." In the ensuing battle with his earthly sovereign, Becket soon suffers the death of a martyr, right before the high altar of Canterbury Cathedral.

The crown of martyrdom gives Becket the final victory. Henry's throne crumbles, and Henry prostrates and scourges himself at the tomb of Becket, already canonized among the saints of the church. The dramatic reversal is complete. Royal supremacy trampling the spiritual now suffers complete abjection before the invincible glow of the church.

Haußleiter argued at length that the historical record of Becket incorporated into the novella had contained its essential drama, the conflict of the two great contradictory forces of human life. Yet, according to Haußleiter, it was Meyer who nevertheless made this drama come alive. Becket's story, as Haußleiter continues, is remembered by a friend, invented by Meyer. This fictional tactic allows Meyer a freedom not enjoyed by the historian: to suffuse historical reality with poetic fantasy. On the very day the church recognizes Becket's joining the company of saints, a feebleminded simple tradesman named Hans recounts the events of Becket's terrestrial life. We are not allowed to forget the manufactured character of this often amusing version of Becket's story, so we must wonder how much history is strained by the tale. There is much inaccuracy, it turns out.

History and fiction thus dovetail, interpenetrating, amplifying each other to support the dramatic conflict of the novella. The invented eyewitness report of the personal friend Hans allows the saint to appear as a real person; yet, Becket's extraordinary combination of sin and sanctity contrasts vividly with the naturalistic, down-to-earth Hans. The reader wonders, which is more concrete: Hans, with his fictive narrative about a historical figure, or history's authenticated saint appearing only in the words of a fictional character claiming to have known him? No matter, for Meyer intends that the inseparable conflicting forces found in the actual historical figure be equally visible in the interlacing of the natural and the supernatural that characterizes the whole of this powerful Poetic Realist exercise.

Continuing the lyric of *Poetischer Realismus*

Like Storm and Keller, Meyer's star also shined bright in the galaxy of great lyricists of Poetic Realism. None other than Julian Schmidt, the theoretical pastor of *Poetischer Realismus* himself, had recognized this. Indeed, for him, Meyer appears to be a truly outstanding lyricist of *Poetischer Realismus*. He found words of praise for Meyer's poetry which he never managed to find for other poets of his time. A vital sense of realism reigns, he says, enhanced by a poetic melody never clouding imagery with too lush orchestration but forceful enough to transfigure the realistic picture, yielding a candid commentary on the timeless aspect of human life.[379]

---

[379] *Preußische Jahrbücher* 53 (1884): 266-71.

In modern times, Schmidt's remarks on Meyer's lyrics have been as blithely overlooked as his comments on Meyer's prose fiction, and this, too, has given rise to a fuzzy understanding of Meyer's historical place in literature. For Heinrich Henel (1905-1981), for instance, Meyer, the lyricist, was not a Poetic Realist but the initiator of a subsequent literary movement known as Symbolism.[380] This thesis, however doggedly argued, has been more often rejected than accepted.[381] Another critic, Friedrich Bruns (1878-1961), has stated that Meyer's poetry "belongs to no school or movement of his day."[382] Such a theory seems as awkward as historically improbable, for it assumes that a segment of literature can exist in vacuo. We have a renewed need to recognize, therefore, that Meyer's verse is no less a part of Poetic Realism than his prose fiction, that it makes up and modifies — together with all the works of the movement — the concept and practice of Poetic Realism as a whole.

"Der römische Brunnen"

The crowning jewel of Meyer's Poetic Realist verse is "Der römische Brunnen" (The Roman Fountain). Heinrich Henel reminded us that it has been interpreted almost to death,[383] a sure proof of its enduring fame:

---

[380] Heinrich Henel, *The Poetry of Conrad Ferdinand Meyer* (Madison: University of Wisconsin Press, 1954), viii, 56.

[381] Werner Oberle, reviewing Henel's book, quickly retorted that Meyer's poetic world was far too strongly orientated toward reality to be connected with the sort of mystical aestheticism that typified the poetry, for example, of a prominent German Symbolist like Rainer Maria Rilke (W. Oberle, "Conrad Ferdinand Meyer, Ein Forschungsbericht," *Germanisch-Romanische Monatsschrift* 37 [1956]: 243). G. Wallis Field said, more bluntly, that the kind of symbolism used by Meyer "does not make Meyer a Symbolist poet" (G. W. Field, *A Literary History of Germany, The Nineteenth Century 1830-1890* [London: Benn, 1975], 143). Paul Böckmann, in the most perceptive essay that has been written in modern times on the German lyric of the nineteenth century, also clearly expressed his doubts as to whether Meyer could be ranked along with the Symbolists (P. Böckmann, "Deutsche Lyrik im 19. Jahrhundert," in *Formkräfte der deutschen Dichtung vom Barock bis zur Gegenwart*, ed. H. Steffen, 2nd ed. [Göttingen: Vandenhoeck & Ruprecht, 1967], 185). Hildegard Emmel, to cite one more instance, found herself unable to include Meyer in her survey of Symbolism printed in *Reallexikon der deutschen Literaturgeschichte*, eds. K. Kanzog & A. Masser, 2nd ed., IV (Berlin: de Gruyter, 1981), 333-44.

[382] Friedrich Bruns, *Die Lese der deutschen Lyrik von Klopstock bis Rilke* (New York: Appleton-Century-Crofts, 1961), 44.

[383] *Gedichte Conrad Ferdinand Meyers, Wege ihrer Vollendung*, ed. H. Henel (Tübingen: Niemeyer, 1962), 171. Particularly perceptive interpretations of this poem are by 1) Wilhelm Schneider in *Liebe zum deutschen Gedicht*, 114-21; 2) Frank G. Ryder, "'Der

> Aufsteigt der Strahl und fallend gießt
> Er voll der Marmorschale Rund,
> Die, sich verschleiernd, überfließt
> In einer zweiten Schale Grund;
> Die zweite giebt, sie wird zu reich,
> Der dritten wallend ihre Flut,
> Und jede nimmt und giebt zugleich
> Und strömt und ruht.[384]

> (Up spurts the stream and falling pours
> Its flood into the marble urn,
> Which, veiled in lacy froth, outpours
> Into a second bowl in turn;
> The second swells, it passes on
> Into a third its seething crest,
> And all receive and give as one
> And flow and rest.)
>
> *Translated by C. A. Bernd*

Biographically, the poem is a plastic recollection of a visit by Meyer in 1858 to the Borghese gardens in Rome. In the lower part of the gardens he saw a fountain that made a profound impression on him. It was a simple, rather austere structure of three weathered marble basins. The waters falling from one basin into another filled the air of the quiet gardens with continuous splashing sounds. Meyer's sister Betsy tells us that he became so intrigued with this fountain that on one of the last evenings before leaving Rome he returned to the gardens and sought there to preserve his impressions in a poem.[385] But these facts only give the background to the verses. Over almost a quarter of a century Meyer revised the poem many times. In the final version (1882), when the memory of the actual visit to Rome had long faded, the poem became a completely different vision of reality. The fountain in the Eternal City became the eternal song of human transience. The incessant flow of water from basin to basin, from beginning to end, figured the current of life from cradle to coffin. This transfigured picture puts Meyer's poem squarely in the lyric tradition of

---

römische Brunnen' — Sound Pattern and Content," *Monatshefte* 52 (1960): 235-41; 3) Thomas Elwood Hart, "Linguistic Patterns, Literary Structure, and the Genesis of C. F. Meyer's 'Der römische Brunnen,'" *Language and Style* 4 (1971): 83-115.

[384] The text is reproduced from the poet's own last important revised edition of his *Gedichte*, 4th enlarged ed. (Leipzig: Haessel, 1891), 152.

[385] Betsy Meyer, *Conrad Ferdinand Meyer in der Erinnerung seiner Schwester* (Berlin: Paetel, 1903), 164.

Storm and Keller: in the two examples of their poetry discussed earlier, we saw precisely the same spectacle of human transience.

Aufsteigt der Strahl gives Meyer's poem a lively start. The heavily intonated first two syllables, deviating from the normal iambic, suggest the energetic gushing from the fountain. But decline follows rise as the water falls again in the antithetical declivity of the second half of the first line. Just as water must obey gravity, so the human being's life must decline toward death. After the first line, a great iambic regularity sets in: life trickles steadily down to the grave, passing through the three basins — youth, middle age, and old age — on its quick journey. Life comes to its appointed end in the last word, *ruht*, that long, deep-voweled, and heavily accented finale indicating the everlasting sleep of the grave (*Hier ruht* [Here rests]).

Between each important stage of life a short pause intervenes. Thus, after life moves forward from line one to line two by enjambment, it halts for a brief moment at the end of line two, meeting there the resistance of both the heavy vowel in *Rund* and the comma. Lines three and four follow a similar pattern: life flows quickly past in a stream of aquatic *ch*, *sch*, and *s* sounds, at times trying to halt (as at the commas in line three), but never able to tarry on its way downstream. The longest pause comes at the end of line four, as if the ritard induced by the semicolon were giving the second, larger basin more time to fill, as if middle age extended over a greater period than did youth. But again, the pause does not last. Life pushes inexorably on and down into the decline of old age, represented by the third and final basin. Commas in the fifth and sixth lines temporarily brake the tempo but never succeed for long. A haunting summary in the penultimate line tells us that life is nothing but a succession of comings and goings. Now we are prepared for the end. As life expires, the quick, rippling flux of iambs draws to a halt, replaced by the slow, choking sounds of four spasmodic breaths:

> Und strömt und ruht.
> (—   —   —   —)
> (And flow and rest.)

The choking of death shrouds itself, at the same time, in the stress of mournful *u* sounds, naturally terminating in the last *ruht*, the everlasting sleep of death.

Once more we have seen the spectacle of human transience. The realities of time and death have been infused into these verses, as into "Meeresstrand" and "Abendlied." Again, there is nothing nebulous or inexact, no enchanted pool of a Romantic wonderland — only the clear and very real flow of life moving surely to death. "Der römische Brunnen" thus essentially duplicates the subject of the two poems by Storm and Keller. But the poetic effects differ: Meyer's poem is sustained neither by Storm's opulent music nor by Keller's richly colorful imagery. Everything is spare, pithy. No descriptive adjectives appear, no references to the surrounding gardens, the verdant foliage, the azure Roman sky, or the glow of the hot Italian sun. There is no gradation of light or shade. The terse eight lines seem as short as life. Realistic vision finds itself cloaked in a poetic mantle stifling all emotion. Dampness, austerity, and chill prevail, like the cold, solid marble of the Roman fountain, damp from the constant trickle of water. The melodious song of sorrow at the passing of life ("Meeresstrand") or of joy in spite of it ("Abendlied") have given way to the bold contours of a cold architectonic.[386] What Storm and Keller orchestrated with warm, pulsating melody, Meyer transposes to a plain, rigid structure of cold marble, hewn into an austere, frozen sculpture of hardened nouns, verbs, sharp commas, and the barest minimum of color and tune. The rigidity and frigidity of Meyer's music give him the advantage of facing ephemerality with cooler, dampened emotions, even with cold indifference to the inevitable. He candidly recognizes the predetermined ending chill of death, and unflinchingly — with neither Keller's joy nor Storm's sorrow — he acquiesces to it.

Did this attitude result from Meyer's Calvinistic upbringing, in which predestination was a cardinal principle? This is open to conjecture, but the poet's cold fatalism is undeniable.

6. The Low German poet: Klaus Groth

The reception of Groth's verse

Modern criticism has let Klaus Groth (1819–1899) drift into a slough of abysmal neglect.[387] But Fritz Martini (1909–1991), the most knowledgeable critic of nineteenth-century German literature in our time, courageously voiced protest. Finding no mention of Groth in a new tome on

---

[386] See Böckmann, "Deutsche Lyrik im 19. Jahrhundert," 185.

[387] The most comprehensive introduction to Groth is the (woefully inadequate) biography by Geert Seelig, *Klaus Groth, Sein Leben und Werden* (Hamburg: Alster, 1924).

the history of German poetry,[388] Martini taunted: "How come Groth is omitted?"[389]

Martini rightly defended Groth against the charge of obscurity. (He subsequently gave the poet meaningful coverage in his own history of German literature in the second half of the nineteenth century.)[390] In 1852 Groth had published his collection of fifty-eight poems entitled *Quickborn* (Living Fountain), a remarkable trophy of Poetic Realist verse that quickly made him famous from the Baltic to as far west as Holland and Flanders. Julian Schmidt spoke of the book's "triumphal march" through Germany.[391] Storm said that these poems had made Groth "a celebrity."[392] One expanded edition followed another. By the end of the century, the volume was in its twenty-fifth edition, containing more than twice as many poems as the first printing. These poems found their way into countless anthologies of the day, and they were frequently reprinted in the many editions of Groth's collected works.

None esteemed Groth more highly than did Theodor Fontane and Johannes Brahms. Fontane called Groth "a splendid poet."[393] When he revised his own anthology, *Deutsches Dichteralbum*, for the fourth and final time in 1858, he let Groth's lyric voice resound louder than any post-1848 poet's but Storm's. In the preface he singled out Groth's poems, citing their intrinsic value as he substituted them for others' verse. Brahms was so impressed with these lyrics that he composed settings for many of them, forever associating Groth's lyric voice with his own immortal music.[394]

---

[388] Johannes Klein, *Geschichte der deutschen Lyrik, Von Luther bis zum Ausgang des zweiten Weltkrieges* (Wiesbaden: Steiner, 1957).

[389] Fritz Martini, "Deutsche Literatur in der Zeit des 'bürgerlichen Realismus,' Ein Literaturbericht," *Deutsche Vierteljahrsschrift für Literaturwissenschaft und Geistesgeschichte* 34 (1960): 619.

[390] Martini, *Deutsche Literatur im bürgerlichen Realismus 1848-1898*, 4th ed. (Stuttgart: Metzler, 1981), 307-12.

[391] Schmidt, *Neue Bilder aus dem geistigen Leben unserer Zeit*, III (Leipzig: Duncker & Humblot, 1873), 149.

[392] *Theodor Storm—Klaus Groth Briefwechsel*, Kritische Ausgabe, ed. B. Hinrichs (Berlin: Erich Schmidt, 1990), 181.

[393] *Storm—Fontane Briefwechsel*, 23.

[394] See Klaus Groth, *Sämtliche Werke*, V, eds. I. Braak & R. Mehlen (Flensburg: Wolff, 1960), 312.

Early verse

Groth was, like Storm, born and raised a subject of the Danish crown. He spent his formative years in Tønder, the surrounding countryside of which was overwhelmingly Danish in language and custom. His ties to the Danish muse were naturally strong, stronger indeed than Storm's; for Groth, unlike Storm, often visited Copenhagen and had close personal ties with many Danish men of letters, including Hans Christian Andersen. Not only did Groth speak and read Danish well, but, as he acknowledged, he also "thought half in Danish."[395]

Unsurprisingly, when Groth began to write verse, he inherited, like Storm, the prevailing musical artistry of Danish poetry. His early verse is filled with the opera of emotion. Typical are these verses of April 1846, in which subjective feeling and song merge in a harmonious tune:

> Von deinen Lippen ist der Ton erklungen,
> Der sonnenwärts mein ganzes Wesen zieht,
> Du hast ihn in die Seele mir gesungen,
> Sieh, was ich denke, wird davon ein Lied.[396]
>
> (Your lips have sent the note of joy a-ringing,
> which sunward pulls my very being on,
> Into my soul you've led its gladsome singing,
> Behold, my thoughts will now become a song.)
> *Translated by Richard D. Hacken*

Groth is composing here, rather obviously, within the orbit of the Danish verse-melody for which Andersen had become famous.

In Groth's pre-1848 "Danish" period a musical imagination prevailed. But this world of comforting poetic melody abruptly crumbled when the fires of 1848 spread to his native Schleswig-Holstein. The bloodstained soil of the twin duchies during their uprising against the Danish crown opened Groth's eyes to harsh reality. He turned to writing political poetry supporting the revolution. Uniquely, he penned these new verses in the Low German spoken by the rebel soldiers. One of the first poems, written in the spring of 1848, bore the title "Dütsche Ehr un Dütsche Eer" (German Honor and German Earth). The opening stanza reads:

---

[395] *Klaus Groths Briefe an seine Braut Doris Finke*, ed. H. Krumm (Braunschweig: Westermann, 1910), 238.

[396] Groth, *Sämtliche Werke*, ed. F. Pauly, I (Flensburg: Wolff, 1952), 24.

Dar keemn Soldaten æwer de Elf,
Hurah, hurah, na't Norn!
Se keemn so dicht as Wagg an Wagg
Un as en Koppel vull Korn.

(There came soldiers across the Elbe,
Hurrah, hurrah, to the North!
They came as thick as wave on wave,
And like a field full of corn.)

Translated by Max Müller[397]

This is a war song, patriotic invective, rhyme and rhythm all pressed into battle for political independence from the Danish crown. With his pen, Groth marched side by side with the German soldiers pushing north in the spring of 1848 in what seemed — in those early months of the rebellion — a successful fight to drive the Danish militia from his homeland.

Most importantly, these verses are written in the Low German tongue of the insurgents. With the spoken vernacular of the rebels the verses could more easily win support for the revolutionary cause. This was a real novelty, for before Groth, Low German was hardly considered a valid medium for poetry. Not since the early sixteenth century, when Burkard Waldis had versified in Low German in support of the Protestant Reformation,[398] had that idiom effectively supported poetry. Much like Waldis three hundred years earlier, Groth thought: only the natural, undistorted idiom of the people could rally the people around his cause. Waldis had protested against a religious wrong, the burning issue of his day; Groth now sought public support for the uprising against the Danish crown.

Groth was truly innovative in his political poetry. Still, he was ill prepared for a vocation limited to writing political pamphlets in verse. His deep roots in the colorful garden of Danish song left him little patience with this narrow concept of realistic poetry, unable to look beyond a current political issue. So he stopped using his pen in the revolutionary cause. Instead, he took up the more enduring poetic form, Danish verse-melody, though now with an eye on the reality to which the revolution had so rudely alerted him.

---

[397] German text and English translation in *Macmillan's Magazine* 10 (1864): 360.

[398] Paul Böckmann, *Formgeschichte der deutschen Dichtung* (Hamburg: Hoffmann & Campe, 1949), 300-5.

Quickborn

It was then that he began *Quickborn*. The book is a melodious composition in the contemporary Danish sense, a felicitous bouquet of buoyant songs, stirring ballads, and rollicking idylls. But for all its high spirits and harmonious tones, the book is no less a moving diorama of real life, graphic proof that Groth could not forget the heat of war, the roar of cannon in the distance, and the armed Danish sentry standing guard in front of his house.[399] Yet, Groth's new poetic presentation of real life is not an illustration of the pitched battles of 1848 like his political poetry. Something breaks through from a deeper level than that of the mind of a conscious political observer. The stern tragedy of the human struggle for life comes to the fore.

Most obviously, these poems offer an accurate view of the land and people of Groth's native countryside, present and past. They describe, with considerable breadth and uncanny truth, the people Groth knew well: the homely folk, farmers and fishers, at work and at play. This portrayal preserves a fidelity of language that gives this slice of real life its only possible genuine expression. As with Groth's political poetry, the real idiom of the Holstein people — whose feelings and manners Groth depicts — adds a touch of local color that makes *Quickborn* come alive. But Groth did not want merely the local characteristics, as Auerbach and Kompert had in their prose. He wanted instead the commonly perceptible truths of human existence, with local features only a means to this end. He said specifically that he wanted to present a "mirror" of real life, a "poetically transfigured" world, where men and women could discover themselves.[400]

Groth is at his best in the *Quickborn* ballads. There, real life and places, the real language of the folk between the North Sea and the Baltic blend most harmoniously with the poetic melody of the Danish lyre. These ballads became exemplary of Poetic Realism. Tellingly, it was the Danish Poetic Realist Bernhard Ingemann who translated the *Quickborn* ballads into Danish.[401] He knew they would find a reading public in Denmark that had acquired a taste for Poetic Realism. Not anomalously, soon after *Quickborn*'s publication, an influential Danish literary critic, Carl Rosen-

---

[399] See the graphic account in Groth, *Die patriotische Wirksamkeit eines schleswig-holsteinischen Privatmannes*, ed. V. Pauls (Neumünster: Wachholtz, 1930), 6-14.

[400] Seelig, 113.

[401] H. Siercks, *Klaus Groth, Sein Leben und seine Werke* (Kiel: Lipsius & Tischer, 1899), 221.

berg (1829–1885)), called Groth an "ally" of Danish culture.[402] Reading *Quickborn*, Hans Christian Andersen sensed a compelling kinship with Groth.[403] By 1857 even the king of Denmark, Frederick VII, offered Groth — notwithstanding the bitterness of the recently quelled revolution — an annuity from the crown coffers.[404]

The *Quickborn* ballads were remarkably attuned to Danish poetic melody, and yet they also possessed a strong penchant for realism. Few have attracted critical attention like "Ol Büsum" (Old Büsum), composed late in 1851. Storm considered it[405] one of the three best poems in the collection:

> Ol Büsen liggt int wille Haff,
> De Floth de keem un wöhl en Graff.
>
> De Floth de keem un spöl un spöl,
> Bet se de Insel ünner wöhl.
>
> Dar blev keen Steen, dar blev keen Pahl,
> Dat Water schœl dat all hendal.
>
> Dar weer keen Beest, dar weer keen Hund,
> De ligt nu all in depen Grund.
>
> Un Allens, wat der lev un lach,
> Dat deck de See mit depe Nach.
>
> Mitünner in de holle Ebb
> So süht man vunne Hüs' de Köpp.
>
> Denn dukt de Thorn herut ut Sand,
> As weert en Finger vun en Hand.
>
> Denn hört man sach de Klocken klingn,
> Denn hört man sach de Kanter singn,

---

[402] C. Rosenberg, "Klaus Groth som plattydsk Digter," *Dansk Maanedsskrift* II (1859): 121.

[403] Groth, *Sämtliche Werke*, eds. I. Braak & R. Mehlem, VIII (Flensburg: Wolff, 1965), 260.

[404] Seelig, 284.

[405] *Storm—Groth Briefwechsel*, 32.

Denn geit dat lisen dœr de Luft:
"Begrabt den Leib in seine Gruft."[406]

(Old Büsum lies 'neath angry wave,
The waters came and scooped its grave.

The stealthy tide crept sure and slow,
Till it had gnawed the island through.

No fence remained, nor stick nor stone,
The waves washed all remorseless down.

Nor dog nor beast again gave sound,
They all lie deep on ocean's ground.

And all who lived and laughed in light,
The sea has covered with black night.

Sometimes at lowest ebb you see
The tops of houses in the sea.

A steeple points from out the sand,
As 'twere the finger of a hand.

Then hears one low the church bells ring,
Then hears one low the cantor sing,

Then sounds the hymn below today:
"This body in the grave we lay.")

Translated by Richard D. Hacken

This ballad displays immediately several characteristics popular with the Danish ballad: the basic narrative foundation, the impersonal tone, the bold dramatic outline, the simple two-line stanza with four accentuated syllables in each verse, and, of course, the plaintive melodic echoing of iambs and rhyming couplets. These balladic features combine with the realistic portrayal of the island of Büsum sinking into the North Sea, an actual historical event.

---

[406] The text is reproduced from Groth, *Gesammelte Werke*, I (Kiel: Lipsius & Tischer, 1893), 117-18. The more recent and more readily available printing of this poem in Groth's *Sämtliche Werke*, eds. I. Braak & R. Mehlem, II (Flensburg: Wolff, 1957), 155, is faulty. Hence, the need to quote from the older edition.

The first three stanzas poetically recreate the erosive action of the restless waves, showing the island's vulnerability before the sea. The fourth and fifth stanzas bemoan the drowning of all living things. Stanzas six and seven speak hauntingly of monuments of man's past habitations jutting through the waves, reminding later generations of how their predecessors perished in the watery depths. The church spire, graphically compared to a human finger reaching up out of the sandy shallows, warns posterity that it, too, will be engulfed inescapably. The final two stanzas appropriately conclude with the death knell from the belfry of the steeple and the eerie chant of a lonely cantor singing the first line of a funeral hymn by the eighteenth-century poet Friedrich Gottlieb Klopstock:

> Begrabt den Leib in seine Gruft.
> (This body in the grave we lay.)

Significantly, this last line deliberately omits Klopstock's subsequent exultant antiphonal song of conquest over death, widely sung in Groth's time in the churches of northern Germany and Denmark. Here is the opening stanza of Klopstock's hymn:

> Begrabt den Leib in seine Gruft,
> Bis ihm des Richters Stimme ruft!
> Wir säen ihn; einst blüht er auf,
> Und steigt verklärt zu Gott hinauf![407]

> (This body in the grave we lay
> There to await that solemn Day!
> When God Himself shall bid it rise
> To mount triumphant to the skies!)
> *Translated by William M. Czamanske*[408]

In Groth's poem this possibility of an afterlife is not raised; nothing remains but the finality of death.

As with Storm's "Meeresstrand," the rich melody orchestrates the tone of the narrative and stirs the emotions, forcing the listener to linger on the tormented meditation on the ephemerality of life. The sound of the Low German folk-speech helps the somber eschatological theme penetrate the ear as a primal cry. The short lines and stanzas suggest natural lamentation, as if advancing dread were interrupted by groans and sighs. The regular iambic beat at once echoes the steady tolling of funeral bells and

---

[407] *Klopstocks sämmtliche Werke*, VII (Leipzig: Göschen, 1823), 210.

[408] From *The Lutheran Hymnal* (St. Louis: Concordia, 1941), 596.

thrusts the narrative forward, emphasizing time's quick passage. The combination of forward movement and interruptive pause, the alternation of short and long stresses, and the consistency of rhymed couplet produce a sense of duality, underscoring the conviction that death unshakably follows life. The unfolding of this agonizing realization cuts to the heart. Not statically but in the constant confrontation of image and meter, the interlocked apparitions of life and death meet in furious but hopeless dialogue. A crescendo of suspense and anxiety overtakes the mortal toward the end of the poem, as the eerie voices from beyond come on stage, announced by the ominously repeated Low German adverb of inexorable time: *Denn* (then).

The final two stanzas abruptly depart from visual imagery, insistently appealing to auditory stimuli. (Life is no longer visible above the waves.) This prepares the ear for the funeral service after the completion of life's cycle, the hymn of death deprived of Klopstock's comforting hope of resurrection.

Life has always been indifferent and fleeting, the ballad reminds us. It was so centuries ago, before the sea swallowed old Büsum; it is so now, as the foam lurks insidiously beyond the rampart of the sandy shallows; and it will be so always.

7. Experimenting with the diary novel: Wilhelm Raabe

Die Chronik der Sperlingsgasse

Wilhelm Raabe (1831–1910), now known for the "experimental attitude" he brought to the craft of narrative,[409] considerably broadened the reach of *Poetischer Realismus* by experimenting with diary fiction. In October 1856 he published the diary novel *Die Chronik der Sperlingsgasse* (The Chronicle of Sparrow Lane). Julian Schmidt rushed to bring it to the attention of the *Grenzboten*'s subscribers.[410] The German reading public of

---

[409] No one has stated this more incisively than Barker Fairley, *Selected Essays on German Literature*, ed. R. Symington (New York: Lang, 1984), 262.

[410] *Die Grenzboten*, 1856, IV, 399. Hermann Kinder has pointed out that Raabe was not aware that the *Grenzboten* had advertised his novel; there was no reason, therefore, for Raabe to have been upset about any lack of recognition on the pages of this critical forum for Poetic Realism. See Kinder, *Poesie als Synthese* (Frankfurt am Main: Athenäum, 1973), 162. Presumably, Raabe had Schmidt's co-editor Freytag in mind when he was upset with the *Grenzboten*. Freytag had indeed snubbed Raabe, but Schmidt had not. This is another

the nineteenth century accepted it enthusiastically. By 1910, the year of Raabe's death, seventy editions had appeared. This hearty reception resembles the way the Danes took to Blicher's diary novel *En Landsbydegns Dagbog*, when *Poetisk Realisme* stood at its zenith in Denmark. During their lifetimes each of these authors' diary novels achieved popular successes never equalled by the rest of their prose fiction.

Did Blicher's early landmark of Poetic Realism inspire Raabe to follow in his Danish forbear's footsteps? He nowhere admits to a dependence on Blicher's diary novel, but he may have been influenced by it. He never acknowledged the debt his subsequent novel *Der Hungerpastor* owed to Gustav Freytag's *Soll und Haben*, yet we know he drew heavily from it.[411]

Surely the genre of diary fiction had entered Raabe's consciousness from somewhere, and Blicher's highly successful diary novel seems a likely source, certainly a more probable source than the second- or third-rate novels of this genre available at the time to a North German reader like Raabe.[412] It is easy, too, to imagine how he could have read Blicher's diary novel. From 1849 to 1853 he had served as an apprentice in a large bookshop in Magdeburg. On the shelves of German bookstores at the time one found the inexpensive volumes of world literature in translation that were published by J. A. Diezmann (1805–1869) in his series *Die belletristische Welt* (The Belletristic World). Much like the Reclam series in modern Germany, these thrifty productions sold easily, so German bookstores universally stocked them. The series included six small volumes of Blicher's novellas, added in 1849. Jeffrey Sammons suggests that Raabe probably took more interest in reading the books of the Magdeburg bookshop than in selling them.[413] Doubtless he continued his reading every evening in his lonely bachelor room after the shop had closed. Given his voracious ap-

example of how greatly the critical opinions of the journal's poorly matched co-editors diverged. See the earlier section "Ludwig not Freytag."

[411] Jeffrey L. Sammons, *Wilhelm Raabe, The Fiction of the Alternative Community* (Princeton: University Press, 1987), 82, 353. This book offers the best introduction to Raabe. See this author's review in *Colloquia Germanica* 23 (1990): 83-85. Other remarkable introductions are by 1) Horst Denkler, *Wilhelm Raabe, Legende — Leben — Literatur* (Tübingen: Niemeyer, 1989); 2) Horst Daemmrich, *Wilhelm Raabe* (Boston: Twayne, 1981); 3) Barker Fairley, *Wilhelm Raabe, An Introduction to his Novels* (Oxford: Clarendon, 1961).

[412] Of the fourteen German diary novels published in the decade prior to the year Raabe began writing *Die Chronik der Sperlingsgasse* (see the list in Lorna Martens, *The Diary Novel* [Cambridge, England: University Press, 1985], 288-89), only one, Adalbert Stifter's *Feldblumen*, could possess any claim to being first-rate. But it was published in a journal in central Hungary, and, as we know from the reception of Franz Grillparzer's *Der arme Spielmann*, that journal did not circulate north of the Austro-Hungarian frontier.

[413] Sammons, 10.

petite for belles lettres, he could hardly have avoided devouring the Blicher novellas he was supposed to sell.

In 1854, only a year after completing his apprenticeship, Raabe moved from Magdeburg to Berlin. He soon began writing his own successor-volume to Blicher's diary novella. Blicher had worked against the backdrop of impoverished, post-Napoleonic-wars' Denmark; Raabe now worked against poverty-stricken, post-1848-wars' Germany. Both works derive their basic energies from the still-smoldering aftereffects of national catastrophe.

When Raabe arrived in Berlin in 1854, tangible reminders of the unsettling events of 1848 were still evident everywhere: the economy had been disrupted, making food scarce, prices high, and unemployment rampant. The destruction wrought by the revolutions had to be paid for: taxes became crippling, and bankruptcies occurred daily. Memories of the terror on the streets of Berlin — of bloody engagements, of the wounded and the dead — were still very much on everyone's mind and lips. Everywhere appeared bedraggled and hungry people. A pall of defeat, frustration, and despair hung over the whole city, and all of Germany. Newspapers gave daily notice of the sad exodus of hapless Germans for greener pastures in the United States, the southern provinces of Brazil, and even the coastal regions of Algeria. Hundreds of thousands fled to escape the poverty brought on by political instability. Beginning in 1848 emigration from German-speaking lands soared exponentially. But the year 1854, when Raabe commenced writing *Die Chronik der Sperlingsgasse*, turned out to be the worst of all. The emigrations of that peak year surpassed every previous exodus of Germans seeking to escape pauperism.[414]

Such was the desperate state of affairs in Germany when Raabe began to compose this novel. Doubtless what he saw greatly moved him, for he addressed himself first to the terrible conditions prevailing in Germany. In the opening lines of the novel we read of scarcity and dearth, of need, sickness, and sorrow: "It is a bad age indeed! Laughter has become dear.... In the distance roll the dark and bloody thunderclouds of war, while, closer-by, disease, hunger, and misery have laid their gloomy veil over the entire area round about...." Realistic allusions of this sort are ba-

---

[414] Helmut Richter, "Die Chronik der Sperlingsgasse," in *Raabe in neuer Sicht*, ed. H. Helmers (Stuttgart: Kohlhammer, 1968), 314. The fullest treatment of this novel is by Charlotte L. Goedsche, *Narrative Structure in Wilhelm Raabe's "Die Chronik der Sperlingsgasse"* (New York: Lang, 1989). Other valuable analyses include 1) William P. Hanson, "Raabes erste Chronik" and 2) Jürgen Brand, "Strukturelle Symmetrien in Raabes 'Die Chronik der Sperlingsgasse,'" both in *Jahrbuch der Raabe-Gesellschaft* (1983): 33-58; 3) Walter Dietze, "Zeitstimmung und Zeitkritik in Wilhelm Raabes 'Chronik der Sperlingsgasse,'" *Monatshefte* 61 (1969): 337-46; 4) Fairley, *Wilhelm Raabe*, 182-95.

sic to the novel's structure. Emigrants fleeing to the United States and elsewhere appear again and again, and the narrator gives clearly their reasons for escape:

> No longer is it the old German sense of adventure and wanderlust which drives people away from hearth and home, cities and countryside, which tears the charcoal burner away from his forest, and the miner away from his dark shaft, which pulls the shepherd down from his Alpine meadows, and which lets them all depart together for the Far West: distress, misery, and oppression are now the things which scourge our citizens and which force them to leave their homeland, with bleeding hearts.

The narrator speaks with the seasoned authority of a sad observer of contemporary reality; the drama of 1848 and, more particularly, its tragic aftereffects as felt in 1854 have become central.

But if the narrator is seeking truth about the reality of his "age of revolution" (as we read on the novel's last page), it seems peculiar that this commentary on the times is confided to the reader by means of a fabricated diary. The narrator pretends he is a diarist, offering reality in the fictional garb of a quotidian record.

On the one hand, the narrator appears to be trying hard to give a scrupulously authentic picture of the economic reality of the day. A diary does not recall a reality that has become blurred, partially forgotten, or distorted by the quirks of a fallible memory; nor is it a belated attempt at self-justification, a mutation of the past, a malicious attempt to remold history to bolster and exalt the recorder's ego. Instead, it gives the faithful description of a specific event on the very day it occurred, committing the moment's happenings to paper in their immediacy, before they become distorted or deliberately truncated and manipulated in the light of later experiences. Written ostensibly for the diarist's eyes alone, the account remains unvarnished by any attempt to make the recorder look better than he was.

But if the narrator's resorting to diary exhibits a strong concern for fidelity to reality, if he seems most anxious to convince the reader that he depicts reality and not fiction — "I am not writing a novel," he states in his first entry — it is strange that the diary form of this novel appears more affected than genuine. The diarist, we quickly notice, only pretends to record life on a diurnal basis; actually, he skips over many days and capriciously manipulates his entries. The absence of regular day-by-day notations renders the diary form merely perfunctory, clearly open to the charge of fictionalization. The narrator reveals himself as too great a master of the art of omission to convince us that he is confiding the true contents of his personal diary. Despite his pretense at setting forth his daily life, convincing factual and homely details about family, love life, daily meals, and even daily work remain conspicuously undisclosed. New Year's Eve, for instance, comes and goes, yet the diarist records nothing of what he experienced. The same holds true for the Easter holidays, likewise omitted. The intimate revelations of the narrator's passions seem lacking: hardly any candid expressions, no honest record of personal obsessions, of successes or failures, no genuine echo of scorn or complaint. For a personal diary, there is an altogether strange omission of inner life, no sweet nothings, no vapid but realistic notes such as "nothing important happened today." In short, we scarcely perceive a human being with a heart that beats and blood that flows.

In addition to these gaps, certain entries strain the bounds of probability. Take for example the story of the actress who must leave the bedside of her dying child for the theater so that the show may go on; when the performance is over, she rushes home to witness the child's death just as she arrives. It is scarcely credible that the child waits to die until the very moment of the mother's return. Furthermore, mundane details are curiously fabricated. For instance, the date given in the diary for the celebration of the queen's birthday is February 28. Readers in Prussia at the time would have known that the birthday of Queen Consort Elisabeth fell on November 13. They must have smiled at Raabe's deliberate distortion of fact.

Thus, the diary form of this novel works as an index of extraordinary fidelity to reality in the revolutionary age, yet finds itself transformed into all-too-obvious fiction. Reality is rendered fully into art; fiction is made to seem real. The reader asks: is *Die Chronik der Sperlingsgasse* actually fiction, or does the narrator's disclaimer (that he is not writing a novel) hold true? Should Raabe's reader react to this diary as if it were a real record or a contrived fictional statement? The margin between fact and fabrication has become tenuous indeed; and that is surely the most disquieting truth about life that this diary — this novel — conveys.

When Raabe published *Die Chronik der Sperlingsgasse*, he did not have his real name printed on the title page but rather a fictitious author's: Jacob Corvinus. Why did Raabe use a pseudonym? He had no good reason, as far as we know, for concealing his true identity. Perhaps just as this novel's diary form points to the perplexity of differentiating between the real and the imaginary, so, too, the fictionalization of the author himself makes it more difficult for the reader to distinguish between fact and fabrication.

Moving away from *Poetischer Realismus*

Raabe was still a young man when he published *Die Chronik der Sperlingsgasse*, only twenty-five years old. His youth, his agile mind, and, doubtless, the experience of reading a great variety of novels at the bookshop in Magdeburg all combined to make him eager to experiment with other forms of narrative. This led him to burst his ties to Poetic Realism. If Raabe's unusually fertile imagination had matured further within the frame of *Poetischer Realismus*, we might now have a novel of Poetic Realism of artistic caliber even higher than Keller's *Der grüne Heinrich*.

This was not to be. Raabe's itch to experiment made him try a variety of shorter forms of prose fiction next. In one of the most famous of these experiments, the novella *Die schwarze Galeere* (The Black Galley, 1860), he gives an absorbing picture of the drama between the Spaniards and Netherlanders in the sixteenth century. Dull history comes alive, but Raabe seems so bent on experimenting with the technique of colorful and entertaining scene-painting that the reality he describes is never transfigured into a poetic message.

Raabe departed further from Poetic Realism in 1862–1863 with a novel of morals, *Der Hungerpastor* (The Hunger Pastor). There he completely sacrifices the real to the ideal. He traces and accentuates the progress of a good boy with a parallel bad boy, subordinating everything in the novel to this bipolar structure. Such moralizing could have proven fatal in the hands of a lesser novelist. Not so with Raabe. Yet, if he succeeded with *Der Hungerpastor* in captivating generations of readers, it was not because of the novel's "poetic" or "realistic" qualities,[415] but because he had learned how to manipulate plot and characters effectively to suit the ethical prepossessions of a large number of readers.

Such easy victory could not, however, satisfy a writer of Raabe's abilities for long. *Der Hungerpastor* (and two succor novels in a similar vein), he wrote to his publisher, had given him "little happiness."[416] In the 1870s, and until the end of his life, his fondness for experiment pushed him to try another style of novel-writing. The school of form critics gathered around Paul Böckmann (1899-1987) at Heidelberg in the 1950s

---

[415] See the apt comment by Robert C. Holub in *Reflections of Realism*, 199: "From the perspective of 'poetry' and 'realism' delineated in *Der Hungerpastor*, the novel itself is impossible."

[416] Wilhelm Raabe, *Sämtliche Werke*, ed. K. Hoppe et al., VIII (Freiburg i.B.: Klemm, 1952), 406.

pinpointed this form, best described as "Polyperspectivism."[417] Central for this final style of Raabe's novel-writing is, as Böckmann's pupil Christa Hebbel says, "a reflexive and at the same time subjective distancing from mere event.... It is not the narrated occurrences that form the continuum of the narrative context, but the consciousness of the narrator."[418] This inward polyperspective style made the late Raabe, as Walter Killy adds, "decidedly an anti-realist."[419] And, of course, it helped bring about the dissolution of Poetic Realism in Germany. Tellingly, Eberhard Geisler has described this in his analysis of one of Raabe's last novels: "The Dissolution of Poetic Realism in Wilhelm Raabe's *Akten des Vogelsangs*."[420]

8. Ringing down the curtain: Theodor Fontane

Fontane's calling to *Poetischer Realismus*

In a blaze of glory, the Prussian writer Theodor Fontane (1819–1898) finally rang down the curtain on Poetic Realism. Yet, this occurred only after he had first contributed significantly to the movement.[421]

His calling to *Poetischer Realismus* was sparked by his experiences in the 1848 uprisings. During the worst fighting on the streets of Berlin, in

---

[417] The two outstanding studies on Raabe which emerged from this school of form criticism (and which sought to debunk the then prevailing opinion that *Der Hungerpastor* was the author's best novel) were 1) the Ph.D. dissertation by Christa Hebbel, "Die Funktion der Erzähler- und Figurenperspektiven in Wilhelm Raabes Ich-Erzählungen," 1960; and 2) the *Habilitationsschrift* by Wolfgang Preisendanz, *Humor als dichterische Einbildungskraft,* 2nd ed. (Munich: Fink, 1976).

[418] Christa Hebbel, 127, 139. English translation by Jeffrey L. Sammons, *Wilhelm Raabe,* 172.

[419] Walter Killy, "Geschichte gegen Geschichte: 'Das Odfeld,'" in *Raabe in neuer Sicht,* 234.

[420] Eberhard Geisler, "Abschied vom Herzensmuseum, Die Auflösung des Poetischen Realismus in Wilhelm Raabes *Akten des Vogelsangs*," in *Wilhelm Raabe, Studien zu seinem Leben und Werk,* eds. L. A. Lensing & H. W. Peter (Braunschweig: pp-Verlag, 1981), 365-80.

[421] The literature on Fontane is vast and growing by leaps and bounds. An indispensable, concise introduction to his life and work is: Charlotte Jolles, *Theodor Fontane,* 4th ed. (Stuttgart: Metzler, 1993). The fullest biography is by Hans-Heinrich Reuter, *Fontane,* 2 vols. (Munich: Nymphenburg, 1968). Excellent background information is contained in Gerhard Friedrich, *Fontanes preußische Welt* (Herford: Mittler, 1988). The most recent general study in English is by William L. Zwiebel, *Theodor Fontane* (New York: Twayne, 1992).

March 1848, he had helped man the barricades and been an eyewitness to much of the death and destruction. These shattering experiences resembled those of his close contemporaries Keller (b. 1819), Groth (b. 1819), and Storm (b. 1817). Later, as a war correspondent for the Prussian press, he also saw the ghastly and sobering results of the insurrections in Schleswig-Holstein against the crown of Denmark.

Realism in art, he thought, was what the new age of revolution demanded, but this realism, he said, needed a poetic power which could transfigure "naked prosaic realism" into a meaningful message.[422] He grew intrigued by the verse of poets who had been baptized by fire in the revolutions. He gave their poetry conspicuous attention in the four editions of the anthology he compiled: *Deutsches Dichteralbum* (1852–1858). Soon, too, he began composing his own Poetic Realist verse. His first volume of poetry, *Gedichte* (Poems), appeared in 1851, and Storm himself commended it in a review in a prominent journal of the day.[423] At the conclusion of the review, Storm offered that perhaps the best from Fontane's pen was yet to come.

Storm was right. But probably it would not have come if Fontane had not then entered into a rewarding association with an unusual group of highly civilized men who shared his shock at the horrors of the 1848 revolutions. Modern criticism has downplayed the import of the Berlin writers' club *Tunnel über der Spree* (Tunnel over the Spree) for Fontane's literary vocation, brushing aside his membership as incidental, irrelevant, indeed even detrimental, to his development. In particular, Fontane's chief modern biographer, Hans-Heinrich Reuter (1923–1978), disparaged this club.[424] Its members, in his opinion, were hardly more than aesthetic snobs governed by rigid rules like those in the sterile musical contests in Richard Wagner's opera *Die Meistersinger*. This unfortunate misjudgment of the club and its members needs correction. In his affiliation with this congenial company, Fontane reaped the benefit of an invaluable literary apprenticeship. Nowhere could the literary schooling of the *Tunnel über der Spree* be matched, except perhaps in the congregation of literati around Hans Christian Andersen in Copenhagen.

Attendance at this club in the early 1850s must have been particularly rewarding. The club at that time brought together some of the best liter-

---

[422] Theodor Fontane, "Unsere lyrische und epische Poesie seit 1848," in *Aufsätze zur Literatur*, ed. K. Schreinert (Munich: Nymphenburg, 1963), 7-33, esp. 8.

[423] Theodor Storm, "Theodor Fontane," now conveniently reprinted in Storm, *Sämtliche Werke*, eds. K. E. Laage & D. Lohmeier, IV (Frankfurt am Main: Deutscher Klassiker Verlag, 1988), 358-67.

[424] Reuter, *Fontane*, I, 170-84.

ary minds in the city (including Storm, who was living then in Potsdam). They met once a week for several hours in the smoke-filled room of a tavern directly behind St. Hedwig's Cathedral, applying their collective intelligence to a literature shipwrecked by revolution. Fontane could present a new specimen of poetry to the group and observe them nodding approval or shaking heads over blunders. Or he could hear a fellow-author read a new poem, take part in the heated but incisive debate, and — after replenishing his glass with cooling beer — calmly vote his uninhibited acceptance or rejection. Fontane learned to orchestrate words, switch details, regulate the overall balance, and avoid irrelevant sallies, all the while adding realistic credibility and poetic meaning to what he wrote. For this circle of fastidious minds, according to its statutes, not only rejected everything that did not correspond to reality but also spurned any exercise in realism that did not have superimposed upon it a poetic "transfiguration" of that reality.[425] Could any apprentice in Poetic Realism have wanted anything more?

"Archibald Douglas"

The finest product of this extraordinary schooling is Fontane's ballad "Archibald Douglas," which he recited before a spellbound audience of *Tunnel*-members on December 3, 1854. The reception accorded to this ballad in the 140 years since its birth confirms its importance. Few anthologies of German poetry have failed to include it. Indeed, no other poem by Fontane before or after has been nearly so persistent.

> "Ich hab' es getragen sieben Jahr
> Und ich kann es nicht tragen mehr,
> Wo immer die Welt am schönsten war,
> Da war sie öd' und leer.
>
> Ich will hintreten vor sein Gesicht
> In dieser Knechtsgestalt,
> Er kann meine Bitte versagen nicht,
> Ich bin ja worden alt.
>
> Und trüg' er noch den alten Groll,
> Frisch wie am ersten Tag,
> So komme, was da kommen soll,

---

[425] Joachim Krueger, "Der Tunnel über der Spree und sein Einfluß auf Theodor Fontane," *Fontane Blätter* 4 (1978): 222.

Und komme, was da mag."

Graf Douglas spricht's. Am Weg ein Stein
Lud ihn zu harter Ruh,
Er sah in Wald und Feld hinein,
Die Augen fielen ihm zu.

Er trug einen Harnisch, rostig und schwer,
Darüber ein Pilgerkleid —
Da horch, vom Waldrand scholl es her.
Wie von Hörnern und Jagdgeleit.

Und Kies und Staub aufwirbelte dicht,
Her jagte Meut' und Mann,
Un ehe der Graf sich aufgericht't,
Waren Roß und Reiter heran.

König Jakob saß auf hohem Roß,
Graf Douglas grüßte tief,
Dem König das Blut in die Wange schoß,
Der Douglas aber rief:

"König Jakob, schaue mich gnädig an
Und höre mich in Geduld,
Was meine Brüder dir angetan,
Es war nicht meine Schuld.

Denk nicht an den alten Douglas-Neid,
Der trotzig dich bekriegt,
Denk lieber an deine Kinderzeit,
Wo ich dich auf den Knien gewiegt.

Denk lieber zurück an Stirling-Schloß,
Wo ich Spielzeug dir geschnitzt,
Dich gehoben auf deines Vaters Roß
Und Pfeile dir zugespitzt.

Denk lieber zurück an Linlithgow,
An den See und den Vogelherd,
Wo ich dich fischen und jagen froh
Und schwimmen und springen gelehrt.

O denk an alles, was einsten war,
Und sänftige deinen Sinn,
Ich hab' es gebüßet sieben Jahr,
Daß ich ein Douglas bin."

"Ich seh' dich nicht, Graf Archibald,
Ich hör' deine Stimme nicht,
Mir ist, als ob ein Rauschen im Wald
Von alten Zeiten spricht.

Mir klingt das Rauschen süß und traut,
Ich lausch' ihm immer noch,
Dazwischen aber klingt es laut:
Er ist ein Douglas doch.

Ich seh' dich nicht, ich höre dich nicht,
Das ist alles, was ich kann,
Ein Douglas vor meinem Angesicht
Wär' ein verlorener Mann."

König Jakob gab seinem Roß den Sporn,
Bergan ging jetzt sein Ritt,
Graf Douglas faßte den Zügel vorn
Und hielt mit dem Könige Schritt.

Der Weg war steil, und die Sonne stach,
Und sein Panzerhemd war schwer,
Doch ob er schier zusammenbrach,
Er lief doch nebenher.

"König Jakob, ich war dein Seneschall,
Ich will es nicht fürder sein,
Ich will nur warten dein Roß im Stall
Und ihm schütten die Körner ein.

Ich will ihm selber machen die Streu
Und es tränken mit eig'ner Hand,
Nur laß mich atmen wieder aufs neu
Die Luft im Vaterland.

Und willst du nicht, so hab' einen Mut,
Und ich will es danken dir,

Und zieh dein Schwert und triff mich gut
Und laß mich sterben hier."

König Jakob sprang herab vom Pferd,
Hell leuchtete sein Gesicht,
Aus der Scheide zog er sein breites Schwert,
Aber fallen ließ er es nicht.

"Nimm's hin, nimm's hin und trag' es neu
Und bewache mir meine Ruh',
Der ist in tiefster Seele treu,
Wer die Heimat liebt wie du.

Zu Roß, wir reiten nach Linlithgow,
Und du reitest an meiner Seit',
Da wollen wir fischen und jagen froh,
Als wie in alter Zeit."[426]

("The life I have borne for seven years,
I can no longer bear,
Wherever the world most fair appears,
Tis bleak and empty there.

To face him as I am is best,
A menial to behold,
He cannot in fairness refuse my request,
For I have grown so old.

And should his grudge and his distrust
Be fresh as they were the first day,
Then happen will, what happen must,
Let happen whatever may."

Thus spoke Lord Douglas. A stone by the way
Invited to hard repose,
He looked out to where field and forest lay,
And his eyes began to close.

His heavy, rusty mail was worn,
Beneath a pilgrim's gown —

---

[426] Text taken from Fontane, *Sämtliche Werke*, XX, 120-23.

But hark! from the wood the sound of the horn
And of huntsmen came floating down.

And chasing along came man and hound
That gravel and dust rose high,
And ere the lord got up from the ground,
The horse and its rider were nigh.

King James, on his stallion proud, stopped dead.
Lord Douglas humbly bowed;
A blush the King's cheeks overspread,
But the Douglas called out aloud:

"King James, oh look on me graciously,
With patience thine ear incline!
Whatever my brothers have done to thee,
The fault has not been mine.

Forget the Douglas' jealous ways,
That they fought thee stubbornly,
But rather remember thy childhood days,
When I rocked thee on my knee.

Recall the Castle of Stirling so fair,
Where I carved for thee many a toy,
Where I lifted thee up on thy father's mare,
And sharpened thy darts when a boy.

The memories of Linlithgow revive,
Of its lake and its fowling place,
Where I taught thee how to swim and dive,
How to fish and to follow the chase.

Oh, think of all that once has been,
Let soften thy heart and relent,
By seven weary years and lean,
I atoned for my Douglas descent."

"I do not see thee, Lord Archibald,
I do not hear thy voice,
But a rustling in the wood recalled
The times when I could rejoice.

A rustling, sweetly familiar,
I listen to it yet,
But in between a dissonant bar,
A Douglas he is! don't forget!

I see thee not, I hear thee not,
That is all I can do for thee.
A Douglas, stood he in this spot,
A man undone would be."

King James thereon set spurs to his horse,
The ride went uphill to the crest,
Lord Douglas gripped the reins with force,
And kept with the king abreast.

The way was steep and hot the day,
And heavily weighed the mail,
Yet though his strength gave almost way,
He ran by the side of the trail.

"To be Master of the Horse again,
My King, I have no call,
But let me pour for thy mount the grain,
And groom him in his stall.

His litter I myself shall strew,
And his bucket to him I shall hand,
But only let me breathe anew
The air in my fatherland.

Yet wilt thou not, then pity discard,
I shall deem it an act of grace,
And draw thy sword and hit me hard
And let me die in this place."

King James he vaulted down from his steed,
His face with joy aglow,
His broadsword he unsheathed indeed,
But he never struck the blow.

"Oh take it, take it into thy trust,

And guard my slumbers anew!
Who loves his homeland the way thou dost,
In his deepest soul he is true.

On horseback I go to Linlithgow with thee,
Thou ridest beside me, nigh,
And there we shall fish and hunt with glee
As we did in days gone by.")

Translated by Helen Kurz Roberts[427]

The starting point for discovering the place this ballad holds in Poetic Realism is the (apparently) actual story of a Scottish king, James V, and a member of a dissenting clan who became brothers in peace and love after having opposed each other in strife and hatred.[428] Two heroes emerge: the one a mighty king who humbles himself to halt a destructive feud, the other a lonely subject whose human qualities give him the strength to tame his sovereign's anger. The story is made to look thoroughly authentic with its appeal to Scottish history and the form of direct discourse it employs. Yet, it also has a ring of distinct artificiality, for the spurious antiquarian framework, the quaintness of remote medieval legend, intrudes on the audience's consciousness, as much as does the narrative of the two starkly delineated characters. The poeticizing of the realistic chronicle comes further to the fore when we notice the superabundance of poetic devices, such as interchanging tetrameter and trimeter stress patterns, alternating rhyme schemes, and varying incantations of iambic and anapestic meter. Obvious balladic rhythm and a sense of factual realism compete for attention. We are forced to wonder: is this a real story from the pages of history or is this imaginatively wrought poetry? On reflection, we realize that we have a blending of authenticity and artificiality, and that this has occurred within the poetic mould of sophisticated balladry.

For the *Tunnel*-audience to which the ballad was addressed, however, it must have also possessed another, realistic dimension. In the tavern in downtown Berlin where the thoughtful men assembled in 1854, the cruel reminders of the events of 1848 were at least as much on their minds and lips as on Raabe's when he commenced writing (in the same year and in

---

[427] From *A Treasury of German Ballads* (New York: Ungar, 1964), 269-75. Reprinted by permission.

[428] Perceptive interpretations of this ballad include 1) W. D. Williams, "Theodor Fontane: 'Archibald Douglas,'" in *Wege zum Gedicht*, eds. R. Hirschenauer & A. Weber, II (Munich: Schnell & Steiner, 1964), 367-76; and 2) Udo Wasmer, "Archibald Douglas," in *Die deutsche Ballade*, ed. K. Bräutigam et al., 4th ed. (Frankfurt am Main: Diesterweg, 1969), 99-107.

the same city) *Die Chronik der Sperlingsgasse*. The *Tunnel*-members were sitting, after all, in an inn located only a few city blocks from the royal palace, in front of which in March 1848 the brutal clash between royal power and the rights of the individual citizen had taken place. Fontane throws the shadow of this contemporary reality across the enchanting verses of his quaint ballad. For him and his *Tunnel*-audience the feudal King James V and the simple, reasoning Scottish clansman were fictionally disguised counterparts of Prussia's autocratic Frederick William IV and the ordinary citizen of Berlin who, in March 1848, had dared to speak out in favor of human rights over arbitrary dynastic rule. As King James's heart had melted in compassion at the pleadings of the clansman, so Frederick William IV in 1848 had been brought to tears and had given in to the implorings of his subjects. Fontane and the *Tunnel*-audience listening to "Archibald Douglas" remembered all too well their sovereign's famed relenting proclamation *An Meine Lieben Berliner* (To My Dear Berliners), in which he extended the hand of reconciliation to those in revolt against him: "Your loving Queen and sincerely true Mother and Friend, who lies prostrate with pain and grief, joins with mine her heartfelt and tearful supplications."[429] The contest between sovereign power and the freedom of the individual, hence, was as much a part of the contextual setting in which Fontane presented the ballad as it was in the feigned Scottish medieval milieu. For us, Fontane's excited participation in the lives of Berlin's populace in the years immediately following 1848 seems to have commingled with colorful poetic artifice.

Encouraged by the stunning success of "Archibald Douglas," Fontane tried his hand at Poetic Realist balladry again and again throughout his life. Each time the poetic rhythm of balladry is so gently compounded with the realism of political or current events that it has always proven difficult to determine, as Manfred Fleischer has shown in regard to "John Maynard" (1886), how and where truth and fiction converge or diverge.[430] The only thing perplexed readers seem to be constantly sure of is the slippery line between fact and fabrication.

---

[429] Raymond Postgate, *Story of a Year: 1848* (New York: Oxford University Press, 1956), 90.

[430] See the (seldom cited) historical account by Manfred Fleischer, "John Maynard — Dichtung und Wahrheit," *Zeitschrift für Religions- und Geistesgeschichte* 16 (1964): 168-73.

"Ausgang"

Fontane also firmly acknowledged the association of his poetry with the lyric of Poetic Realism when composing verse outside the ballad genre. This is so, and especially noticeable, in "Ausgang" (Exit, 1888), a compelling and curiously neglected poem in the extensive body of Fontane criticism:

> Immer enger, leise, leise,
> Ziehen sich die Lebenskreise,
> Schwindet hin, was prahlt und prunkt,
> Schwindet Hoffen, Hassen, Lieben,
> Und ist nichts in Sicht geblieben
> Als der letzte dunkle Punkt.[431]
>
> (Now life's circles gently, lightly,
> Dwindle ever, draw in tightly,
> Vanish all display and show,
> Vanish hoping, hating, loving;
> And there stays in view awaiting
> The dark point at last to know.)
> *Translated by C. Fillingham Coxwell,*
> *revised by C. A. Bernd*[432]

The poem lies squarely in the lyric tradition of Storm, Keller, Meyer, and Groth. It feeds on that tradition and confirms and strengthens it. It offers another chilling meditation on the ephemerality of life: human transience, the specter of impending death, again looms darkly on the poetic horizon. Life is captured in a single sentence, a single stanza. In the background, in the steady stream of trochaic beats, the incessant march of time moves unerringly to the inevitable terminus, to that dark point of final destiny where life irrevocably ends. The brevity of these verses shadows the duration of man's stay on earth. The harrowing truth of the ever-narrowing circles appears here as ruthless as it is compactly stated. Yet, for all its uncompromising realism, this composition is no less poetic: its clear, plaintive sincerity calmly grips our emotions, succinctly reminding us of our own sure mortality.

---

[431] Text taken from Fontane, *Sämtliche Werke*, II, 40.

[432] The unrevised parts of this translation are reprinted, by permission, from C. Fillingham Coxwell, *German Poetry translated into English in the Original Metres* (London: Daniel, 1938), 180.

Was Fontane coming to terms with his life's expected end when he wrote this poem, approaching the age of seventy? If so, he did it by unflinchingly acquiescing to the inevitable. Doubtless, his longstanding affiliation with the French Reformed Church in Berlin had given him an awareness of the psalmist's prophecy, as stated in the Geneva Bible, Psalm 90.10: "La durée de notre vie est de soixante et dix ans" (The duration of our life is seventy years). Fontane now appears to be facing the reality of death much the same way as Meyer in "Der römische Brunnen": with a cold poetic fatalism. We are not surprised: he shared with the Swiss poet the same French Calvinistic heritage.

Transforming *Poetischer Realismus* into social realism

Distinguished as Fontane's contributions to the lyric of Poetic Realism were, his verse alone did not bring him enduring fame. He also produced a dazzling array of novels that overshadowed his accomplishments as a lyricist. But these novels added a social, an alien dimension to Poetic Realism, thus transforming it.

The itch to write these novels had been sparked by Fontane's trips to England. No other German writer before or since had acquired a deeper knowledge of the whole range of British life and letters than he. He spent nearly four years in Britain. Up and down the countryside he went, assessing Britain's assets and liabilities, virtues and foibles for the Prussian press. His British experience set him apart from all the other Poetic Realists. Dickens — never known to be a Poetic Realist — became for him the "*sans pareil* of all living authors."[433]

Influenced by this intense exposure to British culture and the English novel, Fontane introduced to the German literary scene the novel of social forces; man in relation to society became an important concern of his writing. What Fontane then offered German readers was similar to what Dickens had offered British readers: fictional portraits of human beings interlocked in an existing social order and acting in response to the dictates of social custom.[434] Up to that time German fiction, as Thomas Mann has astutely observed, knew and wanted to know nothing of the sociologi-

---

[433] Fontane, *Sämtliche Werke*, V, 206.

[434] For the fullest treatment of this subject see: Walter Müller-Seidel, *Theodor Fontane, Soziale Romankunst in Deutschland* (Stuttgart: Metzler, 1975).

cal.[435] "God forbid," Julian Schmidt once said, "that the novel should attempt to solve social questions."[436]

Unwiederbringlich

Fontane's most incisive move toward a new novel of social awareness came with *Unwiederbringlich* (Beyond Recall) in 1891. Intentionally, we know, the author transferred the setting of that novel away from Germany to Denmark, where Poetic Realism had first come on stage.[437] In the same place Fontane now lets the curtain fall.

The novel begins in the Dano-German duchy of Schleswig, then moves to Copenhagen and the adjacent Danish landscape; on the concluding pages it returns again to Schleswig. Particularly conspicuous is the great abundance of references to the maze of court intrigues attending the Danish king who reigned from 1848 to 1863: the amorous, much-married, much-divorced, gluttonous Frederick VII. This notorious ruler, one of the most colorful monarchs in modern European history, was an object of fascination to his contemporaries. Never before in Denmark's long history had a reigning sovereign's actions provoked such heated discussions in official government circles in so many nations.

The story unfolds against this background of Danish sociopolitical entanglements,[438] as crucial to understanding the novel as the date the author

---

[435] Mann, *Essays of Three Decades*, 370.

[436] Schmidt, *Bilder aus dem geistigen Leben unserer Zeit*, I (Leipzig: Duncker & Humblot, 1871), 411.

[437] Critics have treated the importance of Denmark and Danish letters for Fontane's oeuvre all too gingerly and even erroneously. George C. Schoolfield, long ago, pointed this out. See his comment in "Scandinavian-German Literary Relations," *Yearbook of Comparative and General Literature* 15 (1966): 28. Not too much has changed since Schoolfield made that observation. Nevertheless, a new beginning has been made as a result of the efforts of Sven-Aage Jørgensen. See the afterword in his edition of *Unwiederbringlich* (Stuttgart: Reclam, 1971) and his study "Dekadenz oder Fortschritt? Zum Dänemarkbild in Fontanes Roman 'Unwiederbringlich,'" *Text & Kontext* 2 (1974): 28-49. See also Dieter Lohmeier, "Vor dem Niedergang: Dänemark in Fontanes Roman 'Unwiederbringlich,'" *Skandinavistik* 2 (1972): 27-53; and Karsten Jessen, "Theodor Fontane und Dänemark," *Fontane-Blätter* 4 (1978): 226-45.

[438] Studies on *Unwiederbringlich* have mushroomed since Peter Demetz in his seminal book *Formen des Realismus: Theodor Fontane* (Munich: Hanser, 1964) singled it out as "Fontane's most flawless artwork" (166). The fullest treatment is the (unfortunately) unpublished Ph.D. dissertation by Leckie R. Tuulikki, "Theodor Fontane's Novel 'Unwiederbringlich': Analysis, Interpretation, and Evaluation," Indiana University, 1970. Particularly perceptive readings are by 1) Walter Müller-Seidel, *Theodor Fontane*, 378-93; 2) Alan F. Bance, *Theodor Fontane, The Major Novels* (Cambridge, England: University

chooses for the opening of his narrative: the end of September 1859. In that month the duchy of Schleswig came nearer to tying itself legally and administratively to Denmark than at any other time in its history. The common constitution of Denmark and the twin duchies of Schleswig and Holstein had just been amended to give German-speaking Holstein an independent political existence. As a result, Holstein's historic ties to Schleswig were loosened, and Schleswig was drawn into a closer political union with Denmark. During the final week of September 1859, Frederick VII briefly but ostentatiously moved his court from Copenhagen to Glücksburg in Schleswig to point up this new, closer union.

For the hero of the novel, Count Holk, these events mark the beginning of a new era in his life. A member of Schleswig's landed aristocracy, he is, therefore, automatically a leader within the duchy's ruling caste; with the closer administrative union of Schleswig and Denmark, official duties take him more frequently to the capital city, Copenhagen. He spends prolonged periods away from home, increasingly drawn into a myriad of bizarre allurements characteristic of life in the capital, much to the detriment of his marriage. His wife, Christine, cannot easily accompany him to Copenhagen. In his absence she has to watch over the day-to-day management of the family estate, and, more importantly, she needs to be near her German-speaking teenage children, for whom a transfer to Danish schools in Copenhagen is hardly feasible.

More and more, the marital partners become prisoners of the new sociopolitical circumstances intruding into their family life. The lax moral atmosphere of the royal court at Copenhagen quickly proves irresistible to the lonely Holk. The decadent environment he plunges into makes it easy for him to succumb to the temptations of other women. These extramarital affairs estrange him from his wife, and divorce becomes inevitable.

But the vice-laden conventions of Copenhagen's court, encouraged and promoted by the king's erstwhile mistress and morganatic wife, the voluptuous and glittering actress Countess Danner (1815–1874), also drive the women of Holk's new love life into relationships with other men. Then the disenchanted and depressed Holk yearns to return to his former wife; but in vain, for the pressure of intervening circumstances in Christine's life has also alienated her. Scandalized by her husband's adulteries, she has retreated into a religious solipsism, finding doleful comfort in a

Press, 1982), 103-30; 3) Rolf Christian Zimmermann, "Paradies und Verführung in Fontanes *Unwiederbringlich,* Zur Glücksthematik und Schuldproblematik des Romans," in *In Search of the Poetic Real, Essays in Honor of Clifford Albrecht Bernd,* 289-309; 4) Rolf Christian Zimmermann, "'Unwiederbringlich' — Nichtehen und Scheintriumphe neuer Fontane-Philologie," in *Architectura Poetica, Festschrift für Johannes Rathofer zum 65. Geburtstag,* eds. U. Ernst & B. Sowinski (Cologne: Böhlau, 1990), 471-90.

preoccupation with the prospect of eternal life beyond the grave. Even while Holk lost himself to erotic pleasures in the Paris of the North, she had sealed him off from herself and her dream world. Her shipwrecked marriage has led to such a secure haven in the monastic confinement of her faith that she has no desire to resume the responsibilities of married life when her husband returns from his amorous intrigues hoping to renew their relationship. Still, social conventions in provincial Schleswig — sustained by the local company of family, friends, and clergy — demand a reconciliation. She yields, and the two remarry in the family's parish with all the traditional blessings of church and community. But the ceremony proves hollow. The second wedding is based not on Christine's personal preference but social necessity, custom; her religious integrity cannot remain compromised for long by such deception, and she commits suicide.

Majestically in the background, framing all this novel's scenes, stands the sovereign of both Denmark and Schleswig, Frederick VII. Critics have never really acknowledged his hovering presence within the fiction. Nevertheless, he is never far from the scene of action. Whether holding court at his castle in Glücksburg (one scant mile from the Holk family estate), or residing at his Copenhagen palace as Holk attends court there, or sleeping in Frederiksborg Castle on precisely the same night Holk, in another wing, succumbs to the passionate blandishments of a court lady-in-waiting, the monarch is always evident behind the scenes. And for good reason: his crown symbolizes the impossibility of harmonizing internal and external pressures.

Fontane is here bringing to bear on his story historical circumstances that by analogy deepen the significance of the main plot. Throughout his reign the real Frederick VII was caught up in an impossible political situation. Danish public opinion urged him to incorporate the duchy of Schleswig into Denmark proper through outright annexation. The concert of European nations, on the other hand, steadfastly insisted that such a unilateral Danish action would not be tolerated. What choices lay open? To which influence should he yield: the internal pressure of his subjects or the external, foreign powers? Each alternative spelled disaster. To go against the obvious will of the Danish majority would put his throne in jeopardy. But to ignore the grave warnings of the great powers of Europe would risk a European war, with certain defeat for Denmark. Frederick VII sedulously avoided giving his kingly assent to either alternative. He chose, instead, a route of cowardly indifference. Fleeing political reality and his royal prerogative to initiate diplomatic negotiations on the issue, he elected to take as little interest as possible in vital matters of state, leaving them to unreliable subordinates who shuttled in and out of office. As compensation for his inertia he sought comfort in his infatuation with the adulterous Countess Danner. This adjustment naturally turned the court of Denmark into one where affairs of the bed-chamber took precedence over affairs of state and the distractions of scandal reigned supreme.

Such, then, is the sociopolitical context of the tragic collapse of the marriage of Holk and Christine. The recurring presence of Frederick VII behind the scenes is as integral a part of the novel's composition as are the Holks and the host of subsidiary characters. The royal frame and the inner story complement one another, stressing that the two opposing worlds of the individual and the sociopolitical forces that surround him cannot converge, except in disaster.

Effi Briest

With *Unwiederbringlich* still fresh in his mind, Fontane began to mull over another novel. In fact, he had already completed a first draft when *Unwiederbringlich* came off the press in 1891. Work on the revisions continued for years, and not until October 1895 did the new novel, *Effi Briest*, appear in final form.[439]

In this novel, which Thomas Mann declared one of the six best novels of world literature,[440] Fontane varies a compositional principle he used with considerable effect in *Unwiederbringlich:* the integration of an omnipresent political figure into the fictional web. The regal figure of Frederick VII pervasively influenced the narration of *Unwiederbringlich*. Again and again the narrator placed great stock in telling about Frederick, together with the sociopolitical conditions the monarch had introduced and maintained — to the terrible misfortune of Holk and his wife. In *Effi Briest* the author replaces the kingly figure with a princely figure, namely Prince Otto von Bismarck, the "Iron Chancellor" of Germany from 1871 to 1890. As with Frederick VII in *Unwiederbringlich*, Bismarck appears repeatedly throughout the novel, so often that his personality and characteristics become as much a concern as were the reign and lifestyle of Frederick in the sister novel. For this reason, the two novels are mutually illuminating and should be viewed together (rather than separately as Fontane critics have preferred to look at them).

---

[439] Studies on this work of world literature are unusually numerous. Highly illuminating modern interpretations include 1) Walter Müller-Seidel, *Theodor Fontane*, 351-77; 2) Henry Garland, *The Berlin Novels of Theodor Fontane* (Oxford: Clarendon, 1980), 169-208; 3) Alan F. Bance, *Theodor Fontane, The Major Novels*, 38-77; 4) Roy C. Cowen in *Der Poetische Realismus*, 346-61; 5) Valerie D. Greenberg, "The Resistance of *Effi Briest:* An (Un)told Tale," *PMLA* 103 (1988): 770-81.

[440] Mann, *Gesammelte Werke* (Frankfurt am Main: Fischer, 1960), X, 577.

It comes as no surprise that Bismarck should play such an important role in this new novel. Fontane's success with *Unwiederbringlich* had shown him — precisely as he was conceiving *Effi Briest* — how immensely effective the use of a prominent political figure could be in fiction. The tragedy of the Holks would never have assumed the proportions it did if Frederick were not always waiting to create and manipulate the sociopolitical conditions on which the marriage of his subjects, the Holks, foundered. Fontane, therefore, had good reason to introduce into the new novel another powerful behind-the-scenes political figure. It seemed perfectly logical that this figure should be none other than Bismarck.

Fontane was preoccupied with the composition of *Effi Briest* from 1890 to 1895, the years when the name of Bismarck, that colossal figure who had shaped Germany's destiny for some thirty years, was on the lips of all Germans. An impetuous young emperor, William II, had suddenly forced the veteran chancellor to resign from office on March 18, 1890. The curious circumstances of this dismissal and the polarized public response it engendered immediately became prime topics of the day throughout Germany. Fontane's thoughts in March 1890, and in the ensuing months, like his countrymen's, focused intently on the personality of Bismarck, on his achievements and shortcomings. Fontane's letters offer conclusive evidence of this preoccupation. Any reader of this correspondence will be impressed by the depth of his musings on Bismarck's resignation. For years thereafter the subject of Bismarck's fall remained alive in German conversation — and in Fontane's thoughts as well, as his letters again reveal. The year 1895 marked a particular high point for such conversation. On April 1, 1895, Bismarck celebrated his eightieth birthday, and Germany celebrated with him. This event contributed to an especially widespread renewal of discussion about the Iron Chancellor and the controversy five years earlier.

From March 1890 to April 1895, therefore, the fortunes of Bismarck provided a theme for every kaffeeklatsch and keynote speech in Germany, and Fontane remained as involved in this ongoing conversation as anyone. During the same period Fontane was busy writing and revising *Effi Briest*. Naturally, the two subjects commingled in his mind. It seemed only logical that Bismarck should intrude into the design of the novel. Fontane made no apparent attempt to check this tendency, as the bountifully recurrent references in *Effi Briest* to the chancellor's name reveal. There is even an inn named "Prince Bismarck" in the novel, and, fittingly, conversation at the inn revolves around Bismarck's personality and activities.

But the "Chancellor of Blood and Iron" provides more than just local color in *Effi Briest;* he forms an integral part of the novel's composition. As a leader, Bismarck projected something of a dual public image: a dedicated civil servant on the one hand, with staunch moral and ethical principles, and a sly politician and callous military strategist on the other, a man who could act both ruthlessly and unscrupulously when the need arose. A strict sense of responsibility, deeply rooted in his abiding Lutheran faith, animated his life and work; the sterling quality of a religious imperative of conscientious duty, of performing God's work on earth, motivated his conduct in the business of state. Yet, these same lofty principles carried with them the solemn obligation, as he firmly believed, to protect from all danger the state that God had entrusted to him, using every means at his disposal, no matter how brutal or dishonorable. Bismarck proved himself, therefore, both a champion and a violator of principles at once. No one realized this better than the wise Fontane. "Bismarck is the greatest scorner of principles who ever existed," he wrote to his daughter Martha on January 29, 1894, while working on *Effi Briest*, "and a 'principle' finally brought him down, the same principle that he carried written on his banner all his life and in accordance with which he never acted."[441]

These two opposing faces of Bismarck manifest themselves in the novel as the two contrasting characters who come to be rivals for the love of Effi, the heroine. The first is Baron von Innstetten, Effi's husband. A dedicated official in the higher echelons of the Prussian civil service, he champions all the established values of moral decency and personifies the ethical commitment to duty. Appropriately, none other than Bismarck himself, we are told, had a high regard for him. To make the analogy with Bismarck more complete, the narrator stresses over and over that Innstetten is a "man of principle."

Against this high-minded avatar of the "public" Bismarck stands a character representing his darker side, the dashing officer Major von Crampas. Innstetten, the civil service official, and Crampas, the uniformed officer of the militia, remind us that Bismarck's duality had impelled him to wear a military uniform while performing his duties as a civil official. If Innstetten represents a man of character with a high code of conduct, a conscientious, hardworking, and honorable pillar of irreproachable moral standards, Crampas represents just the opposite. With malicious and ulterior motives, he maneuvers situations to his selfish advantage. Sneering at conventions when they do not further his own designs, he cleverly exploits the weaknesses of others until they succumb to his wishes. Crampas's unscrupulous behavior is most dramatically illustrated in his cunning seduction of Innstetten's wife, Effi. He carefully calculates his moves, taking

---

[441] *Fontanes Briefe in zwei Bänden*, ed. G. Erler, II (Berlin and Weimar: Aufbau, 1968), 316.

advantage of both the husband's absence from home because of official duties and the wife's loneliness and inexperience in order to beguile his hapless prey.

Caught in a crosscurrent between these two men, who together reflect the Janus-faced society that bore the impress of Bismarck's iron fist, is Effi. If Innstetten and Crampas seem stereotypes of the two poles of the social order presided over by Bismarck, Effi exemplifies an individual with an independent personality. In her drab marriage to Innstetten, she never adapts to the rigid codes and conventions of his bureaucratic life. But neither can she adapt to Crampas's salacity. She becomes his victim in lust rather than his partner in love, and inwardly she leaps at the opportunity to free herself from her carnal relationship with him. As much repelled by Crampas's ruthless scorn of ethical principles as by Innstetten's slavish adherence to them, she finds herself trapped. Her mother had imposed marriage to Bismarck's protégé on her when she was a girl of seventeen; the prevailing social order she had been committed to by that marriage is far too rigid to permit any deviation, except in a stolen, dishonorable way. So when Crampas lays amorous siege to the inexperienced young wife, she easily falls prey to his strategy. The adultery runs so thoroughly against the conventions of Bismarckian society that, once discovered, she is not only cut off from her family but ejected from her social environment. Her broken health and early death as a result of her life's disastrous entrapments only finalize the victory of Bismarckian society over her independent spirit.

Bismarckian mores victimize the story's other characters no less. The traditions of the society Innstetten condones so thoroughly predetermine his actions that on learning of his wife's affair he challenges Crampas to a duel. Crampas accepts, equally honor-bound by convention; he is shot and killed. Then Innstetten divorces his wife, sacrificing any possibility of happiness for him or his wife to uphold society's conventional principles. The remarks Fontane made about Bismarck while writing *Effi Briest* — "a 'principle' finally brought him down, the same principle that he carried written on his banner all his life" — apply equally well to the Bismarckian official Innstetten.

A novel of such sociopolitical acuity had little in common with the insulated non-social, non-political compositions of Poetic Realism. In none of these would the characteristics of a contemporary political figure serve as integral parts of the fiction. When Fontane gives a panoramic picture of the *mœurs* of Bismarck's society (or of Frederick VII's society), he has untied his connections to Poetic Realism and aligned himself with the social novelists of nineteenth-century England. His depiction of the society presided over by Bismarck (or by Frederick VII) suggests Dickens's method of acquainting readers with the foibles and liabilities of Queen Victoria's England.

Of course, when Fontane transformed the literary practice of *Poetischer Realismus* into a social realism ultimately at odds with it, he brought to a conclusion the literary movement that had emerged in Denmark, spread over into Sweden and Finland, and found such fertile soil in Germany and Switzerland. He redrew the map of German literature and ushered in a new generation of writers. No less a successor than Thomas Mann was to confirm this truth: "er ist unser Vater" (he is our father).[442]

---

[442] Mann, *Gesammelte Werke*, XIII, 817.

Julian Schmidt
Courtesy of *Bildarchiv Preußischer Kulturbesitz*, Berlin

Otto Ludwig
Courtesy of *Bildarchiv Preußischer Kulturbesitz*, Berlin

Theodor Storm
Courtesy of *Bildarchiv Preußischer Kulturbesitz*, Berlin

Gottfried Keller
Courtesy of *Schweizerische Landesbibliothek*, Berne

Conrad Ferdinand Meyer
Courtesy of *Schweizerische Landesbibliothek*, Berne

Klaus Groth
Courtesy of *Bildarchiv Preußischer Kulturbesitz*, Berlin

Wilhelm Raabe
Courtesy of *Bildarchiv Preußischer Kulturbesitz*, Berlin

Theodor Fontane
Courtesy of *Bildarchiv Preußischer Kulturbesitz*, Berlin

WORKS CONSULTED

Algulin, Ingemar. *A History of Swedish Literature.* Stockholm: Swedish Institute, 1989.

Alker, Ernst. *Die deutsche Literatur im 19. Jahrhundert 1832-1914.* 3rd ed. Stuttgart: Kröner, 1969.

Anderle, Martin. *Deutsche Lyrik des 19. Jahrhunderts. Ihre Bildlichkeit: Metapher — Symbol — Evokation.* Bonn: Bouvier, 1979.

Aspelin, Kurt. *Poesie och verklighet.* Del I: Några huvudlinjer i 1830-talets svenska kritikerdebatt. Göteborg: Akademiförlaget, 1967.

———. *Poesi och verklighet.* Del II: 1830-talets liberala litteraturkritik och den borgerliga realismens problem. Stockholm: Norstedt, 1977.

Aust, Hugo. *Literatur des Realismus.* 2nd ed. Stuttgart: Metzler, 1981.

Bandle, Oskar, et al. *Studien zur dänischen und schwedischen Literatur des 19. Jahrhunderts.* Basel and Stuttgart: Helbing und Lichtenhahn, 1976.

———. "Periodiseringen i nyare nordisk litteraturhistoria." *Samlaren* 105 (1984): 58-77.

Bernd, Clifford Albrecht. *German Poetic Realism.* Boston: Twayne, 1981.

———. "The Anticipation of German Poetic Realism in Danish *Poetisk Realisme.*" *MLN* 97 (1982): 573-89.

———. "Poetischer Realismus, Bürgerlicher Realismus, Programmatischer Realismus — die Kontroverse um die richtige Benennung einer Epoche in der deutschen Literaturgeschichte." In *Akten des VII. Internationalen Germanisten-Kongresses Göttingen 1985.* Edited by A. Schöne. Vol. 9. Tübingen: Niemeyer, 1986. 110-15.

———. Review of *Der Poetische Realismus. Kommentar zu einer Epoche,* by Roy C. Cowen. *MLN* 102 (1987): 678-81.

Böckmann, Paul. "Deutsche Lyrik im 19. Jahrhundert." In *Formkräfte der deutschen Dichtung vom Barock bis zur Gegenwart.* Edited by H. Steffen. 2nd ed. Göttingen: Vandenhoeck & Ruprecht, 1967. 165-86.

Boeschenstein, Hermann. *German Literature of the Nineteenth Century.* London: Arnold; New York: St. Martin's Press, 1969.

Bolckmans, Alex, ed. *Literature and Reality. Creatio versus Mimesis. Problems of Realism in Modern Nordic Literature.* Ghent: Scandinavian Institute, University of Ghent, 1977.

Borum, Poul. *Danish Literature. A Short Critical Survey.* Copenhagen: Det Danske Selskap, 1979.

Böttcher, Kurt, et al. *Die Geschichte der deutschen Literatur von 1830 bis zum Ausgang des 19. Jahrhunderts.* 2 vols. Berlin: Volk und Wissen, 1975.

Bredsdorff, Elias; Mortensen, Brita; Popperwell, Ronald. *An Introduction to Scandinavian Literature.* Copenhagen: Munksgaard, 1951. Reprint, Westport, Conn.: Greenwood Press, 1970.

Brinkmann, Richard, ed. *Begriffsbestimmung des literarischen Realismus.* 3rd ed. Darmstadt: Wissenschaftliche Buchgesellschaft, 1987.

———. *Wirklichkeit und Illusion.* 3rd ed. Tübingen: Niemeyer, 1977.

Brøndsted, Mogens, ed. *Nordische Literaturgeschichte.* Vol. 1: Von den Anfängen bis zum Jahre 1860. Translated by H. K. Mueller. Munich: Fink, 1982.

Bucher, Max, et al. *Realismus und Gründerzeit. Manifeste und Dokumente zur deutschen Literatur 1848-1880.* 2 vols. Stuttgart: Metzler, 1975 & 1976.

Cowen, Roy C. *Neunzehntes Jahrhundert (1830-1880).* Berne and Munich: Francke, 1970.

———. *Der poetische Realismus. Kommentar zu einer Epoche.* Munich: Winkler, 1985.

David, Claude. *Zwischen Romantik und Symbolismus 1820-1885.* Gütersloh: Mohn, 1966.

Dresch, J. "La révolution de 1848 et la littérature allemande." *Revue de littérature comparée* 22 (1948): 176-99.

Eisele, Ulf. Realismus und Ideologie. Zur Kritik der literarischen Theorie nach 1848 am Beispiel des "Deutschen Museums." Stuttgart: Metzler, 1976.

———. "Realismus-Problematik: Überlegungen zur Forschungssituation." *Deutsche Vierteljahrsschrift für Literaturwissenschaft und Geistesgeschichte* 51 (1977): 148-74.

Ermatinger, Emil. *Deutsche Dichter 1750-1900. Eine Geistesgeschichte in Lebensbildern.* 2nd ed. Revised by J. Göres. Frankfurt am Main and Bonn: Athenäum, 1961.

Fehr, Karl. "Realism (1830-1885)." In *German Literature. A Critical Survey.* Edited by B. Boesch. Translated by R. Taylor. London: Methuen, 1971. 254-89.

Fetzer, John F.; Hoermann, Roland; McConnell, Winder, eds. *In Search of the Poetic Real. Essays in Honor of Clifford Albrecht Bernd on the Occasion of his Sixtieth Birthday.* Stuttgarter Arbeiten zur Germanistik 220. Stuttgart: Hans-Dieter Heinz Akademischer Verlag, 1989.

Field, G. Wallis. *A Literary History of Germany. The Nineteenth Century, 1830-1890.* London: Ernest Benn; New York: Barnes and Noble, 1975.

Finney, Gail. "Poetic Realism: Theodor Storm, Gottfried Keller, Conrad Ferdinand Meyer." In *European Writers.* Vol. 6: The Romantic Century. Edited by J. Barzun and G. Stade. New York: Scribner's, 1985. 913-42.

Friis, Oluf. "Den poetiske realismes generation." In *Dansk Litteratur Historie.* Edited by P. H. Traustedt. New ed. Vol. 3. Copenhagen: Politiken, 1976. 11-278.

Fuerst, Norbert. *The Victorian Age of German Literature.* University Park and London: Pennsylvania State University Press, 1966.

Gentikow, Barbara. *Skandinavische und deutsche Literatur. Bibliographie der Schriften zu den literarischen, historischen und kulturgeschichtlichen Wechselbeziehungen.* Neumünster: Wachholtz, 1975.

Gustafson, Alrik. *A History of Swedish Literature.* 3rd printing. Minneapolis: University of Minnesota Press, 1971.

Hermand, Jost. "Zur Literatur der Gründerzeit." *Deutsche Vierteljahrsschrift für Literaturwissenschaft und Geistesgeschichte* 41 (1967): 202-32.

Holub, Robert C. *Reflections of Realism. Paradox, Norm, and Ideology in Nineteenth-Century German Prose.* Detroit: Wayne State University Press, 1991.

Jäger, Hans-Wolf. "Gesellschaftliche Aspekte des bürgerlichen Realismus und seiner Theorie. Bemerkungen zu Julian Schmidt und Gustav Freytag." *Text & Kontext* 2, 3 (1974): 3-41.

Jørgensen, John Chr. *Dansk Realisme 1820-1975.* Copenhagen: Borgen, 1977.

———. *Den sande kunst. Studier i dansk 1800-tals realisme.* Copenhagen: Borgen, 1980.

Kahrmann, Bernd, et al. "Bürgerlicher Realismus." *Wirkendes Wort* 23 (1973): 53-68; 24 (1974): 339-56; 26 (1976): 356-81.

Kinder, Hermann. *Poesie als Synthese. Ausbreitung eines deutschen Realismus-Verständnisses in der Mitte des 19. Jahrhunderts.* Frankfurt am Main: Athenäum, 1973.

Kohlschmidt, Werner. *Geschichte der deutschen Literatur vom Jungen Deutschland bis zum Naturalismus.* Stuttgart: Reclam, 1975.

Kyndrup, Morton and Stæhr, Claus Pico. *Realisme-begrebet i den moderne litteraturteoretiske debat.* 3 vols. Copenhagen: Akademisk Forlag, 1982.

Lauer, Reinhard, et al. *Europäischer Realismus. Neues Handbuch der Literaturwissenschaft.* Edited by K. von See. Vol. 17. Wiesbaden: Akademische Verlagsgesellschaft Athenaion, 1980.

Lönnroth, Lars and Delblane, Sven, eds. *Den Svenska Litteratur. Den liberala genombrotten 1830-1890.* Stockholm: Bonniers, 1988.

Löwith, Karl. *From Hegel to Nietzsche. The Revolution in Nineteenth-Century Thought.* Translated by D. E. Green. New York: Holt, Rinehart and Winston, 1964. Reprint, Garden City, N.Y.: Doubleday, 1967.

Lukács, Georg. *Skizze einer Geschichte der neueren deutschen Literatur.* Neuwied: Luchterhand, 1963. Reprint, 1975.

Markwardt, Bruno. *Geschichte der deutschen Poetik.* Vol. IV: Das neunzehnte Jahrhundert. Berlin: de Gruyter, 1959.

Martini, Fritz. "Deutsche Literatur in der Zeit des 'bürgerlichen Realismus.' Ein Literaturbericht." *Deutsche Vierteljahrsschrift für Literaturwissenschaft und Geistesgeschichte* 34 (1960): 581-666.

———. *Deutsche Literatur im bürgerlichen Realismus 1848-1898.* 4th ed. Stuttgart: Metzler, 1981.

———. "Neue Realismusforschungen: Eine Übersicht." *Zeitschrift für deutsche Philologie* 101 (1982): 262-85.

Mitchell, P. M. *A History of Danish Literature.* 2nd ed. New York: Kraus-Thomson, 1971.

Mortensen, Karl. "Romantikere og poetiske Realister i Danmark." In *Dansk Litteraturhistorie.* Edited by K. Mortensen. 6th ed. Copenhagen: Gyldendal, 1931. 138-88.

Müller, Klaus-Detlef, ed. *Bürgerlicher Realismus. Grundlagen und Interpretationen.* Königstein/Ts.: Athenäum, 1981.

Paul, Fritz. "Romantik und Poetischer Realismus." In *Grundzüge der neueren skandinavischen Literaturen*. Edited by F. Paul. Darmstadt: Wissenschaftliche Buchgesellschaft, 1982. 86-146.

Pettersson, Anders. *Realism som terminologiskt problem. Några definitioner i modern litteraturvetenskap och deras giltighet*. Lund: Gleerup, 1975.

Preisendanz, Wolfgang. *Humor als dichterische Einbildungskraft. Studien zur Erzählkunst des poetischen Realismus*. 2nd ed. Munich: Fink, 1976.

———. *Wege des Realismus. Zur Poetik und Erzählkunst im 19. Jahrhundert*. Munich: Fink, 1977.

Reinhardt, Heinrich. *Die Dichtungstheorie der sogenannten Poetischen Realisten*. Würzburg: Triltsch, 1939.

Ritchie, J. M. "Realism." In *Periods in German Literature*. Edited by J. M. Ritchie. London: Oswald Wolff, 1966. 171-95.

———. "The Ambivalence of 'Realism' in German Literature 1830-1880." *Orbis Litterarum* 15 (1960): 200-17.

———. "Realism in Germany from the Death of Goethe." In *The Age of Realism*. Edited by F. W. J. Hemmings. Harmondsworth, England and Baltimore: Penguin Books, 1974. 218-64.

Roos, Carl. "Die nordischen Literaturen in ihrer Bedeutung für die deutsche." In *Deutsche Philologie im Aufriß*. Edited by W. Stammler. Vol. 3. 2nd ed. Berlin: Erich Schmidt, 1962. 373-406.

Rosenberg, Rainer. "Die deutsche Literatur im Licht des poetischen Realismus." In *Zehn Kapitel zur Geschichte der Germanistik*. Edited by R. Rosenberg. Berlin: Akademie-Verlag, 1981. 78-100.

Rossel, Sven H. "From Romanticism to Realism." In *A History of Danish Literature*. Edited by S. H. Rossel. Lincoln and London: University of Nebraska Press, 1992. 167-259.

Rubow, Paul V. *Dansk Litterær Kritik i det 19. århundrede indtil 1870*. 2nd ed. Copenhagen: Munksgaard, 1970.

Sagarra, Eda. *Tradition and Revolution. German Literature and Society 1830-1890*. London: Weidenfeld and Nicolson; New York: Basic Books, 1971.

Schmitz, Victor A. *Dänische Dichter in ihrer Begegnung mit deutscher Klassik und Romantik*. Frankfurt am Main: Klostermann, 1974.

Schoolfield, George C. "Scandinavian-German Literary Relations." *Yearbook of Comparative and General Literature* 15 (1966): 19-35.

Silz, Walter. *Realism and Reality. Studies in the German Novelle of Poetic Realism*. 4th printing. Chapel Hill: University of North Carolina Press, 1965.

Stahl, E. L. and Yuill, W. E. *German Literature of the Eighteenth and Nineteenth Centuries*. London: Cresset; New York: Barnes and Noble, 1970.

Stern, J. P. *Idylls and Reality. Studies in Nineteenth-Century German Literature*. London: Methuen; New York: Ungar, 1971.

———. "German Literature in the Age of European Realism." In *German Language and Literature: Seven Essays*. Edited by K. Weimar. Englewood Cliffs, N.J.: Prentice-Hall, 1974. 223-306.

Svanberg, Victor. *Medelklassrealism*. Uppsala: Gidlund, 1980.

Svendsen, Hanne Marie and Werner. *Geschichte der dänischen Literatur*. Neumünster: Wachholtz; Copenhagen: Gyldendal, 1964.

Svendsen, Paulus. "Der Ausklang der Romantik im Norden." In *Spätzeiten und Spätzeitlichkeit*. Edited by W. Kohlschmidt. Berne and Munich: Francke, 1962. 73-85.

Swales, Martin. "Zum Problem des deutschen Realismus." In *Akten des VII. Internationalen Germanisten-Kongresses Göttingen 1985*. Edited by A. Schöne. Vol. 9. Tübingen: Niemeyer, 1986. 116-26.

Westling, Christer. "Idealistisk estetik, Poetisk Realism, idealrealism." In *Idealismens estetik*. Stockholm: Westling, 1985. 233-38.

Widhammer, Helmuth. *Realismus und klassizistische Tradition. Zur Theorie der Literatur in Deutschland 1848-1860*. Tübingen: Niemeyer, 1972.

———. *Die Literaturtheorie des deutschen Realismus 1848-1860*. Stuttgart: Metzler, 1977.

Wiese, Benno von, ed. *Deutsche Dichter des 19. Jahrhunderts. Ihr Leben und Werk*. 2nd ed. Berlin: Erich Schmidt, 1979.

Winterscheidt, Friedrich. *Deutsche Unterhaltungsliteratur der Jahre 1850-1860*. Bonn: Bouvier, 1970.

Wittrock, Ulf. "Från Biedermeier och Vormärz till imperialism och symbolism. Periodindelning och syntesförsök inom väst- och östtysk germanistik." *Samlaren* 96 (1975): 72-141.

Wretö, Tore. *Det förklarade ögonblicket. Studier i västerländsk idyll från Theokritos till Strindberg*. Stockholm: Almqvist and Wiksell, 1977.

Index of Names

Abe, Yoshio, 164 n328
Ainsworth, William Harrison, 130
Albertsen, Leif Ludwig, 2 n3, 63, 144
Algulin, Ingemar, 80, 85 n136
Alt, A. Tilo, 144 n282
Andersen, Hans Christian, 54-57, 61, 128, 146, 192, 195, 205
Andersen, Vilhelm, 1, 4 n9, 5 n10 n11, 19 n32
Aspelin, Kurt, 78, 81, 82 n115, 83 n121, 84, 119 n204
Atterbom, Per Daniel Amadeus, 64, 80-85, 89, 104, 119-21, 142
Auerbach, Berthold, 129-30, 164, 194
Augustenburg, Duke of, *see* Christian August, Duke of Augustenburg
Auring, Steffen, 40 n66

Baggesen, August, 106 n164
Baggesen, Jens, 106, 108
Baggesen, Søren, 28 n40
Balzac, Honoré de, 155, 164
Bance, Alan F., 216 n438, 219 n439
Bandle, Oskar, 82 n116
Barz, Paul, 153 n307
Baudelaire, Charles, 156
Beaton, Kenneth Bruce, 136 n254
Becket, Thomas à, 184-86
Bennett, Edwin K., 133 n243, 152 n303, 182
Bentley, Eric, 140, 141 n273
Berg, Ruben G:son, 119 n202 n203
Berman, Russell A., 174 n344
Bernhard, Carl, 46-49, 62, 69, 110-112
Bismarck, Prince Otto von, 54, 219-22
Blicher, Steen Steensen, 22-35, 38, 44, 62, 67, 75, 88, 112, 117, 125, 147, 199-200
Boccaccio, Giovanni, 17-21, 27-28, 35, 38

Böckmann, Paul, 187 n381, 190 n386, 193 n398, 203-04
Boswell, Patricia M., 151 n302, 155 n309, 158 n317
Brahms, Johannes, 191
Bramsen, Henrik, 50 n76
Brand, Jürgen, 200 n414
Brandes, Georg, 27-28, 55, 134, 174
Brask, Peter, 28 n40
Bredsdorff, Elias, 23, 30 n41, 82 n118, 85 n137, 86 n138, 89 n153, 97 n160
Bremer, Fredrika, 76-79, 81, 89, 102
Brenna, Arne, 52 n82
Brinkmann, Richard, 119 n207
Brix, Hans, 5 n13, 19 n32, 28 n40
Broad, C. D., 91-92
Brockhaus, Friedrich & Heinrich, 118-20, 122, 125, 142
Brøndsted, Mogens, 17 n28, 77 n102, 85 n137
Browning, Robert, 155
Bruns, Alken, 55 n87
Bruns, Friedrich, 187
Bufano, Randolph, 87 n140
Burkhard, Marianne, 181 n362

Cervantes, Miguel de, 17
Charles XIV, King of Sweden, 74
Chateaubriand, François René de, 127
Christian VIII, King of Denmark, 54, 56
Christian IX, King of Denmark, 178
Christian August, Duke of Augustenburg, 56
Claudius, Matthias, 157
Corneille, Pierre, 23
Corvinus, Jacob, *see* Raabe, Wilhelm
Coupe, William A., 183 n371
Cowen, Roy C., 151 n302, 154 n307, 183 n371, 219 n439
Coxwell, C. Fillingham, 214
Czamanske, William M., 197

Index of Names

Daemmrich, Horst, 199 n411
Danner, Countess Louise Christine, 217, 219
Demetz, Peter, 216 n438
Denkler, Horst, 199 n411
Dickens, Charles, 155, 215, 222
Dickson, Keith A., 138 n260
Dietze, Walter, 200 n414
Diezmann, Johann August, 199
Dilthey, Wilhelm, 133
Dirckinck-Holmfeld, Baron Constant, 112-15
Dirckinck-Holmfeld, Baron Ulysses, 114
Disraeli, Benjamin, 113
Dostoyevsky, Fëdor, 23, 156
Drachmann, Holger, 175
Droste-Hülshoff, Annette von, 46, 132-33

Ebers, Georg, 183
Eigenbrodt, Wolrad, 90 n155
Elisabeth, Queen Consort of Prussia, 202, 213
Ellis, John M., 153 n307
Elmquist, Adolph Frederik, 24, 30
Elsner, Paul, 26 n37
Emmel, Hildegard, 187 n381
Engels, Friedrich, 145
Euclid, 153

Fabricius, Knud, 146
Fairley, Barker, 198 n409, 199 n411, 200 n414
Falck, Nicolaus, 145
Fenger, Henning, 33 n51 n52, 35 n53, 38
Fich, Brørson, 19 n32
Field, G. Wallis, 187 n381
Finney, Gail, 137, 181
Fischer, Erik, 52 n81
Flaubert, Gustave, 156
Fleischer, Manfred, 213
Flor, Christian, 108, 110
Fontane, Martha, 221
Fontane, Theodor, 137, 144, 148, 156, 166 n337, 174, 181 n364, 191, 204-23, 231
Frederick I, Grand Duke of Baden, 90 n155
Frederick VI, King of Denmark, 37, 106, 109
Frederick VII, King of Denmark, 195, 216-20, 222
Frederick William IV, King of Prussia, 213

Freiligrath, Ferdinand, 131-32, 146-47
Freund, Winfried, 144 n282, 151 n302, 153 n307
Freytag, Gustav, 125, 134-37, 199
Friedrich, Gerhard, 204 n421
Friedrichsen, Peter, 145
Friis, Oluf, 1-2, 5, 16
Frühwald, Wolfgang, 154 n307

Gähler, Adolph von, 114-17
Garland, Henry, 219 n439
Geffroy, A., 121 n211
Geisler, Eberhard, 204
Gervinus, Georg Gottfried, 165-66
Gillhoff, Gerd, 158
Goedsche, Charlotte L., 200 n414
Goethe, Johann Wolfgang von, 17, 23, 147, 156, 164
Goldschmidt, Meïr, 57-59, 61, 125-26
Greenberg, Valerie D., 219 n439
Grenville, J. A. S., 113 n187
Grillparzer, Franz, 199 n412
Grønbech, Bo, 55 n85
Groth, Klaus, 190-98, 205, 214, 229
Grundtvig, Nikolaj Frederik Severin, 56-57, 61-62
Gundolf, Friedrich, 137
Gustafson, Alrik, 85 n137
Gustavus II Adolphus, King of Sweden, 124-25
Gutenberg, Johann, 122
Gutzkow, Karl, 132
Gyllembourg, Thomasine, 33-50, 62, 68, 75-77, 79, 108, 111, 115, 147-48, 161

Hacken, Richard D., 192, 196
Hagberg, Carl August, 118-20, 142
Hannover, Emil, 60 n90
Hansen, Valdemar, 6 n16
Hanson, William P., 200 n414
Hart, Thomas Elwood, 188 n383
Hauch, Carsten, 108
Hausmann, Manfred, 157
Häusser, Ludwig, 163
Haußleiter, Johannes, 184-86
Hebbel, Christa, 204
Hegel, Georg Wilhelm Friedrich, 36-37
Heiberg, Johan Ludvig, 34, 36-39, 46-47, 54, 108, 115
Heiberg, Peter Andreas, 33
Heine, Thomas, 154 n307
Henel, Heinrich, 187
Henningsen, Bernd, 4 n9, 19 n32, 22 n33, 73 n99
Henry II, King of England, 185
Herlth, Paul, 118 n201

Index of Names

Hertling, Gunter H., 183 n371
Hertz, Henrik, 128
Heyse, Paul, 47
Hillyer, Robert Silliman, 10, 14
Hirn, Yrjö, 99 n162
Hirsch, Emanuel, 31, 112 n185
Holander, Reimer Kay, 153 n307
Holub, Robert C., 151 n302, 164 n328, 184 n371, 203 n415
Hornborg, Eirik, 90 n155
Hude, Elisabeth, 38-39, 40 n66, 49

Ingemann, Bernhard Severin, 62-64, 71, 80, 194

Jackson, David A., 144 n282, 148 n293
James V, King of Scotland, 212-13
Jensen, T. Hoyer, 107 n166
Jessen, Karsten, 216 n437
Jillings, Lewis, 32
Jolles, Charlotte, 204 n421
Jones, W. Glyn, 4 n9, 22, 62 n91
Jørgensen, Sven-Aage, 216 n437
Jutikkala, Eino, 87 n142 n143

Kaiser, Gerhard, 161 n320, 164 n328, 170 n339, 174 n343
Keller, Gottfried, 44-46, 132 n240, 133 n243, 161-82, 184, 186, 189-90, 203, 205, 214, 227
Kierkegaard, Søren, 6, 15, 30-31, 33, 35, 112 n185
Killy, Walter, 204
Kinder, Hermann, 198 n410
Kivi, Aleksis, 99-100
Klausen, Gottlieb Ernst, 109-10, 116
Klein, Johannes, 191 n388
Kleist, Heinrich von, 147
Klinge, Matti, 86 n139
Klopstock, Friedrich Gottlieb, 197-98
Klose, Olaf, 110 n172
Købke, Christen, 49-53, 59-61, 70
Kohlschmidt, Werner, 184 n374
Kompert, Leopold, 129-30, 194
Köster, Albert, 150
Köster, Alex, 123 n219
Kristensen, Sven Møller, 17 n28
Krueger, Joachim, 206 n425
Kruse, Laurids, 45
Kuh, Emil, 132
Kulling, Jacob, 81 n114
Kunze, Erich, 117 n197, 121
Kyrre, Hans, 125 n224

Laage, Karl Ernst, 145 n288
Lange, Victor, 181
Lappe, Karl, 120
Larsen, Hanna Astrup, 86 n139
Lassalle, Ferdinand, 125
Leinberg, Gottfried von, 45 n70, 46 n71
Lenk, Heinrich von, 33 n49
Lewes, George Henry, 139, 164, 169
Lillyman, William J., 137 n260
Lindau, Rudolf, 181
Lindsay, J. M., 161 n320
Ling, C., 123 n219
Lobedanz, Edmund, 117-18
Lohmeier, Dieter, 216 n437
Lowrie, Walter, 6 n17
Lübker, Detlev Lorenz, 107 n166, 145
Ludwig, Otto, 119-20, 134-44, 161, 225
Lukács, György, 137 n256, 148, 165n335

Mallarmé, Stéphane, 156
Mann, Thomas, 153, 157, 174, 215-16, 219, 223
Marggraff, Hermann, 134-35
Marker, Frederick J., 18 n30, 38, 55 n84
Martens, Lorna, 199 n412
Martini, Fritz, 190-91
Marx, Karl, 146 n289
McFarlane, James Walter, 72-73
Meinhold, Wilhelm, 129
Merker, Paul, 140, 158 n319
Metternich, Prince Clemens von, 126-27
Meves, Ida, 120-21
Meyer, Betsy, 188
Meyer, Conrad Ferdinand, 181-90, 214-15, 228
Michelangelo, 60
Mis, Léon, 140
Mitchell, P. M., 6 n15, 62
Molbech, Christian, 108
Møller, Poul Martin, 4-25, 27-30, 33-35, 37-38, 57, 61-62, 66, 73-75, 88, 114, 125, 155
Monrad, Kasper, 51
Monten, Karin Carsten, 77 n103
Mortensen, Brita, 23 n35, 82 n118
Mortensen, Karl, 62-63
Mortensen, Klaus P., 38 n55
Müller, Max, 193
Müller-Seidel, Walter, 215 n434, 216 n438, 219 n439
Mynster, Bishop Jakob, 58

Napoleon I, Emperor of France, 2-3, 18-21, 23-27, 29, 33, 39, 50, 53-55, 74-75, 86, 200
Navarre, Marguerite de, 17
Nørgaard, Felix, 28

Nørregård-Nielsen, Hans Edvard, 50 n78, 53 n83
Nørvig, Johs., 26 n37
Nyblom, Carl Rupert, 142

Oberle, Werner, 187 n381
Oehlenschläger, Adam, 2-4, 10, 13-15, 18, 21, 27, 33-34, 36-37, 62, 75-76, 80
Osenbrüggen, Eduard, 116-17
Österling, Anders, 157

Paetel, Elwin & Hermann, 150
Pascal, Roy, 174 n343
Paul, Fritz, 63, 75, 77, 80, 84 n131, 85 n137
Paulin, Roger, 31, 112 n185
Peischl, Margaret T., 154 n307
Petersen, Anne-Marie, 178 n352
Petersen, Lorenz, 178 n352
Petersen, Wilhelm, 178-80
Plato, 82, 84
Polonsky, Y. P., 156
Popperwell, Ronald, 23 n35, 82 n118
Postgate, Raymond, 213 n429
Prawer, S. S., 170 n339, 172
Preisendanz, Wolfgang, 174 n343, 204 n417
Priest, George Madison, 151
Puknat, E. M. & S. B., 164 n332

Raabe, Wilhelm, 198-204, 212, 230
Racine, Jean, 23
Rahbek, Knud Lyne, 16
Reinhardt, Heinrich, 82 n119, 142 n277
Remak, Henry H., 123
Reuter, Hans-Heinrich, 204 n421, 205
Reventlow, Countess Emilie, 153
Richter, Helmut, 200 n414
Rilke, Rainer Maria, 187 n381
Roberts, Helen Kurz, 212
Rodenberg, Julius, 181
Rohweder, Joachim, 145 n287
Rohweder, Jürgen, 107 n165
Romberg, Bertil, 174 n343
Rosenberg, Carl, 194-95
Rößler, Constantin, 123 n218
Rubow, Paul V., 39 n65
Runeberg, Johan Ludvig, 83, 85-101, 105, 116-17, 119-21, 125, 142
Ruppel, Richard R., 161 n320, 174 n343
Ryder, Frank G., 187 n383
Rydqvist, Johan Erik, 77-85, 103, 118-19

Saint-Aubain, Andreas Nicolai de, *see* Bernhard, Carl

Saint-René Taillandier, René-Gaspard-Ernest, 134-35
Sammern-Frankenegg, Fritz Rüdiger, 148 n293
Sammons, Jeffrey L., 135, 199, 204 n418
Santesson, Carl, 79-80
Sautermeister, Gert, 174 n343
Scharff, Alexander, 113 n189
Schelling, Friedrich Wilhelm Joseph, 82-84, 119-120
Schepelern, Jens Bergendahl von, 114-17
Schiller, Friedrich, 23, 143
Schleiermacher, Friedrich, 11-12
Schmidt, Julian, 122-39, 140-46, 161, 164, 174, 182-84, 186-87, 191, 198, 216, 224
Schmitz, Victor A., 31, 112 n185
Schneider, Wilhelm, 158 n319, 170 n339, 187 n383
Schönert, Jörg, 138 n260
Schoolfield, George C., 87 n140, 89 n154, 216 n437
Schwanenflügel, H., 47 n72
Schwarz, Alfred, 141
Seelig, Geert, 190 n387, 194 n400, 195 n404
Sengle, Friedrich, 123
Shakespeare, William, 140-41, 165
Siercks, H., 194 n401
Silman, Tamara, 158 n319
Silz, Walter, 18-19, 142, 181
Simonsen, Anna, 146 n291
Skalberg, Harald, 108 n167, 110 n171
Smith, Alistair, 50
Söderhjelm, Werner, 120 n209
Spielhagen, Friedrich, 137
Steinecke, Hartmut, 134 n247
Stendhal (Henri Beyle), 155
Stern, Adolf, 142
Sternberg, Alexander von, *see* Ungern-Sternberg, Alexander von
Sternhagen, J. P., 107 n166, 109, 111 n178
Stifter, Adalbert, 199 n412
Stork, Charles Wharton, 93, 95-96
Storm, Theodor, 30-32, 44, 63, 112, 137, 144-62, 164-65, 170, 172-74, 179,181-82, 184, 186, 189-92, 195, 197, 205-06, 214, 226
Strodtmann, Adolf, 55
Stuckert, Franz, 31-32, 112 n185
Stutz, Elfriede, 158 n319
Swales, Martin, 164 n328, 174 n343
Swineburne, Algernon Charles, 155

Taillandier, René-Gaspard-Ernest, *see* Saint-René Taillandier, René-Gaspard-Ernest
Tennyson, Alfred, Lord, 155
Thackeray, William Makepeace, 155
Thiele, Adolf, 136 n250
Thomas, Calvin, 151
Thomas, Lionell, 138 n260
Thorvaldsen, Bertel, 59-61
Tieck, Ludwig, 147
Toldberg, Helge, 19 n32
Tolstoy, Count Leo, 23, 156, 164
Topelius, Zacharias, 99
Traustedt, Poul H., 1-2, 33 n50
Trömel, Ferdinand, 153 n304
Turgenev, Ivan Sergeevich, 156
Tuulikki, Leckie R., 216 n438
Tykesson, Elisabeth, 80 n111, 81 n114

Undset, Sigrid, 26 n37
Ungern-Sternberg, Alexander von, 131-32, 146

Verlaine, Paul, 156
Victoria, Queen of England, 155, 223
Viljanen, Lauri, 89 n151

Wachenhusen, Hans, 121
Wagner, Richard, 205
Waldis, Burkard, 193
Walzel, Oskar, 123 n219, 126 n226
Ward, Mark G., 154 n307
Wasmer, Udo, 212 n428
Wellek, René, 119 n207, 142
Wells, G. A., 164 n328
Westling, Christer, 82 n116
Wharton, Edith, 164
White, Alfred D., 154 n307
Wibelius, Olof, 93
Willatzen, Peter Johann, 117
William II, Emperor of Germany, 220
Williams, W. D., 212 n428
Winther, Christian, 26 n37
Wrede, Johan, 89 n154
Wretö, Tore, 87 n140 n141 n144, 88 n145 n147 n149 n150, 89 n154, 92-93
Wright, D. G., 171

Zagari, Luciano, 155 n309, 183 n371
Zimmermann, Rolf Christian, 217 n438
Zuck, Virpi, 87 n140
Zwiebel, William L., 204 n421

OHIO UNIVERSITY LIBRARY
Please return this book as soon as you have finished with it. In order to avoid a fine it must be returned by the latest date stamped below. All books are subject to recall after two weeks or immediately if needed for reserve.

JUL 18 1995